D1685664

Yamaha XS 1100 Fours Owners Workshop Manual

by Pete Shoemark

Models covered

XS1100 E. 1101 cc. Introduced UK 1978, USA 1977
XS1100 F and SF. 1101 cc. Introduced USA 1978
XS1100 G. 1101 cc. Introduced UK and USA 1980
XS1100 SG. 1101 cc. Introduced USA 1979

ISBN 0 85696 483 2

CF

HAYNES PUBLISHING GROUP
SPARKFORD YEOVIL SOMERSET ENGLAND
distributed in the USA by
HAYNES PUBLICATIONS INC
861 LAWRENCE DRIVE
NEWBURY P/ ⸝K
CALIFORNIA
USA

000000761209

Acknowledgements

Our grateful thanks are due to Mitsui Machinery Sales (UK) Limited, who gave permission to use the line drawings used throughout this manual.

Our thanks are also due to R. S. Damarell and Son Ltd., of St. Austell, who supplied the machine featured in this manual.

Finally, we would also like to thank the Avon Rubber Company, who kindly supplied illustrations and advice about tyre fitting, and NGK Spark Plugs (UK) Ltd. who furnished advice about sparking plug conditions.

About this manual

The purpose of this manual is to present the owner with a concise and graphic guide which will enable him to tackle any operation from basic routine maintenance to a major overhaul. It has been assumed that any work would be undertaken without the luxury of a well-equipped workshop and a range of manufacturer's service tools.

To this end, the machine featured in the manual was stripped and rebuilt in our own workshop, by a team comprising a mechanic, a photographer and the author. The resulting photographic sequence depicts events as they took place, the hands shown being those of the author and the mechanic.

The use of specialised, and expensive, service tools was avoided unless their use was considered to be essential due to risk of breakage or injury. There is usually some way of improvising a method of removing a stubborn component, provided that a suitable degree of care is exercised.

The author learnt his motorcycle mechanics over a number of years, faced with the same difficulties and using similar facilities to those encountered by most owners. It is hoped that this practical experience can be passed on through the pages of this manual.

Where possible, a well-used example of the machine is chosen for the workshop project, as this highlights any areas which might be particularly prone to giving rise to problems. In this way, any such difficulties are encountered and resolved before the text is written, and the techniques used to deal with them can be incorporated in the relevant sections. Armed with a working knowledge of the machine, the author undertakes a considerable amount of research in order that the maximum amount of data can be included in this manual.

Each Chapter is divided into numbered sections. Within these sections are numbered paragraphs. Cross reference throughout the manual is quite straightforward and logical. When reference is made 'See Section 6.10' it means Section 6, paragraph 10 in the same Chapter. If another Chapter were intended the reference would read, for example, 'See Chapter 2, Section 6.10'. All the photographs are captioned with a section/paragraph number to which they refer and are relevant to the Chapter text adjacent.

Figures (usually line illustrations) appear in a logical but numerical order, within a given Chapter. Fig. 1.1 therefore refers to the first figure in Chapter 1.

Left-hand and right-hand descriptions of the machines and their components refer to the left and right of a given machine when the rider is seated normally.

Whilst every care is taken to ensure that the information in this manual is correct no liability can be accepted by the author or publishers for loss, damage or injury caused by any errors in or omissions from the information given.

Contents

Note: General descriptions and specifications are given in each Chapter immediately after the list of Contents. Fault diagnosis is given at the end of the Chapter.

Right-hand view of the Yamaha XS1100 E

Close-up of engine/gearbox unit of the Yamaha XS1100 E

Introduction to the Yamaha XS1100 Fours

Although the history of Yamaha can be traced back to the year 1887, when a then very small company commenced manufacture of reed organs, it was not until 1954 that the company became interested in motor cycles. As can be imagined, the problems of marketing a motor cycle against a background of musical instruments manufacture were considerable. Some local racing successes and the use of hitherto unknown bright colour schemes helped achieve the desired results and in July 1955 the Yamaha Motor Company was established as a separate entity, employing a work force of less than 100 and turning out some 300 machines a month.

Competition successes continued and with the advent of tasteful styling that followed Italian trends, Yamaha became established as one of the world's leading motor cycle manufacturers. Part of this success story is the impressive list of Yamaha 'firsts' — a whole string of innovations that include electric starting, pressed steel frame, torque induction and 6 and 8 port engines. There is also the 'Autolube' system of lubrication, in which the engine-driven oil pump is linked to the twist grip throttle, so that lubrication requirements are always in step with engine demands.

Since 1964, Yamaha has gained the World Championship on numerous occasions, in both the 125cc and 250cc classes. Indeed, Yamaha has dominated the lightweight classes in international road racing events to such an extent in recent years that several race promoters are now instituting a special type of event in their programme from which Yamaha machines are barred!

In 1970 Yamaha broke into the four-stroke market with the parallel twin 650cc XS1. This model was soon augmented by a 500cc model and 750cc model of similar configuration. The move from two-strokes to four-strokes was a trend followed by the other large Japanese manufacturers, due to the 'energy crises' and world opinion on pollution. The XS750 D was introduced first to America, where it was available in 1976, as the machine to head the Yamaha range, and so compete in the 'Superbike' market position. The popularity of this machine prompted the introduction of a still larger flagship, the XS1100, which shares many design features with the XS750, including a similar transmission configuration and shaft drive. The original XS1100 E model appeared in touring trim in 1977, to be continued with slight modifications as the F model (1978 US only) and the G model (1980). A further variant in 'custom' trim, the SF (1979) and SG (1980) is available only in the USA.

Model dimensions and weights

	E(UK) and G(UK)	E(US) and F	SF	G(US)	SG
Overall length	2260 mm (89.0 in)	2260 mm (89.0 in)	2275 mm (89.6 in)	2260 mm (89.0 in)	2275 mm (89.6 in)
Overall width	755 mm (29.7 in)	920 mm (36.2 in)	855 mm (33.7 in)	920 mm (36.2 in)	855 mm (33.7 in)
Overall height	1145 mm (45.1 in)	1175 mm (46.3 in)	1230 mm (48.4 in)	1175 mm (46.3 in)	1230 mm (48.4 in)
Wheelbase	1545 mm (60.8 in)	1545 mm (60.8 in)	1545 mm (60.8 in)	1545 mm (60.8 in)	1545 mm (60.8 in)
Seat height	810 mm (31.9 in)	810 mm (31.9 in)	805 mm (31.7 in)	800 mm (31.5 in)	790 mm (31.1 in)
Ground clearance	150 mm (5.9 in)	150 mm (5.9 in)	155 mm (6.1 in)	150 mm (5.9 in)	155 mm (6.1 in)
Dry weight	256 kg (565 lb)	255 kg (562 lb)	252 kg (556 lb)	255 kg (562 lb)	252 kg (556 lb)

Ordering spare parts

When ordering spare parts for the Yamaha XS1100, it is advisable to deal direct with an offical Yamaha agent, who will be able to supply many of the items required ex-stock. Although parts can be ordered from Yamaha direct, it is preferable to route the order via a local agent even if the parts are not available from stock. He is in a better position to specify exactly the parts required and to identify the relevant spare part numbers so that there is less chance of the wrong part being supplied by the manufacturer due to a vague or incomplete description.

When ordering spares, always quote the frame and engine numbers in full, together with any prefixes or suffixes in the form of letters. The frame number is found stamped on the right-hand side of the steering head, in line with the forks. The engine number is stamped on the right-hand side of the upper crankcase, immediately below the right-hand carburettor.

Use only parts of genuine Yamaha manufacture. A few pattern parts are available, sometimes at cheaper prices, but there is no guarantee that they will give such good service as the originals they replace. Retain any worn or broken parts until the replacements have been obtained; they are sometimes needed as a pattern to help identify the correct replacement when design changes have been made during a production run.

Some of the more expendable parts such as spark plugs, bulbs, tyres, oils and greases etc., can be obtained from accessory shops and motor factors, who have convenient opening hours, charge lower prices and can often be found not far from home. It is also possible to obtain parts on a Mail Order basis from a number of specialists who advertise regularly in the motor cycle magazines.

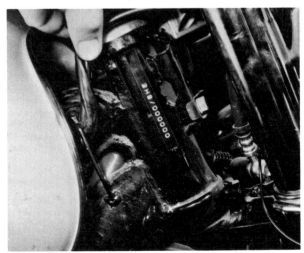

Frame Number Location

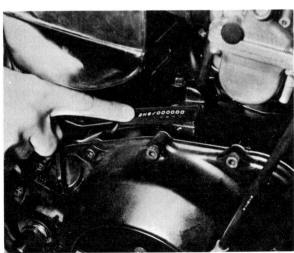

Engine Number Location

Safety First!

Professional motor mechanics are trained in safe working procedures. However enthusiastic you may be about getting on with the job in hand, do take the time to ensure that your safety is not put at risk. A moment's lack of attention can result in an accident, as can failure to observe certain elementary precautions.

There will always be new ways of having accidents, and the following points do not pretend to be a comprehensive list of all dangers; they are intended rather to make you aware of the risks and to encourage a safety-conscious approach to all work you carry out on your vehicle.

Essential DOs and DON'Ts

DON'T start the engine without first ascertaining that the transmission is in neutral.

DON'T suddenly remove the filler cap from a hot cooling system — cover it with a cloth and release the pressure gradually first, or you may get scalded by escaping coolant.

DON'T attempt to drain oil until you are sure it has cooled sufficiently to avoid scalding you.

DON'T grasp any part of the engine, exhaust or silencer without first ascertaining that it is sufficiently cool to avoid burning you.

DON'T syphon toxic liquids such as fuel, brake fluid or antifreeze by mouth, or allow them to remain on your skin.

DON'T inhale brake lining dust — it is injurious to health.

DON'T allow any spilt oil or grease to remain on the floor — wipe it up straight away, before someone slips on it.

DON'T use ill-fitting spanners or other tools which may slip and cause injury.

DON'T attempt to lift a heavy component which may be beyond your capability — get assistance.

DON'T rush to finish a job, or take unverified short cuts.

DON'T allow children or animals in or around an unattended vehicle.

DON'T inflate a tyre to a pressure above the recommended maximum. Apart from overstressing the carcase and wheel rim, in extreme cases the tyre may blow off forcibly.

DO ensure that the machine is supported securely at all times. This is especially important when the machine is blocked up to aid wheel or fork removal.

DO take care when attempting to slacken a stubborn nut or bolt. It is generally better to pull on a spanner, rather than push, so that if slippage occurs you fall away from the machine rather than on to it.

DO wear eye protection when using power tools such as drill, sander, bench grinder etc.

DO use a barrier cream on your hands prior to undertaking dirty jobs — it will protect your skin from infection as well as making the dirt easier to remove afterwards; but make sure your hands aren't left slippery.

DO keep loose clothing (cuffs, tie etc) and long hair well out of the way of moving mechanical parts.

DO remove rings, wristwatch etc, before working on the vehicle — especially the electrical system.

DO keep your work area tidy — it is only too easy to fall over articles left lying around.

DO exercise caution when compressing springs for removal or installation. Ensure that the tension is applied and released in a controlled manner, using suitable tools which preclude the possibility of the spring escaping violently.

DO ensure that any lifting tackle used has a safe working load rating adequate for the job.

DO get someone to check periodically that all is well, when working alone on the vehicle.

DO carry out work in a logical sequence and check that everything is correctly assembled and tightened afterwards.

DO remember that your vehicle's safety affects that of yourself and others. If in doubt on any point, get specialist advice.

IF, in spite of following these precautions, you are unfortunate enough to injure yourself, seek medical attention as soon as possible.

Fire

Remember at all times that petrol (gasoline) is highly flammable. Never smoke, or have any kind of naked flame around, when working on the vehicle. But the risk does not end there — a spark caused by an electrical short-circuit, by two metal surfaces contacting each other, or even by static electricity built up in your body under certain conditions, can ignite petrol vapour, which in a confined space is highly explosive.

Always disconnect the battery earth (ground) terminal before working on any part of the fuel system, and never risk spilling fuel on to a hot engine or exhaust.

It is recommended that a fire extinguisher of a type suitable for fuel and electrical fires is kept handy in the garage or workplace at all times. Never try to extinguish a fuel or electrical fire with water.

Fumes

Certain fumes are highly toxic and can quickly cause unconsciousness and even death if inhaled to any extent. Petrol (gasoline) vapour comes into this category, as do the vapours from certain solvents such as trichloroethylene. Any draining or pouring of such volatile fluids should be done in a well ventilated area.

When using cleaning fluids and solvents, read the instructions carefully. Never use materials from unmarked containers — they may give off poisonous vapours.

Never run the engine of a motor vehicle in an enclosed space such as a garage. Exhaust fumes contain carbon monoxide which is extremely poisonous; if you need to run the engine, always do so in the open air or at least have the rear of the vehicle outside the workplace.

If you are fortunate enough to have the use of an inspection pit, never drain or pour petrol, and never run the engine, while the vehicle is standing over it; the fumes, being heavier than air, will concentrate in the pit with possibly lethal results.

The battery

Never cause a spark, or allow a naked light, near the vehicle's battery. It will normally be giving off a certain amount of hydrogen gas, which is highly explosive.

Always disconnect the battery earth (ground) terminal before working on the fuel or electrical systems.

If possible, loosen the filler plugs or cover when charging the battery from an external source. Do not charge at an excessive rate or the battery may burst.

Take care when topping up and when carrying the battery. The acid electrolyte, even when diluted, is very corrosive and should not be allowed to contact the eyes or skin.

If you ever need to prepare electrolyte yourself, always add the acid slowly to the water, and never the other way round. Protect against splashes by wearing rubber gloves and goggles.

Mains electricity

When using an electric power tool, inspection light etc which works from the mains, always ensure that the appliance is correctly connected to its plug and that, where necessary, it is properly earthed (grounded). Do not use such appliances in damp conditions and, again, beware of creating a spark or applying excessive heat in the vicinity of fuel or fuel vapour.

Ignition HT voltage

A severe electric shock can result from touching certain parts of the ignition system, such as the HT leads, when the engine is running or being cranked, particularly if components are damp or the insulation is defective. Where an electronic ignition system is fitted, the HT voltage is much higher and could prove fatal.

Routine maintenance

Periodic routine maintenance is a continuous process that commences immediately the machine is used and continues until the machine is no longer fit for service. It must be carried out at specified mileage recordings or on a calendar basis if the machine is not used regularly, whichever is the soonest. Maintenance should be regarded as an insurance policy, to help keep the machine in the peak of condition and to ensure long, trouble-free service. It has the additonal benefit of giving early warning of any faults that may develop and will act as a safety check, to the obvious advantage of both rider and machine alike.

The various maintenance tasks are described under their respective mileage and calendar headings. Accompanying photos or diagrams are provided, where necessary. It should be remembered that the interval between the various maintenance tasks serves only as a guide. As the machine gets older, is driven hard, or is used under particularly adverse conditions, it is advisable to reduce the period between each check.

For ease of reference each service operation is described in detail under the relevant heading. However, if further general information is required it can be found within the manual in the relevant Chapter.

Although no special tools are required for routine maintenance (with, perhaps, the exception of a valve adjustment shim removal tool), a good selection of general workshop tools are essential. Included in the tools must be a range of metric ring or combination spanners, and a set of Allen keys (socket wrenches).

Weekly or every 200 miles (320 km)

---

1 Tyre pressures

Check the tyre pressures with a pressure gauge that is known to be accurate. Always check the pressures when the tyres are cold. If the tyres are checked after the machine has travelled a number of miles, the tyres will have become hot and consequently the pressure will have increased, possibly by as much as 8 psi. A false reading will therefore result.

Tyre pressures (cold) — US models only
Up to 198 lb (90 kg) load:
 Front 26 psi (1.8 kg/cm²)
 Rear 28 psi (2.0 kg/cm²)
198 – 337 lb (90 – 153 kg) load:
 Front 28 psi (2.0 kg/cm²)
 Rear 36 psi (2.5 kg/cm²)
337 – 478 lb (153 – 217 kg) load:
 Front 28 psi (2.0 kg/cm²)
 Rear 40 psi (2.8 kg/cm²)
Continuous high-speed riding:
 Front 36 psi (2.5 kg/cm²)
 Rear 40 psi (2.8 kg/cm²)

Tyre pressures (cold) — UK models only
Up to 324 lb (147 kg) load:
 Front 28 psi (2.0 kg/cm²)
 Rear 36 psi (2.5 kg/cm²)
324 – 463 lb (147 – 210 kg) load:
 Front 28 psi (2.0 kg/cm²)
 Rear 40 psi (2.8 kg/cm²)
Continuous high-speed riding:
 Front 36 psi (2.5 kg/cm²)
 Rear 40 psi (2.8 kg/cm²)

2 Engine/transmission oil level

With the engine at its normal operating temperature, place the machine on its centre stand on level ground. The oil level will be visible between the upper and lower level lines marked on the inspection window in the right-hand outer cover. If the level falls below the minimum mark, bring it back to the normal level by adding new oil via the filler orifice above the inspection window. Note that when checking the oil level, the machine should be allowed to stand for a few minutes so that any residual oil can drain down from the crankcase walls.

Yamaha recommend the use of an SAE 20W/40 SE motor oil at temperatures of 5°C (41°F) and above, and SAE 10W/30 SE motor oil at temperatures of 15°C (59°F) and below. Where these overlap, ie between 5°C and 15°C (41°F and 59°F), either grade may be used.

3 Safety check

Give the machine a close visual inspection, checking for loose nuts and fittings, frayed control cables etc. Check the tyres for damage, especially splitting on the sidewalls. Remove any stones or other objects caught between the treads. This is particularly important on the front tyre, where rapid deflation due to penetration of the inner tube will almost certainly cause total loss of control.

4 Legal check

Ensure that the lights, horn and trafficators function correctly, also the speedometer.

Monthly or every 1000 miles (1600 km)

Complete the tasks listed under the weekly/200 mile heading and then carry out the following checks.

1 Hydraulic fluid level

Check the level of the hydraulic fluid in the front brake master cylinder reservoir, on the handlebars, and also the rear brake reservoir, behind the right-hand frame side cover. The level in both reservoirs should lie between the upper and lower level marks. During normal service, it is unlikely that the hydraulic fluid level will fall dramatically, unless a leak has developed in the system. If this occurs, the fault should be remedied AT ONCE. The level will fall slowly as the brake linings wear and the fluid deficiency should be corrected, when required. Always use an hydraulic fluid of DOT 3 or SAE J1703 specification, and if possible do not mix different types of fluid, even if the specifications appear the same. This will preclude the possibility of two incompatible fluids being mixed and the resultant chemical reactions damaging the seals.

If the level in either reservoir has been allowed to fall below the specified limit, and air has entered the system, the brake in question must be bled, as described in Chapter 5, Section 8.

Check the front brake fluid level

The rear fluid reservoir is mounted beneath the right-hand side panel

2   Battery electrolyte level

A GS battery is fitted as standard. This battery is a lead-acid type and has a capacity of 20 Amp hours.

The translucent plastic case of the battery permits the upper and lower levels of the electrolyte to be observed when the battery is lifted from its housing below the dualseat. Maintenance is normally limited to keeping the electrolyte level between the prescribed upper and lower limits and by making sure that the vent pipe is not blocked.

Unless acid is spilt, as may occur if the machine falls over, the electrolyte should always be topped up with distilled water, to restore the correct level. If acid is spilt on

any part of the machine, it should be neutralised with an alkali such as washing soda and washed away with plenty of water, otherwise serious corrosion will occur. Top up with sulphuric acid of the correct specific gravity (1.260-1.280) only when spillage has occurred. Check that the vent pipe is well clear of the frame tubes or any of the other cycle parts, for obvious reasons.

3   Middle gearcase and final drive box oil levels

The oil level in both the middle gear case and the final drive box (at the rear wheel) should be checked at regular intervals. The filler plug on both units accepts an Allen key, the hexagonal recess being protected by a removable rubber bung. The oil level should be checked using the dipstick supplied in the toolkit. Use the long arm (marked middle) for the middle gear case, and the short arm (marked rear) for the final drive box. The oil level in each case should be between the two marked parallel lines. If required, replenish with Hypoid gear oil as follows.

SAE 90EP for use above 5°C (41°F)
SAE 80EP for use below 5°C (41°F)

On US models, Yamaha recommend gear oil conforming to GL-4, GL-5 or GL-6 specifications. This does not apply to UK machines, where any good quality EP Hypoid oil will be satisfactory.

4   Cleaning the air filter element

Access to the filter element is gained by releasing the four wing nuts which secure the lower section of the air filter casing. Lift the element clear of the casing for cleaning and examination. Most of the loose dust can be removed by tapping the element on a hard surface. The remaining dust will be trapped in the filter's porous surface, and can be cleared by blowing compressed air through the element from the inside surface.

No exact interval for element renewal can be given, because this will depend entirely upon the usual operating conditions. Experience will show when the element will require removal. It will be noted that each time the element is cleaned it will become progressively more difficult to dislodge all of the dust. Eventually, after about 6 – 10 cleaning operations, the element will require renewal.

Any obvious damage, such as holes or oil contamination, will necessitate immediate renewal of the element, because the entry of unfiltered air into the engine will cause accelerated wear, and the reduced resistance will result in a weak mixture. Conversely, a badly contaminated filter will obstruct the passage of air through the engine and will lead to an over rich mixture.

Two monthly or every 2000 miles (3200 km)

Complete the checks listed under the Weekly/200 mile and Monthly/1000 mile headings and then carry out the following tasks:

1   Cleaning and adjusting sparking plugs

Remove the sparking plugs and clean them using a wire brush. Clean the electrode points using emery paper or a fine file and then reset the gaps. To reset the gap, bend the outer electrode to bring it closer to or further from the central electrode, until a feeler gauge of the correct size can just be slid between the gap. Never bend the central electrode or the insulator will crack, causing engine damage if the particles fall in whilst the engine is running. The correct plug gap is 0.7 – 0.8 mm (0.028 – 0.032 in). Before replacing the plugs, smear the threads with a small quantity of graphite grease to aid subsequent removal.

2 Carburettors — checking and adjustment

If carburettor malfunction has been indicated by rough running or poor fuel consumption, attention to the carburettor adjustment and synchronisation is likely to be required. This is a somewhat lengthy procedure and requires the use of a set of vacuum gauges to ensure accurate synchronisation. Reference should be made to Chapter 2 for further details.

Three monthly or every 3000 miles (4800 km)

Carry out the operations listed under the previous headings, then perform the following:

1 Engine/gearbox oil change

Place a container of more than 3 litre capacity below the drain plug in the front left-hand wall of the sump. Remove the filler plug from the primary chaincase and then remove the drain plug. The oil should be drained when the engine is hot, preferably after the machine has been on a run, because the lubricant will be thinner and so drain more rapidly and more completely.

When drainage is complete, refit the drain plug and the sealing washer and refill the sump with approximately 3.0 litre (5.28/6.34 Imp/US pint) of the appropriate engine oil (see Recommended Lubricants). Check that the level is between limits in the oil sight glass, then run the engine for a while to circulate the oil. Stop the engine and allow it to stand for a few minutes, then re-check the oil level.

2 Camshaft chain tension

The camshaft drive chain tension should be checked at the intervals specified above and whenever the camshaft drive mechanism appears to be unusually noisy. It should be noted that the engine cannot run properly if there is excessive play in the camshaft drive, because the valve timing accuracy will be lost.

Remove the inspection cover at the left-hand crankshaft end to expose the ignition rotor assembly. Locate the C mark on the rotor periphery, and turn the crankshaft clockwise by means of the large square at the centre until the mark aligns with the fixed pointer. Moving to the tensioner mechanism at the front of the engine unit, slacken the adjuster locknut and bolt to free the spring loaded plunger. The chain will be tensioned automatically as the plunger finds its own level. Secure the bolt and locknut to hold the setting. On no account over-tighten the bolt or locknut because this will only succeed in shearing the bolt. The appropriate torque setting is 4.3 lbf ft (0.6 kgf m) for the bolt and 6.5 lbf ft (0.9 kgf m) for the locknut. Leave the inspection cover off until the ignition timing has been checked as described below.

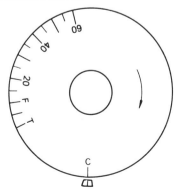

Position of C mark during cam chain tension adjustment

Align the C mark prior to cam chain tensioning

3 Ignition timing check

The ignition timing must be checked using a stroboscopic timing lamp or 'strobe'. Of the two types available, a good quality xenon tube type is preferable to the cheaper neon types, because it will give a more defined image in use, although the latter will usually prove adequate if used in a shaded position. Where a strobe is not available, the timing check must be entrusted to a Yamaha service agent.

Connect the timing lamp to the left-hand (No 1) sparking plug, following the manufacturer's instructions. Start the engine and allow it to idle at 950 – 1050 rpm (US E model), 1050 – 1150 all other models. Direct the lamp at the stationary pointer. If the timing setting is correct, the pulsing lamp will appear to freeze the F mark in line with the pointer. If necessary, stop the engine and make any adjustment by slackening the two baseplate screws and moving the baseplate until the correct setting is achieved. Once set up correctly, the ignition timing will be correct for all four cylinders; there is no facility for individual adjustment.

To check the ignition advance, disconnect the vacuum advance hose and plug the hose end. Start the engine and briefly increase the engine speed to the speed indicated below for the relevant model. The advance should be as shown.

Advance timing
UK models	36° @ 5400 rpm
US models	36° @ 5200 rpm
SF model only	31° @ 5400 rpm

If this is not the case the timing unit will require further attention. See Chapter 3 for details.

Note that on G(US) and SG model the timing baseplate is secured during manufacture by shear-head screws. No adjustment is possible, in the normal sense, and if ignition timing problems occur reference should be made to Chapter 3 for further details.

Four monthly or every 4000 miles (6400 km)

Complete all the tasks under the previous maintenance headings and then:

1 Final driveshaft joint lubrication

The final driveshaft joint should be lubricated with Molybdenum disulphide grease, using a grease gun applied to the nipple provided.

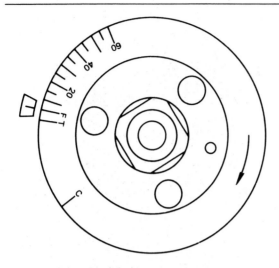

Retarded (idle) ignition timing mark

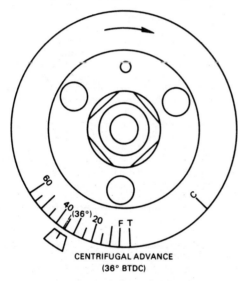

CENTRIFUGAL ADVANCE
(36° BTDC)

XS1100 E, F, G and SG

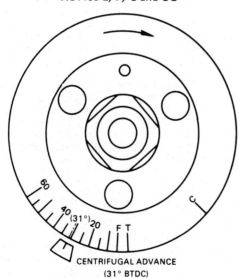

CENTRIFUGAL ADVANCE
(31° BTDC)

Centrifugal advance mark
XS1100 SF

2 Control cable lubrication

Use motor oil or a good general purpose oil to lubricate the control cables. A good method of lubricating cables is shown in the accompanying illustration, using a plasticine funnel. This method has the disadvantage that the cables usually need removing from the machine to allow the oil to drip through. A hydraulic cable oiler which pressurises the lubricant overcomes this problem. Nylon lined cables, which may have been fitted as replacements, should not be lubricated; in some cases the oil will cause the lining to swell leading to cable seizure.

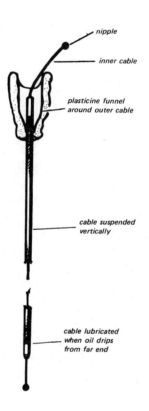

nipple

inner cable

plasticine funnel
around outer cable

cable suspended
vertically

cable lubricated
when oil drips
from far end

Control cable lubrication

Six monthly or every 6000 miles (9600 km)

Complete the operations listed under the previous headings, then carry out the following:

1 Valve clearances

Valve clearances on the XS1100 models are set by fitting hardened steel pads of various thicknesses between the cam follower and lobe. Whilst this results in a rather complicated adjustment sequence, it does allow the engine to run for long periods without the need for adjustment. The valve clearances should be checked at the intervals specified above or whenever the valve gear appears to be unusually noisy.

To gain access to the cylinder head area a certain amount of preliminary dismantling will be necessary. Start by slackening the two extended nuts which secure the seat to the frame. These will be found on the underside of the seat, in line with the grab rail. Once slackened the nuts can be slid forwards until they disengage with the slots in the frame, allowing the seat to be lifted clear.

Remove the single bolt which secures the rear of the fuel tank. Check that the fuel tap is turned off, then remove the petrol pipe, vent pipe and fuel gauge lead from the tank. The latter can then be drawn back, to free it from the mounting rubbers, and removed. With the tank removed, release the ignition ballast resistor and lodge it clear of the cylinder head cover. Remove the bolts which retain the cylinder head cover and lift it away, taking care not to damage the gasket. Remove the left-hand front engine casing to allow the crankshaft to be turned by means of the large square boss at the centre of the ignition rotor.

Before checking the valve clearances, make a rough plan sketch of the cylinder head so that a note of each clearance can be made against the relevant valve. The clearance of each valve should be checked with the appropriate cam lobe at 180° from the cam follower. Check the gap between the cam's base circle and the adjustment shim and note the reading. Repeat this sequence with the remaining valves.

The specified clearance is 0.16–0.20 mm (0.006–0.008 in) for the inlet valve and 0.21–0.25 mm (0.008–0.010 in) for the exhaust valve. If any of the clearances are outside these limits it will be necessary to remove the old pad and fit a new one of a thickness which will restore the correct clearance. This operation entails the use of a special Yamaha tool, part number 90890–01245. It is possible to fabricate a suitable substitute, but in view of the fact that it will be required fairly frequently it is probably as well to obtain the correct item. It is useful to note that an identical tool is used on the XS750 models.

Turn the crankshaft until the valve in question is fully open, having first positioned the slot in the cam follower to point away from the holding tool. Fit the tool in position and retain it with one of the cylinder head cover screws. The crankshaft can now be rotated so that the cam lobe moves clear of the cam follower. It is important that the lobe does not touch the holding tool because this could cause damage to the cylinder head or the camshaft. To this end, rotate the crankshaft so that the inlet camshaft turns clockwise and the exhaust camshaft turns anti-clockwise, as viewed from the left-hand side of the machine.

Remove the adjustment shim by prising it clear with a small screwdriver inserted in the slot or by using a magnet. Pad (shim) selection can now be made following the sequence given below.

1 Note number etched on the shim. This gives its size in millimetres; eg 270 is 2.70 mm, 245 is 2.45 mm, and so on.
2 Using the accompanying chart, trace the point where the installed pad number intersects the measured clearance. This will indicate the new shim required.
3 Fit the new pad and remove the holding tool. Turn the crankshaft through several revolutions and recheck the clearance.
4 If necessary, repeat the sequence until the clearance figure is correct.
5 Repeat the above sequence with the remaining valves.

It should be noted that Yamaha treat the size numbering on the pads as a guide, hence the double check in stages 3 and 4 above. Once the clearance check has been completed, reassemble the cylinder head cover, fuel tank and seat in the reverse order of that given for removal.

2 Sparking plugs

Remove and renew the sparking plugs. Although in general sparking plugs will continue to function after this mileage, their efficiency will have been reduced. The correct plug type is NGK BP-6ES or Champion N-8Y. Before fitting, set the gaps to 0.7–0.8 mm (0.028–0.032 in).

Valve shim size is etched on lower surface

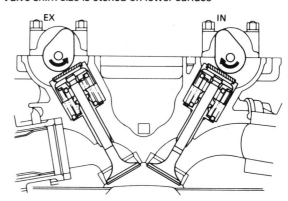
Camshaft position where shim can be removed

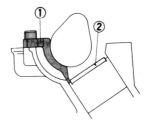
Correct positioning of tappet adjusting tool
1 Adjustment tool   *2 Shim*

3 Middle gear case and final drive box oil change

Place a container below the rear wall of the gearbox. Remove the filler plug from the middle gear casing and then unscrew the drain plug. The drain plug is located in the centre of the middle gear casing rear wall. Drain the final drive box in a similar manner. The two cases must be drained when the oil is warm, thereby ensuring that complete drainage is achieved. The final drive casing particularly takes an extended length of time to warm up and therefore should be drained only after a long run. Replenish the two cases with Hypoid gear oil after checking that the drain plugs have been fitted and tightened. The approximate quantities are as follows:

Middle gear case 360cc (12/13 US/Imp fl oz)
Final drive box   300cc (10/11 US/Imp fl oz)

Check the levels by means of the dipstick before fitting the filler plugs, to prevent overfilling.

MEASURED CLEARANCE	INSTALLED PAD NUMBER*																								
	200	205	210	215	220	225	230	235	240	245	250	255	260	265	270	275	280	285	290	295	300	305	310	315	320
0.00 ~ 0.05			200	205	210	215	220	225	230	235	240	245	250	255	260	265	270	275	280	285	290	295	300	305	310
0.06 ~ 0.10		200	205	210	215	220	225	230	235	240	245	250	255	260	265	270	275	280	285	290	295	300	305	310	315
0.11 ~ 0.15																									
0.16 ~ 0.20	205	210	215	220	225	230	235	240	245	250	255	260	265	270	275	280	285	290	295	300	305	310	315	320	
0.21 ~ 0.25	210	215	220	225	230	235	240	245	250	255	260	265	270	275	280	285	290	295	300	305	310	315	320		
0.26 ~ 0.30	215	220	225	230	235	240	245	250	255	260	265	270	275	280	285	290	295	300	305	310	315	320			
0.31 ~ 0.35	220	225	230	235	240	245	250	255	260	265	270	275	280	285	290	295	300	305	310	315	320				
0.36 ~ 0.40	225	230	235	240	245	250	255	260	265	270	275	280	285	290	295	300	305	310	315	320					
0.41 ~ 0.45	230	235	240	245	250	255	260	265	270	275	280	285	290	295	300	305	310	315	320						
0.46 ~ 0.50	235	240	245	250	255	260	265	270	275	280	285	290	295	300	305	310	315	320							
0.51 ~ 0.55	240	245	250	255	260	265	270	275	280	285	290	295	300	305	310	315	320								
0.56 ~ 0.60	245	250	255	260	265	270	275	280	285	290	295	300	305	310	315	320									
0.61 ~ 0.65	250	255	260	265	270	275	280	285	290	295	300	305	310	315	320										
0.66 ~ 0.70	255	260	265	270	275	280	285	290	295	300	305	310	315	320											
0.71 ~ 0.75	260	265	270	275	280	285	290	295	300	305	310	315	320												
0.76 ~ 0.80	265	270	275	280	285	290	295	300	305	310	315	320													
0.81 ~ 0.85	270	275	280	285	290	295	300	305	310	315	320														
0.86 ~ 0.90	275	280	285	290	295	300	305	310	315	320															
0.91 ~ 0.95	280	285	290	295	300	305	310	315	320																
0.96 ~ 1.00	285	290	295	300	305	310	315	320																	
1.10 ~ 1.05	290	295	300	305	310	315	320																		
1.06 ~ 1.10	295	300	305	310	315	320																			
1.11 ~ 1.15	300	305	310	315	320																				
1.16 ~ 1.20	305	310	315	320																					
1.21 ~ 1.25	310	315	320																						
1.26 ~ 1.30	315	320																							
1.31 ~ 1.35	320																								

VALVE CLEARANCE (engine cold) 0.11 ~ 0.15 mm

Example: Installed is 250
Measured clearance is 0.32 mm
Replace 250 pad with 270

*Pad number (example) Pad No. 250 = 2.50 mm
Pad No. 255 = 2.55 mm
Always install pad with number down.

Inlet valve adjustment pad selection table — G(US) and SG models

MEASURED CLEARANCE	INSTALLED PAD NUMBER*																								
	200	205	210	215	220	225	230	235	240	245	250	255	260	265	270	275	280	285	290	295	300	305	310	315	320
0.00 ~ 0.05				200	205	210	215	220	225	230	235	240	245	250	255	260	265	270	275	280	285	290	295	300	305
0.06 ~ 0.10			200	205	210	215	220	225	230	235	240	245	250	255	260	265	270	275	280	285	290	295	300	305	310
0.11 ~ 0.15		200	205	210	215	220	225	230	235	240	245	250	255	260	265	270	275	280	285	290	295	300	305	310	315
0.16 ~ 0.20																									
0.21 ~ 0.25	205	210	215	220	225	230	235	240	245	250	255	260	265	270	275	280	285	290	295	300	305	310	315	320	
0.26 ~ 0.30	210	215	220	225	230	235	240	245	250	255	260	265	270	275	280	285	290	295	300	305	310	315	320		
0.31 ~ 0.35	215	220	225	230	235	240	245	250	255	260	265	270	275	280	285	290	295	300	305	310	315	320			
0.36 ~ 0.40	220	225	230	235	240	245	250	255	260	265	270	275	280	285	290	295	300	305	310	315	320				
0.41 ~ 0.45	225	230	235	240	245	250	255	260	265	270	275	280	285	290	295	300	305	310	315	320					
0.46 ~ 0.50	230	235	240	245	250	255	260	265	270	275	280	285	290	295	300	305	310	315	320						
0.51 ~ 0.55	235	240	245	250	255	260	265	270	275	280	285	290	295	300	305	310	315	320							
0.56 ~ 0.60	240	245	250	255	260	265	270	275	280	285	290	295	300	305	310	315	320								
0.61 ~ 0.65	245	250	255	260	265	270	275	280	285	290	295	300	305	310	315	320									
0.66 ~ 0.70	250	255	260	265	270	275	280	285	290	295	300	305	310	315	320										
0.71 ~ 0.75	255	260	265	270	275	280	285	290	295	300	305	310	315	320											
0.76 ~ 0.80	260	265	270	275	280	285	290	295	300	305	310	315	320												
0.81 ~ 0.85	265	270	275	280	285	290	295	300	305	310	315	320													
0.86 ~ 0.90	270	275	280	285	290	295	300	305	310	315	320														
0.91 ~ 0.95	275	280	285	290	295	300	305	310	315	320															
0.96 ~ 1.00	280	285	290	295	300	305	310	315	320																
1.10 ~ 1.05	285	290	295	300	305	310	315	320																	
1.06 ~ 1.10	290	295	300	305	310	315	320																		
1.11 ~ 1.15	295	300	305	310	315	320																			
1.16 ~ 1.20	300	305	310	315	320																				
1.21 ~ 1.25	305	310	315	320																					
1.26 ~ 1.30	310	315	320																						
1.31 ~ 1.35	315	320																							
1.36 ~ 1.40	320																								

VALVE CLEARANCE (Engine cold): 0.16~0.20 mm
* Pad number is thickness in millimeter.
(Example: pad No. 250 = 2.50 mm)
Always install pad with number down.

Inlet valve adjustment pad selection table — except G(US) and SG models

INSTALLED PAD NUMBER*

MEASURED CLEARANCE	200	205	210	215	220	225	230	235	240	245	250	255	260	265	270	275	280	285	290	295	300	305	310	315	320
0.00 ~ 0.05					200	205	210	215	220	225	230	235	240	245	250	255	260	265	270	275	280	285	290	295	300
0.06 ~ 0.10				200	205	210	215	220	225	230	235	240	245	250	255	260	265	270	275	280	285	290	295	300	305
0.11 ~ 0.15			200	205	210	215	220	225	230	235	240	245	250	255	260	265	270	275	280	285	290	295	300	305	310
0.16 ~ 0.20		200	205	210	215	220	225	230	235	240	245	250	255	260	265	270	275	280	285	290	295	300	305	310	315
0.21 ~ 0.25																									
0.26 ~ 0.30	205	210	215	220	225	230	235	240	245	250	255	260	265	270	275	280	285	290	295	300	305	310	315	320	
0.31 ~ 0.35	210	215	220	225	230	235	240	245	250	255	260	265	270	275	280	285	290	295	300	305	310	315	320		
0.36 ~ 0.40	215	220	225	230	235	240	245	250	255	260	265	270	275	280	285	290	295	300	305	310	315	320			
0.41 ~ 0.45	220	225	230	235	240	245	250	255	260	265	270	275	280	285	290	295	300	305	310	315	320				
0.46 ~ 0.50	225	230	235	240	245	250	255	260	265	270	275	280	285	290	295	300	305	310	315	320					
0.51 ~ 0.55	230	235	240	245	250	255	260	265	270	275	280	285	290	295	300	305	310	315	320						
0.56 ~ 0.60	235	240	245	250	255	260	265	270	275	280	285	290	295	300	305	310	315	320							
0.61 ~ 0.65	240	245	250	255	260	265	270	275	280	285	290	295	300	305	310	315	320								
0.66 ~ 0.70	245	250	255	260	265	270	275	280	285	290	295	300	305	310	315	320									
0.71 ~ 0.75	250	255	260	265	270	275	280	285	290	295	300	305	310	315	320										
0.76 ~ 0.80	255	260	265	270	275	280	285	290	295	300	305	310	315	320											
0.81 ~ 0.85	260	265	270	275	280	285	290	295	300	305	310	315	320												
0.86 ~ 0.90	265	270	275	280	285	290	295	300	305	310	315	320													
0.91 ~ 0.95	270	275	280	285	290	295	300	305	310	35	320														
0.96 ~ 1.00	275	280	285	290	295	300	305	310	315	320															
1.01 ~ 1.05	280	285	290	295	300	305	310	315	320																
1.06 ~ 1.10	285	290	295	300	305	310	315	320																	
1.11 ~ 1.15	290	295	300	305	310	315	320																		
1.16 ~ 1.20	295	300	305	310	315	320																			
1.21 ~ 1.25	300	305	310	315	320																				
1.26 ~ 1.30	305	310	315	320																					
1.31 ~ 1.35	310	315	320																						
1.36 ~ 1.40	315	320																							
1.41 ~ 1.45	320																								

VALVE CLEARANCE (Engine cold): 0.21~0.25 mm
* Pad number is thickness in millimeter.
  (Example: pad No. 250 = 2.50 mm)
  Always install pad with number down.

Exhaust valve adjustment pad selection table – All models

4   Engine oil filter renewal

At this service interval, ie every second oil change, the engine oil filter should be renewed. The oil filter, which is of the corrugated paper type, is contained within a chamber fitted to the underside of the sump. Access to the filter element is made by unscrewing the filter chamber centre bolt, which will bring with it the chamber and element. Place a container below the sump to catch any oil contained in the chamber.

When renewing the element, it is wise to renew the chamber O-ring to prevent possible leaks. Note that the filter chamber should be primed whenever a new filter is fitted. This is accomplished by adding about half a pint of engine oil prior to fitting the filter assembly to the underside of the crankcase. Do not overtighten the filter centre bolt; the correct torque figure is 3.2 kgf in (23 lbf ft).

Discard old filter element and clean housing

Annually or every 8000 miles (12800 km)

Carry out the operations listed under the previous headings, then complete the following:

1   Changing the front fork oil

The damping oil in each fork leg should be drained and replenished one leg at a time, so that the fork spring remaining in the undisturbed leg will support the machine.

Place the machine on the centre stand and remove the rubber cap from the fork top bolt (E, F and G(UK) models). On machines fitted with air-assisted forks remove the valve cap and depress the valve for a few seconds to bleed off the air pressure. Slacken and remove the fork top bolt and unscrew the drain plug from the fork lower leg, allowing the oil to drain into a suitable container. Pump the forks up and down a few times to expel any remaining oil, and refit the drain plug and washer. Replenish the fork leg with the specified quantity of SAE 10W/30 motor oil (UK models), SAE 10 motor or fork oil (US models).

Fork oil capacity (per leg)
E, F and G(UK)	*212 cc*
SF	*225 cc*
G(US)	*241 cc*
SG	*210 cc*

Refit the top bolt and repeat the procedure for the second fork leg. On completion the fork legs should be

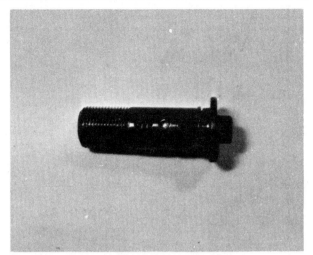

Check that bypass valve operates smoothly

repressurised (where appropriate), within the range 0-36 psi (0 – 2.5 kg/cm²). Refer to Chapter 4 for details.

2   Fuel filter cleaning

Before either petrol tap is removed for filter cleaning or for attention to the lever, the petrol tank must be drained. Detach the petrol feed pipes and substitute a longer length of suitable piping through which to drain the fuel. Turn the tap to the 'Prime' position to allow the petrol to flow freely.

To remove either tap, loosen evenly the two screws which pass through the flange into the petrol tank and withdraw the tap, complete with filter tower. The filter is a push fit on the hollow T-piece which projects from the top of the tap.

The filter should be cleaned at regular intervals to remove any entrapped matter. Use clean petrol and a soft brush.

3   Checking the steering head bearings

Place the machine on the centre stand so that the front wheel is clear of the ground. If necessary, place blocks below the crankcase to prevent the motorcycle from tipping forwards.

Dismantle the steering head assembly as described in Chapter 4 to permit a thorough examination of the bearings. Reassemble, packing the bearings with medium-weight grease, then adjust the free play as described below.

Grasp the front fork legs near the wheel spindle and push and pull firmly in a fore and aft direction. If play is evident between the upper and lower steering yokes and the head lug casting, the steering head bearings are in need of adjustment. Imprecise handling or a tendency for the front forks to judder may be caused by this fault.

To adjust the bearings, loosen the pinch bolt which passes through the rear of the upper yoke. Immediately below the upper yoke, on the steering stem, are two peg nuts, the upper being a locknut and the lower the adjuster nut. Using a C-spanner loosen the upper nut. Tighten the lower peg nut a little at a time until all play is taken up. Do not overtighten the nut. It is possible to place a pressure of several tons on the head bearings by overtightening even though the handlebars may seem to turn quite freely. Overtight bearings will cause the machine to roll at low speeds and give imprecise steering. Adjustment is correct if there is no play in the bearings and the handlebars swing to full lock either side when the machine is on the centre stand with the front wheel clear of the ground. Only a light tap on each end should cause the handlebars to swing.

Fit new element. Note spring and washer

Prime filter housing and then refit to engine

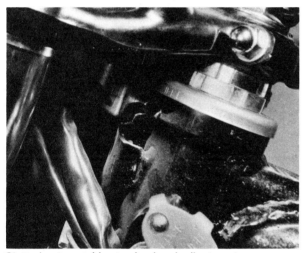

Slotted nuts provide steering head adjustment

4   Swinging arm pivot bearings

Dismantle the swinging arm assembly as described in Chapter 4 Section 10 and remove the pivot bearings for cleaning and examination. If wear, damage or corrosion is evident the bearings should be renewed. Install the bearings after packing with medium weight grease.

5   Wheel bearings

Dismantle and check the wheel bearings as described in Chapter 5 Sections 9 and 11.

Lubricate the bearings with a medium weight high melting point grease, taking care not to over-pack them. Clean and re-pack the speedometer drive gearbox with a lithium-based grease.

General adjustments and examination

---

1   Clutch adjustment

The intervals at which the clutch should be adjusted will depend on the style of riding and the conditions under which the machine is used.

Adjust the clutch in two stages to ensure smooth operation as follows:

Remove the clutch adjustment cover after releasing its two retaining screws. Loosen the locknut on the handlebar adjuster and screw the adjuster in to give plenty of slack in the cable. Slacken the locknut on the clutch adjuster screw in the lifting mechanism and screw the adjuster inwards until a small amount of resistance is felt, then back off the adjuster by a quarter turn. Tighten the locknut without turning the adjuster screw. The play between the clutch operating pushrod and the lifter mechanism is now correct. Refit the cover. Adjust the cable until there is about 2 – 3 mm (0.08 – 0.12 in) free play measured between the handlebar control lever stock and the control lever itself.

2   Checking brake pad wear

Brake pad wear depends largely on the conditions in which the machine is ridden and at what speed. It is difficult therefore to give precise inspection intervals, but it follows that pad wear should be checked more frequently on a hard ridden machine.

The condition of each pad can be checked easily whilst still in situ on the machine. The pads have a red groove around their outer periphery which can be seen if the small inspection cover in each caliper is lifted. If wear has reduced either or both pads in one caliper down to the red line the pads should be renewed as a pair. In practice, if one set of front pads requires renewal, it will be necessary to renew the other pair. The rear disc brake pads should be checked for wear in the same way as that adopted for the front brakes. The renewal procedure is similar also.

Each set of pads may be removed with the wheel in place by detaching the caliper. There is no need to disconnect the brake hose. Unscrew the two bolts which pass through the fork leg into the caliper support bracket. Lift the assembly off the brake disc and remove the single bolt which holds the caliper unit to the bracket. Unscrew the single crosshead screw from the inner face of the caliper, noting that this screw acts as a locator for the pads. Pull the support bracket from the main unit and lift out the pads. Note the various shims and their positions. The anti-chatter spring fitted between the pad and piston is fitted with the arrow pointing in the direction of wheel rotation.

Fit new pads by reversing the dismantling procedure. If difficulty is encountered when fitting the caliper over the disc, due to the reduced distance between the pads, use a wooden lever to push the piston side pad inwards.

Front pads can be removed as shown

Rear caliper released to expose pads

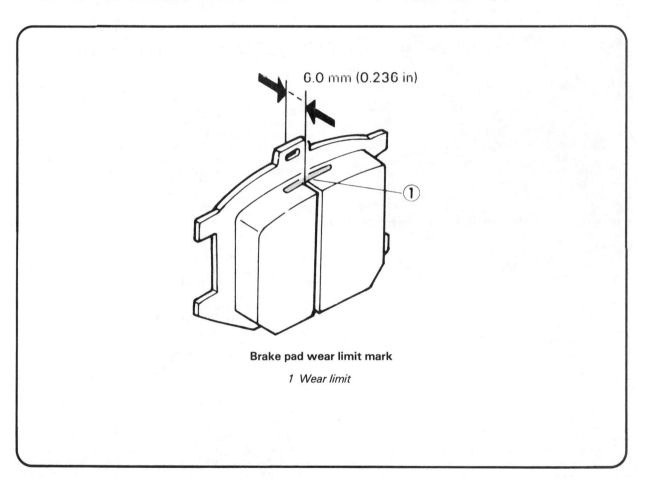

6.0 mm (0.236 in)

①

Brake pad wear limit mark

1 Wear limit

Quick glance
maintenance adjustments and capacities

Engine/transmission oil capacity
Dry:
    UK models .... 4.2 lit (7.39 Imp pint)
    US models* .... 4.0 lit (8.46 US pint)
At oil change:
    UK models .... 3.2 lit (5.63 Imp pint)
    US models* .... 3.0 lit (6.34 US pint)
At oil and filter change:
    UK models .... 3.7 lit (6.51 Imp pint)
    US models* .... 3.5 lit (7.40 US pint)
US models fitted with oil coolers should use UK capacities.

Middle gear case capacity .... 0.36 lit (12/13 US/Imp fl oz)

Final drive box capacity .... 0.30 lit (10/11 US/Imp fl oz)

Sparking plug
    Type .... NGK BP8ES or Champion N-8Y
    Gap .... 0.7 – 0.8 mm (0.028 – 0.032 in)

Front forks
Oil capacity (per leg):
    E, F and G (UK) .... 212 cc
    G (US) .... 241 cc
    SF .... 225 cc
    SG .... 210 cc
Air pressure:
    Standard .... 5.7 psi (0.4 kg/cm²)
    Range .... 0 – 36 psi (0 – 2.5 kg/cm²)

Tyre pressures

	Front	Rear
US models:		
Up to 198 lb (90 kg) load	26 psi (1.8 kg/cm²)	28 psi (2.0 kg/cm²)
198 – 337 lb (90 – 153 kg) load	28 psi (2.0 kg/cm²)	36 psi (2.5 kg/cm²)
337 – 478 lb (153 – 217 kg) load	28 psi (2.0 kg/cm²)	40 psi (2.8 kg/cm²)
Continuous high-speed riding	36 psi (2.5 kg/cm²)	40 psi (2.8 kg/cm²)
UK models:		
Up to 324 lb (147 kg) load	28 psi (2.0 kg/cm²)	36 psi (2.5 kg/cm²)
324 – 463 lb (147 – 210 kg) load	28 psi (2.0 kg/cm²)	40 psi (2.8 kg/cm²)
Continuous high-speed riding	36 psi (2.5 kg/cm²)	40 psi (2.8 kg/cm²)

Recommended lubricants

Component	Lubricant
Engine/transmission	
Not below 5°C (40°F)	SAE 20W/40 SE motor oil
Not above 15°C (60°F)	SAE 10W/30 SE motor oil
Middle gear case and final drive box	
Not below 5°C (40°F)	SAE 90 hypoid gear oil
Not above 15°C (60°F)	SAE 80 hypoid gear oil
All weather	SAE 80W/90 hypoid gear oil
Front forks	
UK models	SAE 10W/30 motor oil
US models	SAE 10 motor or fork oil or equivalent
Drive shaft joint	Molybdenum disulphide grease, type NLG1 – 2M or equivalent
Swinging arm bearings	Medium-weight wheel bearing grease
Wheel bearings	Medium-weight wheel bearing grease
Steering head bearings	Medium-weight wheel bearing grease
General lubrication	Light machine oil

Castrol Lubricants

Castrol Engine Oils

Castrol Grand Prix

Castrol Grand Prix 10W/40 four stroke motorcycle oil is a superior quality lubricant designed for air or water cooled four stroke motorcycle engines, operating under all conditions.

Castrol TT Two Stroke Oil

Castrol TT Two Stroke oil is a high quality lubricant specially formulated for both air and water cooled two stroke motorcycle engines. It is readily miscible with fuel and is designed to protect against malfunction of sparking plugs, build up of combustion chamber deposits, seizure and scuffing of pistons and exhaust port blocking.

Castrol R40

Castrol R40 is a castor-based lubricant specially designed for racing and high speed rallying, providing the ultimate in lubrication. Castrol R40 should never be mixed with mineral-based oils, and further additives are unnecessary and undesirable. A specialist oil for limited applications.

Castrol Gear Oils

Castrol Hypoy EP90

An SAE 90 mineral-based extreme pressure multi-purpose gear oil, primarily recommended for the lubrication of conventional hypoid differential units operating under moderate service conditions. Suitable also for some gearbox applications.

Castrol Hypoy Light EP 80W

A mineral-based extreme pressure multi-purpose gear oil with similar applications to Castrol Hypoy but an SAE rating of 80W and suitable where the average ambient temperatures are between 32°F and 10°F. Also recommended for manual transmissions where manufacturers specify an extreme pressure SAE 80 gear oil.

Castrol Hypoy B EP80 and B EP90

Are mineral-based extreme pressure multi-purpose gear oils with similar applications to Castrol Hypoy, operating in average ambient temperatures between 90°F and 32°F. The Castrol Hypoy B range provides added protection for gears operating under very stringent service conditions.

Castrol Greases

Castrol LM Grease

A multi-purpose high melting point lithium-based grease suitable for most automotive applications, including chassis and wheel bearing lubrication.

Castrol MS3 Grease

A high melting point lithium-based grease containing molybdenum disulphide. Suitable for heavy duty chassis application and some CV joints where a lithium-based grease is specified.

Castrol BNS Grease

A bentone-based non melting high temperature grease for ultra severe applications such as race and rally car front wheel bearings.

Other Castrol Products

Castrol Girling Universal Brake and Clutch Fluid

A special high performance brake and clutch fluid with an advanced vapour lock performance. It is the only fluid recommended by Girling Limited and surpasses the performance requirements of the current SAE J1703 Specification and the United States Federal Motor Vehicle Safety Standard No. 116 DOT 3 Specification.
In addition, Castrol Girling Universal Brake and Clutch fluid fully meets the requirements of the major vehicle manufacturers.

Castrol Fork Oil

A specially formulated fluid for the front forks of motorcycles, providing excellent damping and load carrying properties.

Castrol Chain Lubricant

A specially developed motorcycle chain lubricant containing non-drip, anti corrosion and water resistant additives which afford excellent penetration, lubrication and protection of exposed chains.

Castrol Everyman Oil

A light-bodied machine oil containing anti-corrosion additives for both household use and cycle lubrication.

Castrol DWF

A de-watering fluid which displaces moisture, lubricates and protects against corrosion of all metals. Innumerable uses in both car and home. Available in 400gm and 200gm aerosol cans.

Castrol Easing Fluid

A rust releasing fluid for corroded nuts, locks, hinges and all mechanical joints. Also available in 250ml tins.

Castrol Antifreeze

Contains anti-corrosion additives with ethylene glycol. Recommended for the cooling system of all petrol and diesel engines.

Working conditions and tools

When a major overhaul is contemplated, it is important that a clean, well-lit working space is available, equipped with a workbench and vice, and with space for laying out or storing the dismantled assemblies in an orderly manner where they are unlikely to be disturbed. The use of a good workshop will give the satisfaction of work done in comfort and without haste, where there is little chance of the machine being dismantled and reassembled in anything other than clean surroundings. Unfortunately, these ideal working conditions are not always practicable and under these latter circumstances when improvisation is called for, extra care and time will be needed.

The other essential requirement is a comprehensive set of good quality tools. Quality is of prime importance since cheap tools will prove expensive in the long run if they slip or break and damage the components to which they are applied. A good quality tool will last a long time, and more than justify the cost. The basis of any tool kit is a set of open-ended spanners, which can be used on almost any part of the machine to which there is reasonable access. A set of ring spanners makes a useful addition, since they can be used on nuts that are very tight or where access is restricted. Where the cost has to be kept within reasonable bounds, a compromise can be effected with a set of combination spanners – open-ended at one end and having a ring of the same size on the other end. Socket spanners may also be considered a good investment, a basic $\frac{3}{8}$ in or $\frac{1}{2}$ in drive kit comprising a ratchet handle and a small number of socket heads, if money is limited. Additional sockets can be purchased, as and when they are required. Provided they are slim in profile, sockets will reach nuts or bolts that are deeply recessed. When purchasing spanners of any kind, make sure the correct size standard is purchased. Almost all machines manufactured outside the UK and the USA have metric nuts and bolts, whilst those produced in Britain have BSF or BSW sizes. The standard used in the USA is AF, which is also found on some of the later British machines. Other tools that should be included in the kit are a range of crosshead screwdrivers, a pair of pliers and a hammer.

When considering the purchase of tools, it should be remembered that by carrying out the work oneself, a large proportion of the normal repair cost, made up by labour charges, will be saved. The economy made on even a minor overhaul will go a long way towards the improvement of a tool kit.

In addition to the basic tool kit, certain additional tools can prove invaluable when they are close to hand, to help speed up a multitude of repetitive jobs. For example, an impact screwdriver will ease the removal of screws that have been tightened by a similar tool during assembly, without risk of damaging the screw heads. And, of course, it can be used again to retighten the screws, to ensure an oil or airtight seal results. Circlip pliers have their uses too, since gear pinions, shafts and similar components are frequently retained by circlips that are not too easily displaced by a screwdriver. There are two types of circlip pliers, one for internal and one for external circlips. They may also have straight or right-angled jaws.

One of the most useful of all tools is the torque wrench, a form of spanner that can be adjusted to slip when a measured amount of force is applied to any bolt or nut. Torque wrench settings are given in almost every modern workshop or service manual, where the extent is given to which a complex component, such as a cylinder head, can be tightened without fear of distortion or leakage. The tightening of bearing caps is yet another example. Overtightening will stretch or even break bolts, necessitating extra work to extract the broken portions.

As may be expected, the more sophisticated the machine, the greater is the number of tools likely to be required if it is to be kept in first class condition by the home mechanic. Unfortunately there are certain jobs which cannot be accomplished successfully without the correct equipment and although there is invariably a specialist who will undertake the work for a fee, the home mechanic will have to dig more deeply in his pocket for the purchase of similar equipment if he does not wish to employ the services of others. Here a word of caution is necessary, since some of these jobs are best left to the expert. Although an electrical multimeter of the Avo type will prove helpful in tracing electrical faults, in inexperienced hands it may irrevocably damage some of the electrical components if a test current is passed through them in the wrong direction. This can apply to the synchronisation of twin or multiple carburettors too, where a certain amount of expertise is needed when setting them up with vacuum gauges. These are, however, exceptions. Some instruments, such as a strobe lamp, are virtually essential when checking the timing of a machine powered by a CDI ignition system. In short, do not purchase any of these special items unless you have the experience to use them correctly.

Although this manual shows how components can be removed and replaced without the use of special service tools (unless absolutely essential), it is worthwhile giving consideration to the purchase of the more commonly used tools if the machine is regarded as a long term purchase. Whilst the alternative methods suggested will remove and replace parts without risk of damage, the use of the special tools recommended and sold by the manufacturer will invariably save time.

Chapter 1 Engine, clutch and gearbox

Contents

Specifications

Engine

Type	Four cylinder, dohc, air cooled four-stroke
Bore	71.5 mm (2.815 in)
Stroke	68.6 mm (2.701 in)
Capacity	1102cc (67.25 cu in)
Compression ratio:	
G/SG(US) models	9.0 : 1
All others	9.2 : 1

Cylinder block
Type .... Aluminium alloy, cast iron liners
Standard bore .... 71.5 – 71.52 mm (2.8150 – 2.8158 in)
Wear limit .... 71.6 mm (2.8189 in)
Taper limit .... 0.05 mm (0.0020 in)
Ovality limit .... 0.01 mm (0.0004 in)
Bore to piston clearance:
    G/SG(US) models .... 0.050 – 0.055 mm (0.0020 – 0.0022 in)
    All others .... 0.040 – 0.045 mm (0.0016 – 0.0018 in)
Wear limit .... 0.1 mm (0.0039 in)

Pistons
1st oversize .... 71.75 mm (2.8248 in)
2nd oversize .... 72.00 mm (2.8346 in)
3rd oversize .... 72.25 mm (2.8445 in)
4th oversize .... 72.50 mm (2.8543 in)

Piston rings
Type:
    Top .... Plain
    2nd .... Tapered
    Oil 2-rail
End gap (installed):
    Top .... 0.2 – 0.4 mm (0.0079 – 0.016 in)
    Wear limit .... 1.0 mm (0.0394 in)
    2nd .... 0.2 – 0.4 mm (0.0079 – 0.016 in)
    Wear limit .... 1.0 mm (0.0394 in)
    Oil .... 0.2 – 0.9 mm (0.0079 – 0.0035 in)
    Wear limit .... 1.5 mm (0.0591 in)
Side clearance (ring to groove)
    Top .... 0.04 – 0.08 mm (0.0016 – 0.0031 in)
    Wear limit .... 0.15 mm (0.0059 in)
    2nd .... 0.03 – 0.07 mm (0.0012 – 0.0028 in)
    Wear limit .... 0.15 mm (0.0059 in)
    Oil .... not applicable

Valves
Inlet head diameter:
    G/SG(US) models .... 38.0 mm (1.496 in)
    All others .... 36.0 – 36.2 mm (1.4173 – 1.4253 in)

Exhaust head diameter:
    G/SG(US) models .... 32.0 mm (1.260 in)
    All others .... 31.0 – 31.2 mm (1.2205 – 1.2285 in)

Valve stem outside diameter
    Inlet .... $7.0\,{}^{-0.010}_{-0.025}$ mm $(0.2756\,{}^{-0.0004}_{-0.0010}$ in)
    Exhaust .... $7.0\,{}^{-0.025}_{-0.040}$ mm $(0.2756\,{}^{-0.0010}_{-0.0016}$ in)

Valve guide internal bore
    Inlet .... 7.0 – 7.015 mm (0.2756 – 0.2762 in)
    Exhaust .... 7.0 – 7.015 mm (0.2756 – 0.2762 in)
Stem to guide clearance
    Inlet .... 0.010 – 0.040 mm (0.0004 – 0.0016 in)
    Wear limit .... 0.10 mm (0.004 in)
    Exhaust .... 0.025 – 0.055 mm (0.0010 – 0.0022 in)
    Wear limit .... 0.12 mm (0.005 in)
Valve clearance (engine cold)
    Inlet:
        G(US)/SG models .... 0.11 – 0.15 mm (0.004 – 0.006 in)
        All others .... 0.16 – 0.20 mm (0.006 – 0.008 in)
        Exhaust .... 0.21 – 0.25 mm (0.008 – 0.010 in)

Valve springs
Free length:
    Inner .... 35.6 mm (1.402 in)
    Outer .... 39.9 mm (1.571 in)

Adjustment pads (shims)
Available sizes .... 2.00 – 3.20 mm (0.079 – 0.126 in)
                                       in 0.05 mm (0.002 in) increments

Camshafts

Overall height:

Inlet	36.805 ± 0.05 mm (1.449 ± 0.002 in)
Wear limit	36.65 mm (1.443 in)

Exhaust:

G/SG(US) models	36.80 ± 0.05 mm (1.449 ± 0.002 in)
Wear limit	36.65 mm (1.443 in)
All others	36.305 ± 0.05 mm (1.429 ± 0.002 in)
Wear limit	36.15 mm (1.423 in)

Base circle diameter

Inlet and exhaust:

G/SG(US) models	28.310 ± 0.05 mm (1.115 ± 0.002 in)
Wear limit	28.19 mm (1.110 in)
All others	28.341 ± 0.05 mm (1.116 ± 0.002 in)
Wear limit	28.19 mm (1.110 in)

Cam lift:

Inlet	8.805 mm (0.347 in)

Exhaust:

G/SG(US) models	8.800 mm (0.347 in)
All others	8.305 mm (0.327 in)
Bearing surface diameter	24.967 – 24.980 mm (0.9830 – 0.9835 in)
Camshaft to bearing cap clearance	0.020 – 0.054 mm (0.0008 – 0.0021 in)
Wear limit	0.160 mm (0.006 in)
Camshaft runout (maximum)	0.1 mm (0.004 in)

Crankshaft

Main bearing clearance	0.035 – 0.059 mm (0.0014 – 0.0023 in)
Big-end bearing clearance	0.035 – 0.059 mm (0.0014 – 0.0023 in)
Small-end clearance	0.042 – 0.064 mm (0.0017 – 0.0025 in)
Maximum crankshaft runout	0.04 mm (0.0016 in)

Clutch

Number of plates:

Plain	7
Friction	8 (SF model, 7)
Number of springs	6

Friction plate thickness:

SF model	2.6 mm (0.10 in)
Wear limit	2.4 mm (0.09 in)
All others	3.0 mm (0.12 in)
Wear limit	2.8 mm (0.11 in)
Plain plate maximum warpage	0.1 mm (0.0039 in)
Spring free length	42.8 mm (1.685 in)
Wear limit	41.8 mm (1.646 in)

Gearbox

Type	5-speed constant mesh

Ratios:

1st	2.235 : 1 (38/17)
2nd	1.625 : 1 (39/24)
3rd	1.285 : 1 (36/28)
4th	1.032 : 1 (32/31)
5th	0.882 : 1 (30/34)

Primary drive

Type	Hy-Vo chain and gear

Teeth ratio:

Chain	25/25
Gear	58/35
Overall primary ratio	1.657 : 1

Secondary drive

Type	Shaft

Ratios:

Spur gear	0.936 : 1 (44/47)
Middle gear case	1.056 : 1 (19/18)
Final drive case	3.3 : 1 (33/10)

Torque wrench settings

Component	kgf m	lbf ft
Camshaft cap nuts	1.0	7.2
Cylinder head nuts	3.5	25.3
Cylinder head lower nuts	2.0	14.5
Cylinder head cover bolts	1.0	7.2
Cam sprocket bolts	2.0	14.5
Connecting rod bolts	3.9	28.2
Sparking plugs	2.0	14.5
Crankcase bolts:		
6 mm	1.2	8.7
8 mm	2.4	17.5
Alternator rotor bolt	6.5	47.0
Alternator stator bolts	1.0	7.2
Clutch nut	7.0	50.6
Primary drive pinion	7.0	50.6
Oil filter centre bolt	3.2	23.0
Engine drain plug	4.3	31.0
Middle gear drain plug	4.3	31.0
Oil pipe union bolts	2.0	14.5
Oil pressure switch	2.0	14.5
Neutral gear switch	2.0	14.5
Engine mounting bolts:		
Front	6.7	48.5
Rear	10.0	72.3

1 General description

The engine unit fitted to the various XS1100 models is a double overhead camshaft transverse four cylinder, built in unit with the primary transmission and gearbox. The cylinder head is of conventional light alloy construction featuring two valves per cylinder operated directly from the two camshafts via bucket type cam followers with shim adjustment pads. The camshafts run in plain bearing surfaces formed by detachable caps and by the cylinder head material itself. The camshafts are driven by a central Hy-Vo camshaft chain running from the crankshaft centre through a tunnel between cylinders 2 and 3.

The horizontally split crankcase incorporates a one-piece forged crankshaft supported by five renewable plain main bearings. The connecting rods have split big-end eyes, also with renewable bearing shells. A broad Hy-Vo primary chain runs from the centre of the crankshaft to a primary shaft mounted to the rear of, and parallel to, the cylinder block.

A gear mounted on the end of the primary shaft drives a corresponding gear on the outside of the clutch outer drum. The wet multiplate clutch runs on the end of the gearbox mainshaft. Power is transmitted through the clutch to the five-speed constant mesh gearbox. The layshaft drives a short output shaft and gear which is splined internally to accept the shaft from the intermediate, or middle, gearbox.

The latter is a self-contained unit which can be removed independently of the rest of the crankcase internals. Heavy bevel gears turn the drive through 90° so that a connection to the final drive shaft can be made.

2 Operations with engine/gearbox in frame

It is not necessary to remove the engine unit from the frame in order to dismantle the following items:
1 Right and left crankcase covers.
2 Clutch assembly and gear selector components (external).
3 Oil pump and filter.
4 Alternator and starter motor.
5 Cylinder head and cylinder head cover.
6 Cylinder block, pistons and rings.

7 Ignition pickup and starter motor clutch.
8 Middle gear casing assembly.

It should be noted that where a number of the above items require attention it can often be easier to remove the engine unit and carry out the dismantling work with the unit on a workbench.

3 Operations with engine/gearbox unit removed from frame

As previously described the crankshaft and gearbox assemblies are housed within a common casing. Any work carried out on either of these two major assemblies will necessitate removal of the engine from the frame so that the crankcases can be separated.

4 Removing the engine/gearbox unit

1 Place the machine on its centre stand making sure that it is standing firmly. Although by no means essential it is useful to raise the machine a number of feet above floor level by placing it on a long bench or horizontal ramp. This will enable most of the work to be carried out in an upright position, which is eminently more comfortable than crouching or kneeling in a puddle of sump oil.
2 Place a suitable receptacle below the crankcase and drain off the engine oil. The sump plug lies just to the rear of the oil filter housing. The oil will drain at a higher rate if the engine has been warmed up previously, thereby heating and thinning the oil. Approximately 5½ pints (3 litres) should drain out. Undo the oil filter chamber bolt and remove the chamber and filter, noting that the chamber holds approximately 1 pint. If the middle gear case is to be removed this too should be drained. The drain plug is in the casing rear wall.
3 Slacken the two sleeve nuts which retain the dual seat and slide them forward to free the bolts. The seat can now be lifted clear. Separate the fuel gauge (or lamp) sender lead at the connector at the rear of the tank and release the breather and fuel feed pipes from their stubs. Slacken the single rubber-mounted bolt at the rear of the tank and lift it upwards and rearwards to clear the front mounting rubbers. Place the tank in a safe place to avoid any risk of damage to the paint finish.

4   It will be necessary to remove the ignition ballast resistor and horn from the underside of the top frame tubes because these would otherwise foul the engine. The ballast resistor is retained by a single bolt to a small lug on the frame and can be lodged clear of the engine once released. The single horn is suspended between the frame tubes and should be removed in a similar manner. On machines fitted with twin horns, the two units should be removed complete with their mounting bracket. Note that this entails the removal of the oil cooler, where fitted. See paragraph 13. Disconnect the sparking plug caps and lodge them clear of the engine.

5   Remove the two side panels, noting that the left-hand panel is locked to the frame, whilst the right-hand item is a simple push-fit. Isolate the electrical system by disconnecting one of the battery leads. The battery need not be removed unless it is expected that the machine is to be unused for an extended length of time. If this is the case, the battery should be stored safely and given an external charge every two weeks. Note the breather pipe which is a push fit on the union at the left of the battery.

6   Locate the brake light switch which is mounted inboard of the right-hand footrest mounting plate and disconnect the switch operating spring. It will now be necessary to release the alloy footrest plates from the machine. These are secured by bolts, one of which doubles as the engine rear mounting bolt. Note that the rearmost bolt on each side passes through a rubber mounting to the silencer support bracket. The right-hand footrest plate carries the rear brake pedal assembly, and this can be removed along with the plate. As the assembly is removed the brake operating rod will drop clear of the master cylinder and remain attached to the brake pedal.

7   Slacken the clip which secures the two halves of the collector box. This runs beneath the frame and connects the two halves of the exhaust system. Release the clamps which secure the centre pair of exhaust pipes to the main system. Release the two nuts which secure each of the exhaust pipe retainers to the cylinder head. Once freed, disengage the inner pair of pipes (cylinders 2 and 3) and remove them from the machine.

8   The two halves of the system can now be removed by lowering the silencers and pulling the assembly apart at the collector box joint. If necessary, the system can be released with the inner pair of pipes attached, though it will be necessary to place the side stand down to facilitate removal of the left-hand system.

9   Release the four wing bolts that pass up through the base of the air cleaner casing and lift it away together with the filter element. Slacken the four hose clips which secure the air cleaner hoses to the carburettor intakes. Release the single central bolt which secures the air cleaner support bracket to the upper frame tubes, followed by the bolt at each side of the rear of the air cleaner casing. Pull off the crankcase breather hose and the carburettor vent pipes which are connected to the air cleaner casing. The casing will now be free to be pulled back to clear the carburettors if necessary, this position can be held by securing the upper mounting bolt.

10   Pull off the vacuum advance pipe where it joins the No 2 carburettor adaptor and release the clutch cable from its retaining clip on the right-hand side of the carburettor bank. Slacken the carburettor mounting clips and pull the instruments back to clear the intake adaptors. Manoeuvre the bank of instruments to one side until the throttle cable becomes accessible. Disengage the cable and place the carburettors to one side. Although it is not essential, it was found more convenient to remove the upper section of the air cleaner casing to provide more manoeuvring room.

11   Release the clutch release mechanism inspection cover from the right-hand outer casing. Slacken off the clutch cable adjustment to give plenty of free play in the cable. If necessary, the cable can be disconnected at the handlebar lever. Release the lower end of the cable at the actuating arm, noting that the small metal tang which prevents its escape in normal operation should be bent clear. Lodge the cable clear of the engine.

12   Trace the heavy starter motor cable back to the solenoid terminal on the right-hand side of the machine. Displace the protective boot and release the cable from the solenoid terminal. The cable should be pushed back through to the engine and arranged so that it will not foul during removal. Trace the ignition and alternator harnesses back to their connector blocks. These reside behind the panel which carries the fuse holders, and this can be removed after releasing its three mounting bolts, if desired. In practice, it was found simpler to pull the connectors clear of the frame to allow the wiring to be separated. Position the harness carefully, noting that a check should be made to ensure that it will not become fouled during removal. Release the engine earth strap which runs from the rear of the crankcase, near the drive shaft gaiter, to the adjacent frame brace tube. The earth strap is best released at the frame end where it is held by a single cross-head screw.

13   On machines fitted with an oil cooler it will be necessary to release the union blocks at the crankcase. These are located on the front underside of the engine, each being retained by two Allen bolts. Note that a drain tray will be required to catch the residual oil which will be released as the unions are freed. It may prove helpful to remove the oil cooler and hoses completely, although this is by no means essential.

14   Roll back the spring retainer which secures the rubber gaiter between the middle gear case and the drive shaft casing. The gaiter can now be displaced to expose the four retaining bolts. Mark the flange edges as an aid to re-assembly. Turn the rear wheel until one of the bolts is within reach, then ask an assistant to apply fully the rear brake whilst the bolt is removed. Repeat this operation with the three remaining bolts to free the drive coupling.

15   Remove the single upper and two lower engine front mounting bolts to allow the engine to rest in the frame cradle. Note that the single rear bolt will have been removed when the footrest plates were detached. Dismantle the front engine plates to provide the extra clearance necessary during the removal operation. A minimum of two people will be required to lift the engine unit clear of the frame. The engine unit is no lightweight and its bulk and restricted manoeuvring room compound the problem. Position a stout wooden crate or a similar support to the right-hand side of the machine so that the unit can be swung clear of the frame and rested. Make one final check to ensure that nothing will impede removal, then lift the engine out to the right-hand side.

4.2 Sump drain plug is located adjacent to oil filter

4.3a Seat is retained by two extended nuts (arrowed)

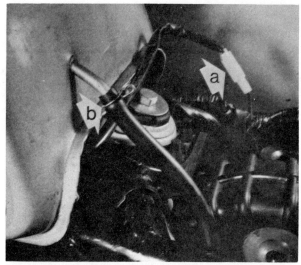

4.3b A: Fuel gauge connector B: Fuel tank breather pipe (arrowed)

4.3c Tank is secured by a single rubber-mounted bolt

4.3d Release vacuum and fuel feed pipes from tap

4.6 Disconnect brake switch spring and release pedal assembly

4.9a Air filter casing is retained by four wing bolts (arrowed)

4.9b Slacken upper bolt and slide casing rearwards (arrowed)

4.10 Disengage carburettors and release operating cable

4.11 Remove inspection cover and release clutch cable

4.12a Separate wiring at connector blocks

4.12b Release single screw to free engine earth strap (arrowed)

4.13a Release oil cooler unions (where fitted) ...

4.13b ... and remove oil cooler and pipes from machine (arrowed)

4.14 Release gaiter and remove drive shaft flange bolts

4.15a Remove engine lower front mounting bolts ...

4.15b ... and dismantle upper bolt and engine plates

5   Dismantling the engine/gearbox unit: general

1   Before commencing work on the engine unit, the external surfaces should be cleaned thoroughly. A motorcycle has very little protection from road grit and other foreign matter which sooner or later will find its way into the dismantled engine if this simple precaution is not carried out.
2   One of the proprietary cleaning compounds such as Gunk or Jizer can be used to good effect, especially if the compound is worked into the film of grease and oil before it is washed away. In the USA Gumout degreaser is an alternative.
3   It is essential when washing down to make sure that water does not enter the carburettors or the electrics particularly now that these parts are more vulnerable.
4   Collect together an adequate set of tools in addition to those of the tool roll carried under the seat.
5   Avoid force in any of the operations. There is generally a good reason why an item is difficult to remove, probably due to the use of the wrong procedure or sequence of operations.

6   Dismantling will be made easier if a simple engine stand is constructed that will correspond with the engine mounting points. This arrangement will permit the complete unit to be clamped rigidly to the workbench, leaving both hands free for dismantling.

6   Dismantling the engine/gearbox unit: removing the cylinder head cover and camshafts

1   The camshafts may be removed with the engine removed from the frame and on a workbench, or with the unit installed in the frame. In the latter case it will be necessary to remove the fuel tank, ignition ballast resistor and horn assembly as described in Section 4 paragraphs 3 and 4.
2   Slacken the 20 Allen screws which secure the cylinder head cover, noting that the centre rear screw also secures the throttle cable clip. Note its position as an aid during reassembly. The cover may now be removed. Where

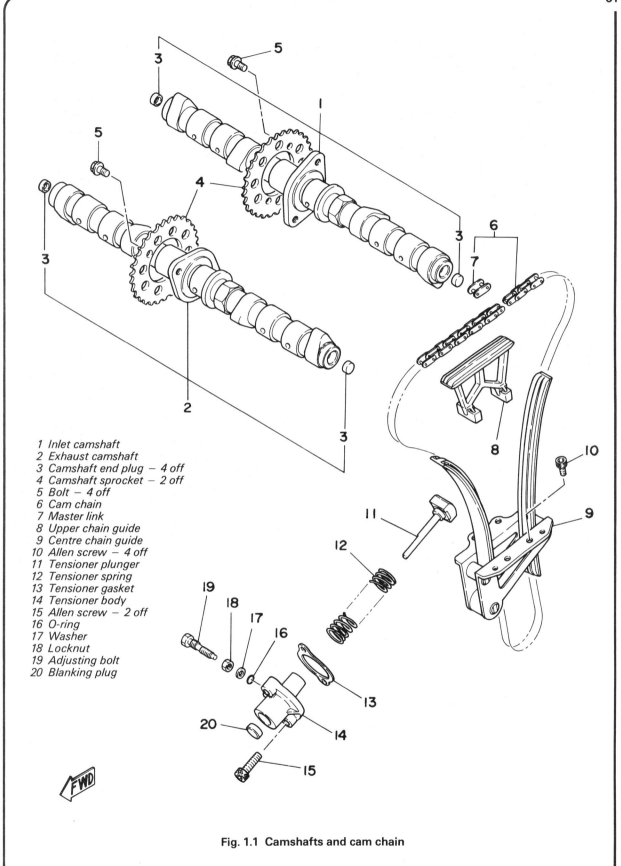

1 Inlet camshaft
2 Exhaust camshaft
3 Camshaft end plug — 4 off
4 Camshaft sprocket — 2 off
5 Bolt — 4 off
6 Cam chain
7 Master link
8 Upper chain guide
9 Centre chain guide
10 Allen screw — 4 off
11 Tensioner plunger
12 Tensioner spring
13 Tensioner gasket
14 Tensioner body
15 Allen screw — 2 off
16 O-ring
17 Washer
18 Locknut
19 Adjusting bolt
20 Blanking plug

Fig. 1.1 Camshafts and cam chain

necessary, tap around the gasket face with a soft-faced mallet to aid separation. Remove the timing inspection cover from the crankshaft left-hand end. This exposes a large square boss which is provided to allow the crankshaft to be turned for timing purposes, using a 19 mm open-ended spanner. Note that the XS1100 engine runs 'backwards'; that is, clockwise when viewed from the left-hand end.

3   Remove the cam chain tensioner plunger assembly from the centre of the tunnel. It is secured by two bolts. Turn the crankshaft until two of the four camshaft sprocket bolts are visible and remove them. Repeat the procedure for the remaining pair of bolts, thus freeing the sprockets. Note that the crankshaft must not be turned after this stage has been reached. Some of the valves will be open, and it is possible for the pistons to contact them, bending the valve stems.

4   Displace the sprockets to the right so that they drop free of the shouldered portion of the camshafts. The resulting slack will allow the central chain guide to be removed from between the two sprockets.

5   The camshafts are retained by five bearing caps each, these being marked I-1 to I-5 in the case of the inlet camshaft, and E-1 to E-5 for the exhaust camshaft. An arrow on each cap faces towards the alternator (right-hand) side of the engine. Slacken the camshaft cap bolts evenly and progressively in a diagonal sequence to release each camshaft. Disengage each camshaft from its sprocket and remove both components. Take great care not to allow the camshaft chain to drop into the crankcase. The chain may be secured by slipping a screwdriver or a length of wire through the end of the loop.

6   Great care must be taken at this stage to prevent the cam followers and shims from becoming mixed up. If they are to be removed, obtain eight small boxes or bags, marking each one to denote the valve and its position (E-1, E-2 and so on). Alternatively, if the cylinder head components do not need to be disturbed, two lengths of dowel can be fitted as shown in the accompanying photograph to preclude the accidental loss of shims.

6.3a Remove cam chain tensioner assembly

6.3b Release cam sprockets and remove bearing caps

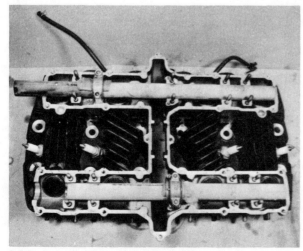

6.6 Fit lengths of dowel to retain shims

7   Dismantling the engine/gearbox unit: removing the cylinder head

1   The cylinder head can be removed with the engine unit in or out of the frame. In the former instance, refer to the opening remarks in Section 6 of this Chapter. In both cases, the camshafts must be removed as described in Section 6. Slacken the banjo union bolts which secure the camshaft oil feed pipe to the cylinder head and crankcase. Lift the pipe away, taking care not to lose the copper sealing washers which can be re-used if in good condition.

2   The cylinder head is secured by a total of 14 nuts, two of which are fitted from the underside of the cylinder head, at the centre of the cam chain tunnel. These should be removed first, and then the remaining twelve slackened in the reverse order shown in the accompanying illustration. Slacken each nut by half a turn to start with, then repeat the sequence until all twelve are slack. This gradual slackening is essential if cylinder head distortion is to be avoided. Run all the nuts off their studs.

3   The cylinder head may prove to be firmly stuck to the cylinder block by the gasket, in which case the area around the joint can be carefully tapped with a soft-faced mallet to encourage separation. Take great care not to damage the fragile cooling fins.

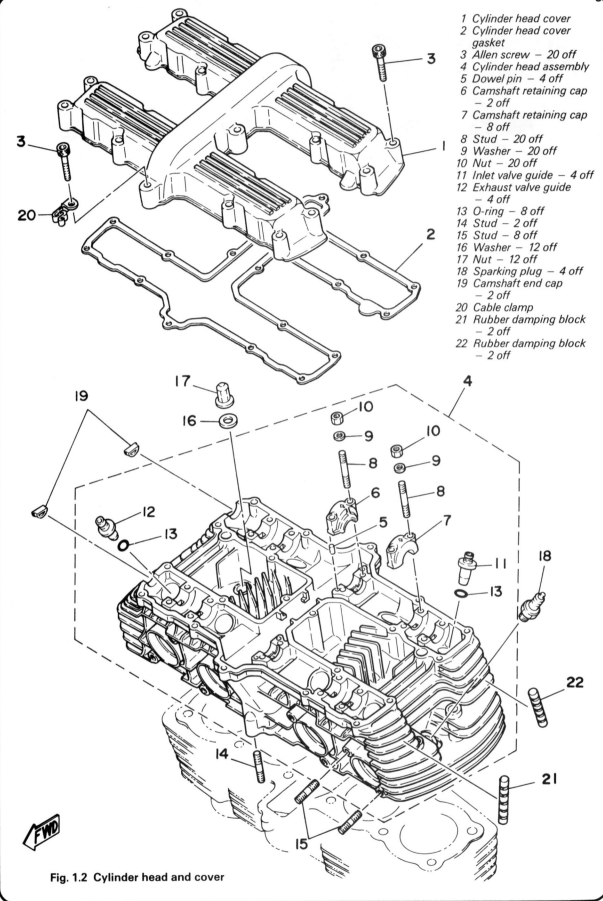

1 Cylinder head cover
2 Cylinder head cover gasket
3 Allen screw – 20 off
4 Cylinder head assembly
5 Dowel pin – 4 off
6 Camshaft retaining cap – 2 off
7 Camshaft retaining cap – 8 off
8 Stud – 20 off
9 Washer – 20 off
10 Nut – 20 off
11 Inlet valve guide – 4 off
12 Exhaust valve guide – 4 off
13 O-ring – 8 off
14 Stud – 2 off
15 Stud – 8 off
16 Washer – 12 off
17 Nut – 12 off
18 Sparking plug – 4 off
19 Camshaft end cap – 2 off
20 Cable clamp
21 Rubber damping block – 2 off
22 Rubber damping block – 2 off

Fig. 1.2 Cylinder head and cover

7.1 Disconnect cylinder head oil feed pipe (arrowed)

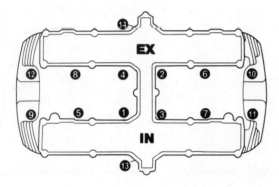

Fig. 1.3 Cylinder head nut loosening sequence

Start from highest number

8   Dismantling the engine/gearbox unit: removing the cylinder block and pistons

1   The cylinder block can be removed after the camshafts and cylinder head have been released as described in the preceding sections. Separate the cylinder block from the base gasket, using the rawhide mallet. If required, a screwdriver may be inserted into the two slots provided in the front of the barrel, to separate the two components. DO NOT use screwdrivers or other levers between the mating surfaces; this will certainly lead to oil leaks.

2   Lift the cylinder block upwards off the pistons. At this juncture a second person should be present to support each piston as it leaves the cylinder barrel spigot. To prevent broken particles of piston ring dropping in, and subsequently other foreign matter, the crankcase mouths should be padded with clean rag. This must be done before the rings leave the confines of the cylinder bores. Endeavour to lift the cylinder block squarely, so that pistons do not bind in the bores.

3   Before removing the pistons, mark each on the inside of the skirt to aid identification. It is important that the pistons are refitted to their original cylinders on reassembly. An arrow mark on each piston crown indicates the front, the pistons must therefore be fitted with the arrow facing forwards. Remove the outer circlip from one of the outermost pistons and push out the gudgeon pin. Lift the piston off the connecting rod. The gudgeon pins are a light push fit in the piston bosses so they can be removed with ease. If any difficulty is encountered, apply to the offending piston crown a rag over which boiling water has just been poured. This will give the necessary temporary expansion to the piston bosses to allow the gudgeon pin to be pushed out.

4   Each piston is fitted with two compression rings and an oil control ring. It is wise to leave the rings in place on the pistons until the time comes for their examination or renewal in order to avoid confusing their correct order.

5   Remove the remaining pistons, using a similar procedure.

6   The camshaft chain tensioner assembly should be removed to prevent it from becoming damaged during subsequent dismantling operations. It is secured by four Allen screws to the crankcase.

8.2 Slide cylinder block off crankcase holding studs

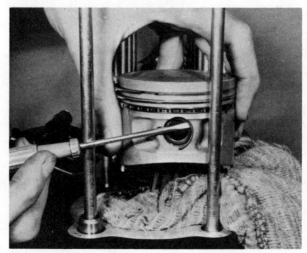

8.3 Use screwdriver blade to displace circlips

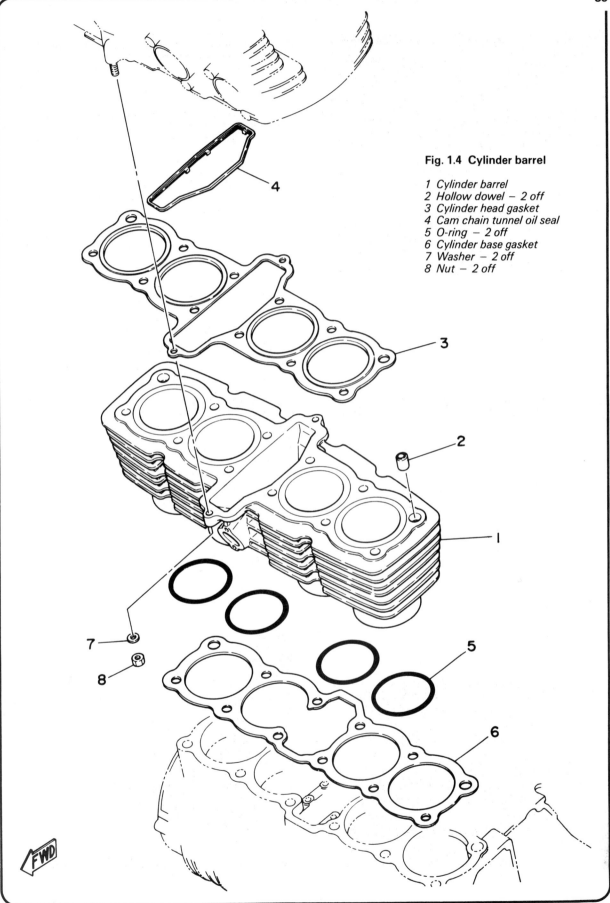

Fig. 1.4 Cylinder barrel

1 Cylinder barrel
2 Hollow dowel – 2 off
3 Cylinder head gasket
4 Cam chain tunnel oil seal
5 O-ring – 2 off
6 Cylinder base gasket
7 Washer – 2 off
8 Nut – 2 off

9 Dismantling the engine/gearbox unit: removing the alternator assembly

1　Release the five Allen bolts which secure the front right-hand outer cover, noting that two different lengths of bolt are used. Lift the cover away complete with the alternator stator assembly. The alternator wiring passes through clips on the side of the crankcase and must be disengaged as it is lifted clear. If the alternator unit is being removed with the engine unit in the frame, trace the alternator leads back to the connector block behind the main fuse-board, and disconnect them to free the stator.

2　Slacken the rotor securing bolt, holding the crankshaft at the opposite end to prevent it from turning. The rotor must now be drawn off its taper, using the Yamaha extractor bolt, part number 90890-01080. The rotor is threaded to accept a special bolt which, when tightened, will push the complete unit from position. If a metric bolt of equivalent size and thread pitch is to hand, this may be used in place of the special service tool. To protect the crankshaft end and the internal thread into which the alternator centre bolt normally screws, a plug or button should be inserted before fitting and tightening the extractor bolt. The plug can be fashioned from a suitable small bolt. A standard two or three legged sprocket puller may also be used to remove the rotor. In this instance insert the centre bolt before fitting the puller. The bolt should be screwed in lightly. Under no circumstances should levers be used in an attempt to remove the rotor. Such an approach will almost certainly lead to damage of the rotor or to the adjacent casings.

10 Dismantling the engine/gearbox unit: removing the clutch, primary drive gear and kickstart mechanism

1　Release the rear right-hand casing after removing the 13 Allen bolts which secure it. In the case of models fitted with an emergency kickstart mechanism, it will first be necessary to pull off the black plastic kickstart shaft cover. Note that a small amount of residual oil may be released, and some provision must be made to catch this.

2　Slacken the six bolts which retain the clutch release plate, and remove it together with the bearing and mushroom-headed pushrod. Knock back the tab washer which locks the clutch centre nut.

3　It will be necessary to devise some means of holding the clutch centre whilst the nut is removed. Yamaha produce a special holding tool for this purpose; part number 90890-04007. In the absence of this, the clutch assembly can be locked by fitting two or three of the springs and bolts, but using plain washers in place of the pressure plate. With the clutch held in this manner, it can be held in position by immobilising the crankshaft via the large square on the left-hand end. Alternatively, if the cylinder block and pistons have been removed, slide a close-fitting round section bar through one of the connecting rod eyes, arranging it so that each end is supported by a wood block resting on the crankcase.

4　A holding tool can be fabricated, given basic workshop facilities, as shown in the accompanying figure. The tool is retained by three of the clutch pressure plate bolts passed through the tubular spacers. If the official holding tool or a home-made version is used, note that it is essential that the three bolts are secured to avoid damage to the clutch centre.

5　With the clutch suitably restrained, slacken the clutch centre nut. The clutch centre can be removed as a unit with the clutch plates and the pressure plate, by pulling on the projecting bosses of the latter. If the holding tool was used it can be left attached to the assembled unit unless specific attention is required. Similarly, the spring and plain washer arrangement can be left undisturbed if required.

6　Remove the plain thrust washer which fits between the clutch centre and the outer drum. Slide off the drum, followed by the bush if this remains on the shaft, and the second thrust washer.

7　The kickstart mechanism can be removed after the return spring tension has been released. Grasp the anchored end of the spring with a pair of pointed-nose pliers, twist it slightly and disengage it from the casing. Release the spring carefully. The complete mechanism can now be disengaged and removed from the casing. Note that on certain later models the emergency kickstart mechanism is omitted and the hole in the outer cover blanked off.

8　If the primary shaft is to be removed at a later stage, the primary shaft gear can be removed now if desired. It should be noted that this is by no means essential, because the gear is easily removed after crankcase separation, if necessary. The gear is retained by a nut which itself is secured by a tab washer. After bending back the locking tab, it will be necessary to prevent the primary shaft from turning whilst the nut is slackened.

9　Several methods are available for this purpose, such as locking the crankshaft with a round bar, as described earlier, or by holding it via the large square on the left-hand end. Alternatively, a special notched rib is provided on the casing, immediately adjacent to the gear. This allows a screwdriver blade to be wedged between the casing and the gear to prevent it from turning. The notch is at the eleven o'clock position when viewed from the right-hand side of the casing.

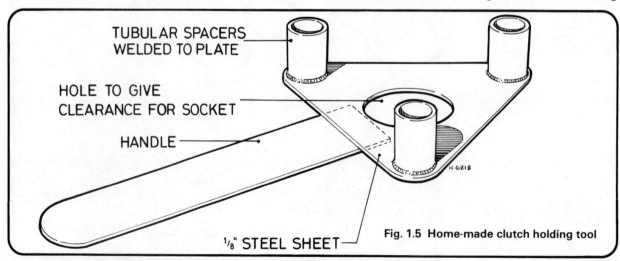

TUBULAR SPACERS WELDED TO PLATE

HOLE TO GIVE CLEARANCE FOR SOCKET

HANDLE

⅛" STEEL SHEET

Fig. 1.5 Home-made clutch holding tool

9.1 Release cover bolts and remove stator assembly

9.2 Two-legged puller can be used to free rotor

10.1 Release right-hand outer casing as shown

10.2 Remove pressure plate and centre assembly ...

10.6 ... followed by clutch outer drum

10.7 Free spring and remove kickstart mechanism

10.9 Slot in casing allows pinion to be locked with screwdriver (arrowed)

11   Dismantling the engine/gearbox unit: removing the ignition pickup assembly

1   Hold the crankshaft by means of the 19 mm flats on the timing plate, and slacken the central Allen bolt. The timing plate can now be lifted away to expose the pickup stator. Check that the projection on the central reluctor aligns with the clearance slot in the pickup stator. If necessary, temporarily refit the timing plate so that the crankshaft can be rotated to the correct position.
2   The stator assembly is retained by two screws which pass through elongated holes in the edge lugs. Release these to free the stator, but do not touch the remaining screws. The stator assembly can be lifted away together with the vacuum advance unit. The vacuum pipe must be pulled clear of the casing as the stator is lifted clear.
3   Remove the automatic timing unit (ATU) from the crankshaft end, noting that it has an offset locating pin to ensure that it is refitted in the correct position.
4   Yamaha recommend that the crankcase-mounted timing pointer should be removed to prevent damage during subsequent dismantling operations. This is sound advice, but it does assume the availability of a dial gauge for re-alignment purposes. If a dial gauge is not to hand, it is preferable to leave the pointer in position and exercise care to avoid damage. This latter course of action was chosen with the example dismantled during the workshop project, and proved no great disadvantage.
5   It will be noted that the ignition baseplate of the G(US) models is retained by shear-head Torx bolts as an 'anti-tamper' measure to comply with US legal requirements. The removal of the stator poses something of a problem on these models, and reference should be made to Chapter 3 for further details.

12   Dismantling the engine/gearbox unit: removing the starter motor and middle gear case

1   Slacken and remove the three bolts which secure the starter motor cover to the upper crankcase half. The two bolts at the left-hand end pass through lugs in the motor end cover, holding it in position. Lift the cover away to expose the starter motor. The latter can now be pulled out of the casing and removed. Note that it will be necessary to release the oil pressure switch lead if this is still in place.
2   The middle gear case can be removed with the engine in or out of the frame, noting that in the former instance it will

first be necessary to release the drive flange bolts as described in Section 4.14. Slacken and remove the six retaining bolts, then lift the middle gear case unit clear of the crankcase. Note that it is necessary to remove the middle gear case before its crankcase halves can be separated.

13   Dismantling the engine/gearbox unit: removing the gear selector mechanism

1   The gear selector mechanism components are housed behind a flat cover on the left-hand side of the crankcase. The cover is retained by a total of nine Allen screws. Slacken and remove the screws, then lift the cover away whilst holding the projecting shaft end against the unit to prevent it from becoming displaced.
2   Before removing any of the selector components, note that the two toothed quadrants have alignment marks stamped on their outer faces, providing a guide to the correct positions during reassembly. Grasp the splined end of the gearchange shaft and lift it clear of the casing. As it is removed the two ends of the centring spring will drop clear of the locating pin in the casing.
3   At this point a decision should be made as to whether further dismantling is required. If the selector mechanism is being dismantled as a precursor to crankcase separation the only other job requiring attention in this area is the removal of the oil feed plate which bridges the crankcase joint. The remaining components can be left in place, or removed as follows.
4   Remove the circlip from the shaft which supports the remaining toothed quadrant. Lift the spring-loaded operating claw clear of the end of the selector drum and pull the assembly off its shaft. The selector drum components need not be disturbed at this stage.
5   The oil feed plate mentioned above, plus an alloy bearing housing are each secured to the crankcase by means of countersunk screws with a star-shaped internal hole, known as Torx screws.
6   The best way to deal with these screws is to obtain the obscurely-named 'drive axle wrench', part number 90890-05245, from a Yamaha dealer. Alternatively, a few minutes work with a hacksaw and file on a suitable Allen key will produce an acceptable home-made equivalent as shown in the accompanying figure.
7   Slacken the three screws which secure the oil feed plate and lift it away, together with the small O-ring. The bearing retainer, which is similarly retained below the oil feed plate, can be left in place for the moment.

11.2 Remove ignition pickup assembly from crankcase

12.2 Middle gear case is retained by six bolts

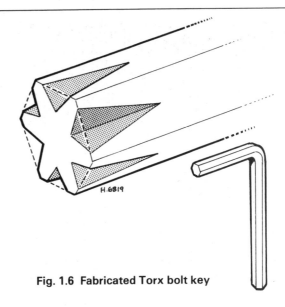

Fig. 1.6 Fabricated Torx bolt key

13.2a Release selector claw assembly ...

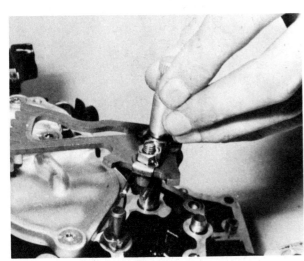

13.2b ... and selector shaft and segment

14 Dismantling the engine/gearbox unit: removing the sump and oil pump

1   Slacken and remove the fourteen Allen bolts which retain the sump to the underside of the crankcase. The sump will usually lift away quite easily, but if necessary it can be tapped around the gasket face with a soft-faced mallet to assist in separation.
2   The oil pump is retained by three Allen screws as shown in the accompanying photograph. Slacken the screws and lift the pump away.

15 Dismantling the engine/gearbox unit: separating the crankcase halves

1   The crankcase halves are secured by a total of 34 bolts. The bolts and their locations are shown in the accompanying figure, together with the loosening sequence which should be followed to help prevent distortion. Starting on the upper crankcase half, slacken each bolt by half a turn. Note that the bolt numbered 32 in the diagram is housed inside the crankcase breather chamber necessitating the removal of its cover before the bolt can be reached. Once all twelve of the upper crankcase bolts have been dealt with, go through the sequence again, slackening and removing each one.
2   Turn the engine unit over, taking care not to damage the timing pointer if this is still in position. Arrange wooden blocks under the rear of the crankcase so that the crankcase is level, resting squarely on the ends of the studs. Do not allow undue sideways pressure on the studs or damage may result. Slacken the lower crankcase bolts, once more in the correct loosening sequence and by half a turn at a time. Do not overlook bolts 1 and 2 which pass up through the oil filter housing.
3   The crankcase halves are now ready for separation, this being accomplished by lifting the **lower** casing half off the upper half, the latter remaining supported on the bench. Separation may be impaired by the jointing compound and the locating dowels, both of which will resist separation until some initial movement has been made. It helps to tap around the joint with a soft-faced mallet, taking care not to strike the more fragile parts of the casing.
4   As the lower crankcase half is freed, check that the gearbox mainshaft and the crankshaft and primary shaft remain in the upper casing. The remaining gearbox components will come away with the lower crankcase half.

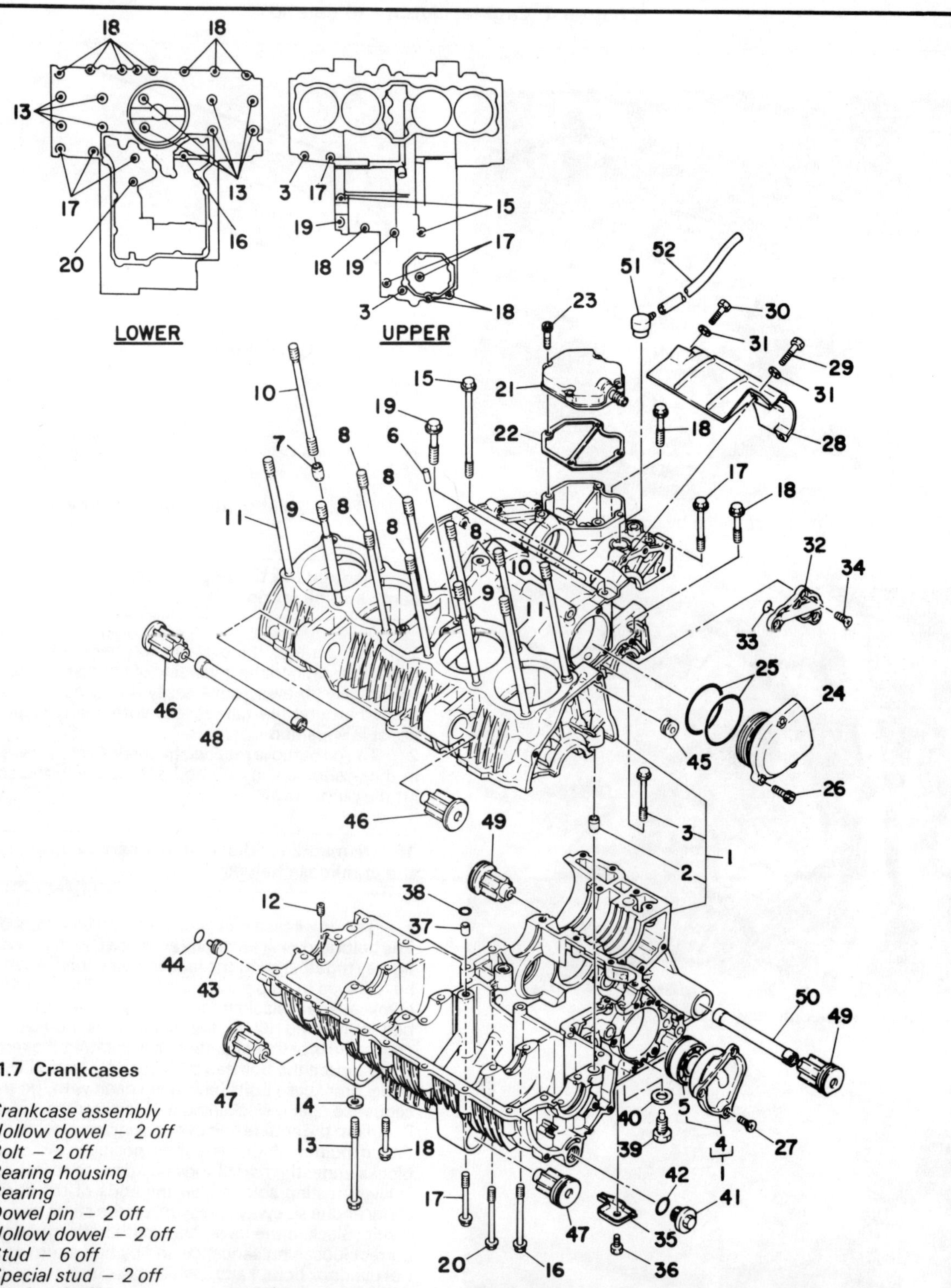

LOWER

UPPER

Fig. 1.7 Crankcases

1 Crankcase assembly
2 Hollow dowel – 2 off
3 Bolt – 2 off
4 Bearing housing
5 Bearing
6 Dowel pin – 2 off
7 Hollow dowel – 2 off
8 Stud – 6 off
9 Special stud – 2 off
10 Stud – 2 off
11 Stud – 2 off
12 Dowel/oilway – 3 off
13 Bolt – 10 off
14 Washer – 8 off
15 Bolt – 2 off
16 Bolt
17 Bolt – 6 off
18 Bolt – 11 off
19 Bolt – 2 off
20 Bolt
21 Breather cover

22 Breather cover gasket
23 Allen screw – 4 off
24 Bearing housing
25 O-ring – 2 off
26 Allen screw – 3 off
27 Screw – 3 off
28 Starter motor cover
29 Bolt – 2 off
30 Bolt
31 Washer – 3 off
32 Oil distributor
33 O-ring

34 Screw – 3 off
35 Oil distributor
36 Bolt
37 Dowel pin
38 O-ring
39 Bolt
40 Gasket
41 Oil chamber plug
42 O-ring
43 Plug
44 O-ring
45 Grommet

46 Upper engine
mounting damper
– 2 off
47 Lower engine
mounting damper
– 2 off
48 Spacer
49 Rear engine mounting
damper – 2 off
50 Spacer
51 Breather cap
52 Breather hose

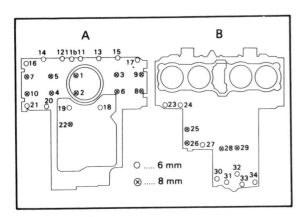

Fig. 1.8 Crankcase bolt loosening sequence

14.2 Oil pump is retained by three screws (arrowed)

15.1 Note crankcase bolt (arrowed) 'hidden' in oil separator ...

15.2 ... and two bolts inside filter housing

16 Dismantling the engine/gearbox unit: removing the crankcase components

1   Lift the middle driven gear assembly from the inverted upper crankcase half. If necessary, tap the assembly a few times to free the bearings from their supporting bosses. The gearbox mainshaft can be removed next, and placed to one side to await further attention.

2   Release the gear pinion from the end of the primary shaft after locking the shaft to prevent its rotation. This is facilitated by a small slotted lug provided for the purpose, the lug allowing a screwdriver blade to be wedged between the lug and a pair of gear teeth whilst the securing nut is removed.

3   Bend back the tab washer and remove the securing nut as described above, followed by the Belville washer that is fitted behind it. Slide off the pinion and spacer.

4   Moving to the opposite end of the primary shaft, remove the three screws which retain the bearing housing and remove the housing together with the bearing. The primary shaft can now be displaced by tapping it through from the right-hand (pinion) end. This will allow the shaft to be withdrawn, leaving the primary chain sprocket/starter clutch unit in position. Once the shaft is clear, disengage the

15.4 Lift lower casing half off upper crankcase

primary chain sprocket unit from the Hy-Vo chain and place it to one side.

5   Grasp the crankshaft at each end and lift it clear of the bearing bosses. If it proves reluctant to move, tap each end upwards until it comes free of the bearing shells. The crankshaft can now be placed to one side and the primary chain and cam chain removed. The primary chain should be marked so that, if it is to be reused, it can be refitted to run in the same direction. Reversing the direction of a partially worn Hy-Vo chain will cause excessive noise and vibration. The bearing shells will probably stay firmly in place in the casing, but if any do fall free they should be cleaned and marked with a felt-tipped pen to indicate their position in relation to the crankcase.

6   Slacken the three bolts which retain the kickstart idler mechanism to the crankcase, the assembly can now be removed and placed to one side.

7   Moving on to the lower casing half, remove the circlip which secures the end of the selector fork shaft on the left-hand side of the casing. Withdraw the shaft from the right-hand side by pulling on the oil pump idler gear. Note carefully the position of each fork and, after the shaft has been removed, refit the forks in the correct order as an aid to reassembly.

8   Identify the selector drum detent assembly which will be found near the right-hand end of the selector drum. Knock back the tab washer and unscrew the large hexagon-headed plunger body. This will enable the detent spring and plunger to be removed, a small magnet proving useful in this task.

9   The opposite end of the selector drum is located by a guide pin which engages in a plain groove around the drum. To remove the guide pin, slacken the bolt which secures the retainer plate. The pin can now be displaced and removed. Release the neutral indicator switch from the left-hand side of the casing. The switch is located in a small external recess directly below the selector drum end.

10   Push the selector drum to the left until the stopper plate prevents further movement. It is necessary to release the stopper plate at this juncture by removing the large circlip which retains it to the drum. Slide the drum completely clear of the casing.

11   To facilitate removal of the gearbox layshaft it will be necessary to use the 'drive shaft wrench' described in Section 13, or its home-made equivalent. Additionally, a layshaft holding tool, part number 90890-04009 will be needed to hold the layshaft whilst the large flanged bolt is unscrewed from the right-hand end. In the absence of this latter tool it may be possible to arrange a strap wrench around one of the gear pinions to hold the shaft. In this case, slacken the flange bolt **before** the bearing retainer is removed.

12   Slacken and remove the three special countersunk screws which retain the cast alloy bearing retainer at the left-hand end of the layshaft. Withdraw the retainer and fit the holding tool, arranging the projecting tang so that it bears upon the eccentric pin adjacent to the bearing boss. Slacken and remove the flanged bolt, then remove the holding tool. Slide the layshaft assembly to the left-hand side of the casing to free the opposite end. The shaft can now be manoeuvred clear of the crankcase.

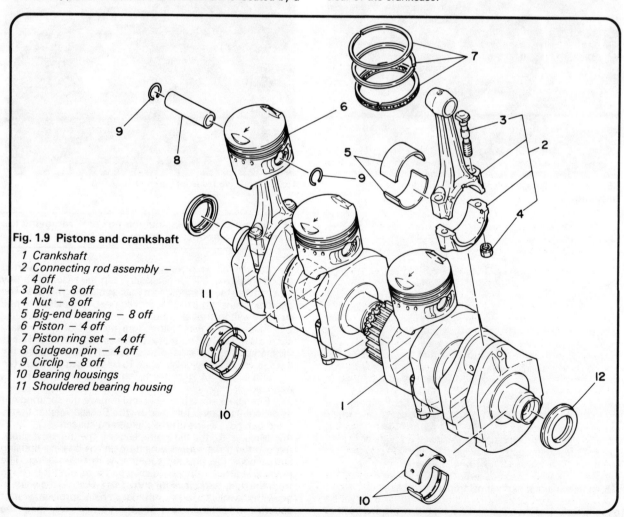

Fig. 1.9 Pistons and crankshaft

1 *Crankshaft*
2 *Connecting rod assembly –*
  4 off
3 *Bolt – 8 off*
4 *Nut – 8 off*
5 *Big-end bearing – 8 off*
6 *Piston – 4 off*
7 *Piston ring set – 4 off*
8 *Gudgeon pin – 4 off*
9 *Circlip – 8 off*
10 *Bearing housings*
11 *Shouldered bearing housing*

16.1 Lift middle gear shaft clear of crankcase

17 Examination and renovation: general

1   Before examining the component parts of the dismantled engine/gear unit for wear, it is essential that they should be cleaned thoroughly. Use a paraffin/petrol mix to remove all traces of oil and sludge which may have accumulated within the engine.
2   Examine the crankcase castings for cracks or other signs of damage. If a crack is discovered, it will require professional attention or in an extreme case, renewal of the casting.
3   Examine carefully each part to determine the extent of wear. If in doubt, check with the tolerance figures whenever they are quoted in the text. The following sections will indicate what type of wear can be expected and in many cases, the acceptable limits.
4   Use clean, lint-free rags for cleaning and drying the various components, otherwise there is a risk of small particles obstructing the internal oilways.

18 Examination and renovation: main bearings and big-end bearings

1   The Yamaha XS1100 models are fitted with shell type bearings on the crankshaft and the big-end assemblies.
2   Bearing shells are relatively inexpensive and it is prudent to renew the entire set of main bearing shells when the engine is dismantled completely, especially in view of the amount of work which will be necessary at a later date if any of the bearings fail. Always renew all five sets of main bearings together. Note that the bearing shell second from the right in the upper casing half differs in form from the remainder. This shell, in addition to serving as a bearing in the normal manner, also controls crankshaft end float.
3   Wear is usually evident in the form of scuffing or score marks in the bearing surface. It is not possible to polish these marks out in view of the very soft nature of the bearing surface and the increased clearance that will result. If wear of this nature is detected, the crankshaft must be checked for ovality as described in the following Section.
4   Failure of the big-end bearings is invariably accompanied by a pronounced knock within the crankcase. The knock will become progressively worse and vibration will also be experienced. It is essential that bearing failure is attended to

without delay because if the engine is used in this condition there is a risk of breaking a connecting rod or even the crankshaft, causing more extensive damage.
5   Before the big-end bearings can be examined the bearing caps must be removed from each connecting rod. Each cap is retained by two high tensile bolts. Before removal, mark each cap in relation to its connecting rod so that it may be replaced correctly. As with the main bearings, wear will be evident as scuffing or scoring and the bearing shells must be replaced as complete sets.
6   Replacement bearing shells for either the big-end or main bearings are supplied on a selected fit basis (ie; bearings are selected for correct tolerance to fit the original journal diameter), and it is essential that the parts to be used for renewal are of identical size. Code numbers stamped on various components are used to identify the correct replacement bearings for both the crankshaft, main bearing and the big-end journals. The journal size numbers are stamped on the crankshaft left-hand outside web; the block of four numbers are for the big-end bearing journals and the block of five numbers for the main bearing journals. The main bearing housing numbers are stamped on the front mating surface of the upper crankcase half. To ascertain which main bearing insert is required, subtract the crankcase number for that particular bearing from the crankshaft journal number. The resultant figure should be compared against the following table, in order to select the correct colour code of shell bearing:

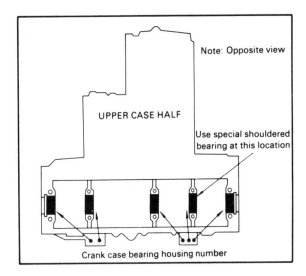

INSERT COLOR CODE	
No. 1	Blue
No. 2	Black
No. 3	Brown
No. 4	Green
No. 5	Yellow

Fig. 1.10 Main bearing housing code number location

A similar method is used to select the correct big-end shell bearings. Each connecting rod is marked in ink on the rod and the cap. Subtract the big-end journal number from the appropriate connecting rod number, and use the number obtained to select the correct colour coded bearing shell set from the table. In practice, provided the coded numbers are quoted correctly, the Yamaha specialist supplying the replacement parts will make the necessary calculations.

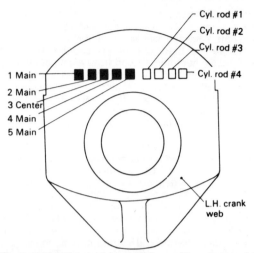

Fig. 1.11 Main bearing and big-end bearing code positions

Note: *position of set of 5 (main) and 4 (big-end) code number locations may be transposed on web face*

18.2 Bearing shell sizes are marked as shown

18.5 Remove connecting rod caps to expose bearing shells

18.6a Note journal coding letters marked on crankshaft

18.6b Connecting rod codes are etched on side

19 Examination and renovation: crankshaft assembly

1   If wear has necessitated the renewal of the big-end and/or main bearing shells, the crankshaft should be checked with a micrometer to verify whether ovality has occurred. If the reading on any one journal varies by more than 0.04 mm (0.0015 in) the crankshaft should be renewed.

2   Mount the crankshaft by supporting both ends on V-blocks or between centres on a lathe and check the run-out at the centre main bearing surfaces by means of a dial gauge. The run-out will be half that of the gauge reading indicated. A measured run-out of more than 0.03 mm (0.001 in) indicates the need for crankshaft renewal. It is wise, however, before taking such drastic (and expensive) action, to consult a Yamaha specialist.

3   The clearance between any set of bearings and their respective journal may be checked by the use of plastigauge (press gauge). Plastigauge is a graduated strip of plastic material that can be compressed between two mating surfaces. The resulting width of the material when measured with a micrometer will give the amount of clearance. For

example if the clearance in the big-end bearing was to be measured, plastigauge should be used in the following manner.

Cut a strip of plastigauge to the width across the bearing to be measured. Place the plastigauge strip across the bearing journal so that it is parallel with the crankshaft. Place the connecting rod complete with its half shell on the journal and then carefully replace the bearing cap complete with half shell onto the connecting rod bolts. Replace and tighten the retaining nuts to the correct torque and then loosen and remove the nuts and the bearing cap. Without bending or pressing the plastigauge strip, place it at its thickest point between a micrometer and read off the measurement. This will indicate the precise clearance. The original size and wear limit of the crankshaft journals and the standard and service limit clearance between all the bearings is given in the Specifications at the beginning of this Chapter. Clearances may be checked also by direct measurement of each journal and bearing using external and internal micrometers.

4   The crankshaft has drilled oil passages which allow oil to be fed under pressure to the working surfaces. Blow the passages out with a high pressure air line to ensure they are absolutely free. Blanking plugs in the form of small steel balls are fitted in each web, to close off the outer ends of the passages. Check that these balls, which are peened into place, are not loose. A plug coming free in service will cause oil pressure loss and resultant bearing and journal damage.

5   When refitting the connecting rods and shell bearings, note that under no circumstances should the shells be adjusted with a shim, 'scraped in' or the fit 'corrected' by filing the connecting rod and bearing cap or by applying emery cloth to the bearing surface. Treatment such as this will end in disaster; if the bearing fit is not good, the parts concerned have not been assembled correctly. This advice also applies to main bearing shells. Use new big-end bolts too – the originals may have stretched and weakened.

6   Oil the bearing surfaces before reassembly takes place and make sure the tags of the bearing shells are located correctly. After the initial tightening of the connecting rod nuts, check that each connecting rod revolves freely, then tighten to a torque setting of 3.9 kgf m (28 lbf ft). Check again for ease of rotation.

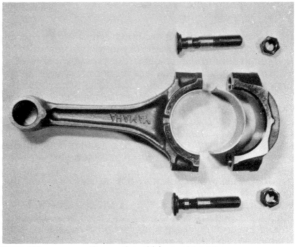

19.5a The connecting rod and big-end bearing

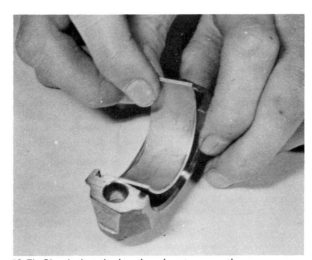

19.5b Check that the bearings locate correctly

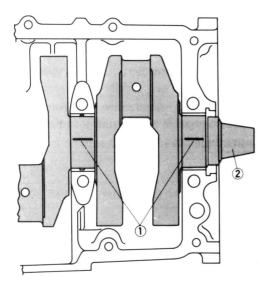

Fig. 1.12 Use of Plastigage to determine crankshaft journal clearance

1 Plastigage
2 Crankshaft

19.6 Torque big end bolts to specified setting

20 Examination and renewal: oil seals

1   The crankcase halves are fitted with a number of oil seals which prevent the escape of the engine/transmission oil through the various bearings. Each seal consists of a metal case to which the seal face is bonded. A small garter spring is fitted around the seal lip to hold it against its shaft.
2   In time the seal face will wear and weaken allowing oil to find its way past. Although the seals themselves are relatively inexpensive, a considerable amount of dismantling work is necessary should one fail in service. For this reason it is advisable to renew all oil seals in the event of a full engine overhaul. In any case, a seal which looks remotely suspect should be renewed.
3   Seal wear or damage may not be very obvious, the finest scoring allowing oil seepage. It follows that the seal will require renewal if any marking is evident. Oil seals fitted within a housing in a casing are a light drive fit and may be drifted from position, using a tubular drift of suitable outside diameter. When fitting a new seal, ensure that it is driven in squarely. As a general rule the spring garter side of the seal should face towards the fluid to be contained.

21 Examination and renovation: connecting rods

1   It is unlikely that any of the connecting rods will become damaged during normal usage unless an unusual occurrence such as a dropped valve causes the engine to lock. This may well bend the connecting rod in that cylinder. Carelessness when removing a tight gudgeon pin can also give rise to a similar problem. It is not advisable to straighten a bent connecting rod; renewal is the only satisfactory solution.
2   The bearing surface of each small-end eye is provided by a cold-metal-sprayed coating with a bronze base. If the small-end eye wears, the connecting rod in question must be renewed. If the clearance between a gudgeon pin and small-end is excessive, check first that the wear is in the eye and not the gudgeon pin. This will prevent the unnecessary renewal of a sound component. Always check that the oil hole in the small-end eye is not blocked since if the oil supply is cut off, the bearing surfaces will wear very rapidly.

22 Examination and renovation: cylinder bores

1   The usual indication of badly worn cylinder bores and pistons is excessive smoking from the exhausts, high crankcase compression which causes oil leaks, and piston slap, a metallic rattle that occurs when there is little or no load on the engine. If the top of the cylinder bore is examined carefully, it will be found that there is a ridge at the front and back the depth of which will indicate the amount of wear which has taken place. This ridge marks the limit of travel of the top piston ring.
2   Since there is a difference in cylinder wear in different directions, side to side and back to front measurements should be made. Take measurements at three different points down the length of the cylinder bore, starting just below the top piston ring ridge, then about 60 mm (2½ in) below the top of the bore and the last measurements about 25 mm (1 in) from the bottom of the cylinder bore. The cylinder measurement as standard and the service limit are as follows:

Standard Cylinder bore	Service limit
71.5 mm	71.6 mm
(2.815 in)	(2.819 in)

If any of the cylinder bore inside diameter measurements exceed the service limit the cylinder must be bored out to take the next size of piston. If there is a difference of more than 0.05 mm (0.002 in) between any two measurements the cylinder should, in any case, be rebored.
3   Oversize pistons are available in four oversizes: 0.25 mm (0.010 in); 0.50 mm (0.020 in); 0.75 mm (0.030 in) and 1.0 mm (0.040 in).
4   Check that the surface of the cylinder bore is free from score marks or other damage that may have resulted from an earlier engine seizure or a displaced gudgeon pin. A rebore will be necessary to remove any deep scores, irrespective of the amount of bore wear that has taken place, otherwise a compression leak will occur.
5   Make sure the external cooling fins of the cylinder block are not clogged with oil or road dirt which will prevent the free flow of air and cause the engine to overheat.
6   If removed for any reason, the cylinder block and cylinder head holding down studs are removed from the crankcase, they should be smeared with Loctite before they are reinserted.

22.4 Examine bore surface for wear ridge or scoring

23 Examination and renovation: pistons and piston rings

1   Attention to the pistons and piston rings can be overlooked if a rebore is necessary, since new components will be fitted.
2   If a rebore is not necessary, examine each piston carefully. Reject pistons that are scored or badly discoloured as the result of exhaust gases by-passing the rings.
3   Remove all carbon from the piston crowns, using a blunt scraper, which will not damage the surface of the piston. Clean away carbon deposits from the valve cutaways and finish off with metal polish so that a smooth, shining surface is achieved. Carbon will not adhere so readily to a polished surface.
4   Small high spots on the back and front areas of the piston can be carefully eased back with a fine swiss file. Dipping the file in methylated spirits or rubbing its teeth with chalk will prevent the file clogging and eventually scoring the piston. Only very small quantities of material should be removed, and never enough to interfere with the correct tolerances. Never use emery paper or cloth to clean the piston skirt; the fine particles of emery are inclined to embed themselves in the soft aluminium and consequently accelerate the rate of wear between bore and piston.

5   Measure the outside diameter of the piston about 10 mm (0.4 in) up from the skirt at right angles to the line of the gudgeon pin. To determine the piston/cylinder barrel clearance, subtract the maximum piston measurement from the minimum bore measurement. If the clearance exceeds 0.1 mm (0.004 in), the piston should ideally be renewed (given that the cylinder bore is within limits). This however, is seeking perfection, and an additional clearance of perhaps 0.025 mm (0.001 in) will not reduce engine performance dramatically.

6   Check that the gudgeon pin bosses are not worn or the circlip grooves damaged. Check that the piston ring grooves are not enlarged. Side float should not exceed 0.08 mm (0.003 in) for the top ring and 0.07 mm (0.0028 in) for the second ring. Side play on the oil control ring is not measurable.

7   Piston ring wear can be measured by inserting the rings in the bore from the top and pushing them down with the base of the piston so that they are square with the bore and close to the bottom of the bore where the cylinder wear is least. Place a feeler gauge between the ring end. If the clearance exceeds the service limit the ring should be renewed. The expander band of the oil control ring cannot be measured. In practice, if wear of the two side rails exceeds the limit, the three components should be renewed. It is advised that, provided new rings have not been fitted recently, a complete set of rings be fitted as a matter of course whenever the engine is dismantled. This action will ensure maintenance of compression and performance. If new rings are to be fitted to cylinder bores which are in good condition and do not require a rebore, it is essential to have the surface of the bores honed lightly. This operation is known as glazebusting and as the name suggests, it removes the mirror smooth surface which has been produced by the previous innumerable up and down strokes of the piston and rings. If the glaze is not removed, the new rings will glide over the surface, making the running-in process unnecessarily protracted. Note that new rings should not be fitted to a part-worn cylinder bore, as the resulting wear ridge may break the top ring, particularly at high engine speeds. The resulting debris could have very expensive results.

8   Check that there is no build up of carbon either in the ring grooves or the inner surfaces of the rings. Any carbon deposits should be carefully scraped away. A short length of old piston ring fitted with a handle and sharpened at one end to a chisel point is ideal for scraping out encrusted piston ring grooves.

9   All pistons have their size stamped on the piston crown, original pistons being stamped standard (STD) and oversize pistons having the amount of oversize indicated. Similarly oversize piston rings are stamped on the upper edge.

24 Examination and renovation: cylinder head and valves

1   Before dismantling the valve gear proper lift out each of the six bucket type cam followers, together with the adjustment pads. Ensure that each follower is marked clearly, so that it may be replaced in the original recess in the cylinder head. It is good practice to obtain eight marked boxes or bags so that the appropriate valve components can be kept separate. It is best to remove all carbon deposits from the combustion chambers before removing the valves for inspection and grinding-in. Use a blunt ended chisel or scraper so that the surfaces are not damaged. Finish off with a metal polish to achieve a smooth, shining surface. If a mirror finish is required, a high speed felt mop and polishing soap may be used. A chuck attached to a flexible drive will facilitate the polishing operation.

2   A valve spring compression tool must be used to compress each set of valve springs in turn, thereby allowing the split collets to be removed from the valve cap and the valve springs and caps to be freed. Keep each set of parts separate and mark each valve so that it can be replaced in the correct combustion chamber. There is no danger of inadvertently replacing an inlet valve in an exhaust position, or vice-versa, as the valve heads are of different sizes. The normal method of marking valves for later identification is by centre punching them on the valve head. This method is not recommended on valves, or any other highly stressed components, as it will produce high stress points and may lead to early failure. Tie-on labels, suitably inscribed, or a spirit-based marker, are ideal for the purpose. Because of the cylinder head design, modification of an existing valve spring compressor may be necessary so that it clears the high walls of the cam and valve spring compartments. Remove the oil seal cap from each valve guide. As each valve is removed, check that it will pass through the guide bore without resistance. After high mileages have been covered it is possible that the collet groove will have spread and if this increased diameter is pulled through the guide bore it will enlarge it. If any resistance is encountered, relieve the high spots with fine abrasive paper until the valve can be removed easily.

3   Before giving the valves and valve seats further attention, check the clearance between each valve stem and the guide in which it operates. Clearances are as follows:

Standard	*Service limit*
Inlet valve/guide clearance	
0.010 – 0.040 mm	*0.10 mm (0.004 in)*
(0.0004 – 0.0016 in)	
Exhaust valve/guide clearance	
0.025 – 0.055 mm	*0.12 mm (0.005 in)*
(0.0010 – 0.0022 in)	

The valve stem/guide clearance can be measured with the use of a dial gauge and a new valve. Place the new valve into the guide and measure the amount of shake with the dial gauge tip resting against the top of the stem. If the amount of wear is greater than the wear limit, the guide must be renewed.

4   To remove an old valve guide, place the cylinder head in an oven and heat it to about 100°C (212°F). The old guide can now be tapped out from the cylinder side. The correct drift should be shouldered with the smaller diameter the same size as the valve stem and the larger diameter slightly smaller than the OD of the valve guide. If a suitable drift is not available a plain brass drift may be utilised with great care. Even heating is essential, if warpage of the cylinder head is to be avoided. Before removing old guides scrape away any carbon deposits which have accumulated on the guide where it projects into the port. Removal of carbon will ease guide movement and help prevent broaching of the guide bore in the cylinder head. If in doubt, seek the advice of a Yamaha specialist. Each valve guide is fitted with an O-ring to ensure perfect sealing. The O-rings must be replaced with new components. New guides should be fitted with the head at the same heat as for removal, following which the seat must be recut to centre the seat with the guide axis.

5   Valve grinding is a simple task. Commence by smearing a trace of fine valve grinding compound (carborundum paste) on the valve seat and apply a suction tool to the head of the valve. Oil the valve stem and insert the valve in the guide so that the two surfaces to be ground in make contact with one another. With a semi-rotary motion, grind in the valve head to the seat, using a backward and forward action. Lift the valve occasionally so that the grinding compound is distributed evenly. Repeat the application until an unbroken ring of light grey matt finish is obtained on both valve and seat. This denotes the grinding operation is now complete. Before passing to the next valve, make sure that all traces of

the valve grinding compound have been removed from both the valve and its seat and that none has entered the valve guide. If this precaution is not observed, rapid wear will take place due to the highly abrasive nature of the carborundum base.

6   When deep pits are encountered, it will be necessary to use a valve refacing machine and a valve seat cutter, set to an angle of 45°. If, after recutting the seat, it is found that the seat width exceeds 2.0 mm (0.08 in) further cuts with 30° and 60° cutters must be made to reduce the seat width to the standard of 1.3 mm (0.05 in). In view of the high cost of the seat cutters and of the expertise involved it is suggested that this work be carried out by a Yamaha Service Agent or other specialist. Never resort to excessive grinding because this will only pocket the valves in the head and lead to reduced engine efficiency. If there is any doubt about the condition of a valve, fit a new one.

7   Examine the condition of the valve collets and the groove on the valve stem in which they seat. If there is any sign of damage, new parts should be fitted. Check that the valve spring collar is not cracked. If the collets work loose or the collar splits whilst the engine is running, a valve could drop into the cylinder and cause extensive damage.

8   Check the free length of each of the valve springs. The springs have reached their serviceable limit when they have compressed to the limit readings given in the Specifications Section of this Chapter.

9   Reassemble the valve and valve springs by reversing the dismantling procedure. Fit new oil seals to each valve guide and oil both the valve stem and the valve guide, prior to reassembly. Take special care to ensure the valve guide oil seal is not damaged when the valve is inserted. As a final check after assembly, give the end of each valve stem a light tap with a hammer, to make sure the split collets have located correctly.

10   Check the cylinder head for straightness, especially if it has shown a tendency to leak oil at the cylinder head joint. If there is any evidence of warpage, provided it is not too great, the gasket face may be lapped on a surface plate or a sheet of plate glass. Place a sheet of 400 or 600 grit abrasive paper on the surface plate. Lay the cylinder head, gasket-face down, on the paper and gently rub it with an oscillating motion to remove any high spots. Lift the head at frequent intervals to inspect the progress of the operation, and take care to remove the minimum amount of material necessary to restore a flat sealing surface.

11   In extreme cases, the above method may prove inadequate, necessitating the re-machining or renewal of the cylinder head casting. In this case, the advice of a Yamaha Service Agent or a competent machinist should be sought. It should be remembered that most cases of cylinder head warpage can be traced to unequal tensioning of the cylinder head nuts and bolts by tightening them in incorrect sequence or using incorrect or unmeasured torque settings.

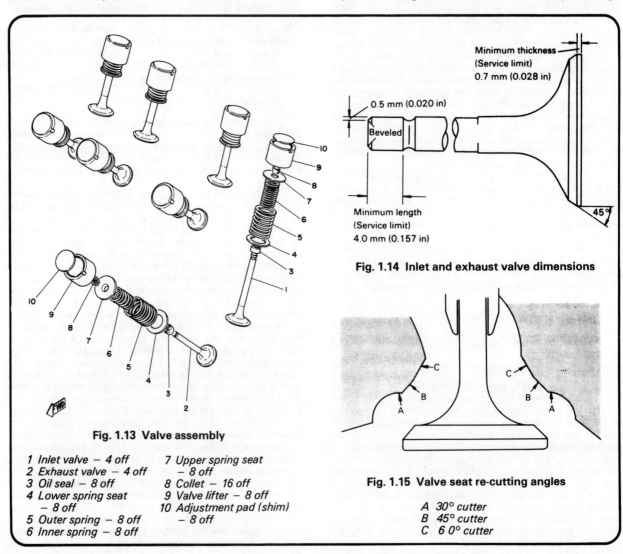

Fig. 1.13 Valve assembly

1 Inlet valve – 4 off
2 Exhaust valve – 4 off
3 Oil seal – 8 off
4 Lower spring seat – 8 off
5 Outer spring – 8 off
6 Inner spring – 8 off
7 Upper spring seat – 8 off
8 Collet – 16 off
9 Valve lifter – 8 off
10 Adjustment pad (shim) – 8 off

Fig. 1.14 Inlet and exhaust valve dimensions

Minimum thickness (Service limit) 0.7 mm (0.028 in)
0.5 mm (0.020 in)
Beveled
Minimum length (Service limit) 4.0 mm (0.157 in)
45°

Fig. 1.15 Valve seat re-cutting angles

A 30° cutter
B 45° cutter
C 60° cutter

24.1a Remove adjustment pad (shim) ...

24.1b ... and cam follower. Place in numbered bag

24.2a Compress valve springs and remove split collet

24.2b Remove compressor and lift away spring seat

24.2c Remove inner and outer valve springs

24.2d Displace and remove valve

24.2e Remove lower valve spring seat from recess

24.2f Note valve stem oil seal on top of guide

25 Examination and renovation: camshafts, camshaft bearings and cam followers

1   The camshafts should be examined visually for wear, which will probably be most evident on the ramps of each cam and where the cam contour changes sharply. Also check the bearing surfaces for obvious wear and scoring. Cam lift can be checked by measuring the height of the cam from the bottom of the base circle to the top of the lobe. If the measurement is less than the service limit given in the Specifications the opening of that particular valve will be reduced resulting in poor performance. Measure the diameter of each bearing journal with a micrometer or vernier gauge. If the diameter is less than the service limit, renew the camshaft.

2   The camshaft bears directly on the cylinder head material and that of the bearing caps, there being no separate bearings. Check the bearing surfaces for wear and scoring. The clearance between the camshaft bearing journals and the aluminium bearing surfaces may be checked using plastigauge (press gauge) material in the same manner as described for crankshaft bearing clearance in Section 19.3 of this Chapter. If the clearance is greater than given for the service limit the recommended course is to replace the camshaft. If bad scuffing, is evident on the camshaft bearing surfaces, due to a lubrication failure, the only remedy is to renew the cylinder head and bearing caps and the camshaft if it transpires that it has been damaged also.

3   Inspect the outer surface of the cam followers for evidence of scoring or other damage. If a cam follower is in poor condition, it is probable that the bore in which it works is also damaged. In extreme cases this may necessitate renewal of both the follower and the cylinder head. Check for clearance between the followers and their bores. If excessive slack is evident, renew the follower.

26 Examination and renovation: camshaft chain, drive sprockets and tensioner blades

1   Check the camshaft drive chain for wear and chipped or broken rollers and links. The cam chain operates under almost ideal conditions and unless oil starvation or prolonged tension adjustment neglect has occurred, it will have a long life. If excessive wear is apparent, or cam chain adjustment has been difficult to maintain correctly, renew the chain.

2   The chain is tensioned via a steel-backed rubber blade by means of a spring loaded plunger. In addition, there is a second blade at the front of the cam chain tunnel which acts as a guide, and a cast bridge piece fitted between the camshaft sprockets which supports the chain upper run. If the rubber material of the guides or blades is worn, the damaged component should be renewed. Extreme wear may indicate a worn drive chain.

3   The cam chain drive sprockets are secured directly to the centre of each camshaft and in consequence are easily renewable if the teeth become hooked, worn, chipped or broken. The lower sprocket is integral with the crankshaft and if any of these defects are evident, the complete crankshaft assembly must be renewed. Fortunately, this drastic course of action is rarely necessary since the parts concerned are fully enclosed and well lubricated, working under ideal conditions.

4   If the sprockets are renewed, the chain should be renewed at the same time. It is bad practice to run old and new parts together since the rate of wear will be accelerated.

27 Examination and renovation: primary chain and sprockets

1   The primary chain is of the Hy-Vo inverted tooth type and runs around broad sprockets on the primary shaft and crankshaft, the latter being integral with the crankshaft itself. Check the chain for damage or loose link plates and pivot pins. This type of chain is very durable and in the normal course of events should have a long service life. Premature wear is unlikely to occur except due to oil starvation. If damage is evident, renew the chain at once. A primary chain which breaks in service will invariably cause extensive engine damage.

2   The service life of the primary chain sprockets is in keeping with that of the chain itself. After considerable use the sprockets may become indented, requiring the renewal of both components. The drive sprocket is an integral part of the crankshaft, and in common with the cam drive sprocket, if wear develops, the crankshaft must be renewed.

28 Examination and renovation: primary shaft assembly

1   The primary shaft assembly conducts drive from the crankshaft to the clutch outer drum. Its main purpose is to keep the width of the engine unit within manageable proportions and also allows the incorporation of a shock absorber unit to absorb transmission snatch.

2   The shock absorber is of the face cam type and is tensioned by five pairs of conical plates which form diaphragm springs. If a shock loading is applied to the unit, the twisting motion forces the cam faces apart. The resulting spring compression and friction serve to absorb the shock.

3   It is unlikely that the unit will require attention during the normal life of the engine, unless the cam faces or springs sustain damage. In this case it will be necessary to dismantle the shock absorber for further attention. To accomplish this task it will be necessary to use a special compressor tool, part number 90890-04011 or a home-made equivalent. The tool takes the form of a U-shaped steel section, the ends of which bear upon the outermost diaphragm spring. The shaft should be arranged in a suitable press and slight movement exerted via the compressor tool to relieve tension on the retaining collar and circlip. The latter can then be removed and the springs and cam dismantled.

4   It must be noted that the springs exert considerable pressure, even though their range of movement is limited. For this reason, no attempt to dismantle the shock absorber should be made unless the unit is safely and adequately compressed. Although it may be possible to contrive some alternative means of compression which avoids the need for a proper press, this course of action cannot be recommended in view of the risk of damage or injury in the event of an accident. If in doubt as to the unit's condition, it is advised that the complete primary shaft should be taken to a Yamaha dealer for inspection or repair.

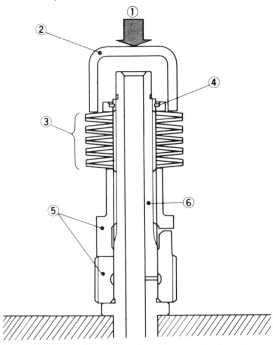

Fig. 1.16 Special tool used to dismantle the primary shaft shock absorber

1 Pressure	4 Circlip
2 Shock absorber	5 Cam
compressing tool	6 Primary shaft
3 Spring	

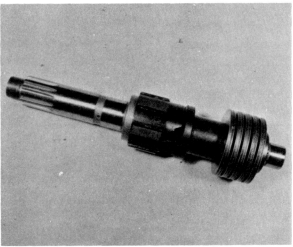

28.2 Primary shaft incorporates cam-type shock absorber

29   Examination and renovation: clutch assembly

1   After an extended period of service the clutch linings will wear and promote clutch slip. The limit of wear measured across each inserted plate and the standard measurement is given in the Specifications. When the overall width reaches the limit, the inserted plates must be renewed, preferably as a complete set.

2   The plain plates should not show any excess heating (blueing). Check the warpage of each plate using plate glass or surface plate and a feeler gauge. The maximum allowable warpage is 0.1 mm (0.004 in).

3   Check the free length of each clutch spring with a vernier gauge. After considerable use the springs will take a permanent set thereby reducing the pressure applied to the clutch plates. The correct measurements are as follows:

Clutch springs
Standard	*Service limit*
42.8 mm	*41.8 mm*
(1.685 in)	*(1.646 in)*

4   Examine the clutch assembly for burrs or indentation on the edges of the protruding tongues of the inserted plates and slots worn in the edges of the outer drum with which they engage. Similar wear can occur between the inner tongues of the plain clutch plates and the slots in the clutch inner drum. Wear of this nature will cause clutch drag and slow disengagement during gear changes, since the plates will become trapped and will not free fully when the clutch is withdrawn. A small amount of wear can be corrected by dressing with a fine file; more extensive wear will necessitate renewal of the worn parts.

5   Check the condition of the spacer upon which the clutch outer drum rotates. If the clearance between the spacer and drum or shaft is excessive the spacer should be renewed. Note that the spacer and drum are a matched pair, and if either component requires renewal a suitable replacement of compatible size must be fitted. As can be seen in the accompanying illustration each item is marked either by a single or double scribed line, this identifies the correct matching part as shown in the table.

6   The clutch release mechanism is mounted inside the right-hand outer casing. As the operating lever is pulled, a retainer housing containing three steel balls turns in relation to an adjacent housing. The housing has three shaped

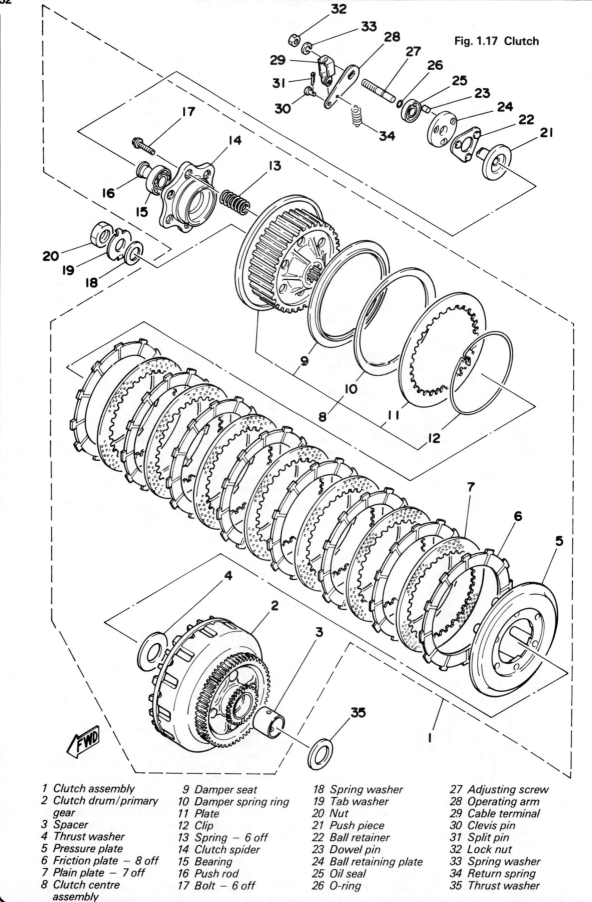

Fig. 1.17 Clutch

1 Clutch assembly	9 Damper seat	18 Spring washer	27 Adjusting screw
2 Clutch drum/primary gear	10 Damper spring ring	19 Tab washer	28 Operating arm
3 Spacer	11 Plate	20 Nut	29 Cable terminal
4 Thrust washer	12 Clip	21 Push piece	30 Clevis pin
5 Pressure plate	13 Spring – 6 off	22 Ball retainer	31 Split pin
6 Friction plate – 8 off	14 Clutch spider	23 Dowel pin	32 Lock nut
7 Plain plate – 7 off	15 Bearing	24 Ball retaining plate	33 Spring washer
8 Clutch centre assembly	16 Push rod	25 Oil seal	34 Return spring
	17 Bolt – 6 off	26 O-ring	35 Thrust washer

recesses which correspond with the balls, and the balls are made, in effect, to run up small ramps. In this way the two parts are pushed apart, thus converting rotary motion to a linear form which can be used to free the clutch.

7   The mechanism is quite robust and will not normally require attention unless obviously damaged. If necessary, the mechanism can be dismantled to facilitate the renewal of worn or broken parts. The order of assembly is shown in the accompanying figure.

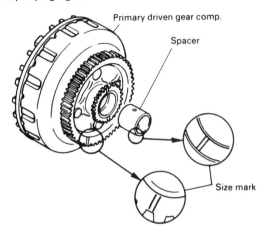

Primary driven gear mark	Spacer mark
I	→ I (or II)
II	→ II only

Fig. 1.18 Correct fitting of primary drive gear and spacer

29.5 Clutch release mechanism is mounted inside cover

30   Examination and renovation: gearbox components

1   The gearbox on Yamaha XS1100 models comprises two main shafts carrying the necessary pinions to provide the five gearbox ratios. The mainshaft (input shaft) protrudes from the right-hand side of the crankcase and carries the clutch assembly. Power from the crankshaft is transmitted through the clutch to the mainshaft, the selected gear pinion transferring motion to its counterpart on the layshaft (output shaft). An additional pinion on the left-hand end of the layshaft drives the middle gear assembly which forms the take-off point for the middle gear case. The latter is a separate, self-contained unit which is dealt with in Section 32.

2   The gearbox is a substantial assembly and does not normally suffer much wear. Light general wear may be expected after extremely high mileages, but the usual causes of accelerated wear or damage can invariably be traced to misuse or poor lubrication. Initial examination can be carried out with the shafts intact, and should be directed at the pinion teeth. Damaged teeth will be self-evident and will of course demand renewal of the component(s) concerned.

3   Look for signs of general wear at the points of contact between the gear teeth. These should normally present a smooth, highly polished profile if in good condition. Pitting of the hardened faces will necessitate renewal of the affected pinions. This type of damage will often be most pronounced on the intermediate (2nd, 3rd and 4th gear) pinions and can be caused by water contamination due to condensation. This is only likely where the machine has been used for frequent short trips which may have prevented the engine unit reaching full operating temperature. Alternatively, neglected oil changes and the resulting thinned and dirty oil can have the same consequences. Pinions with chipped or pitted teeth must always be renewed, there being a real danger of breakage if re-used. In view of the risk of extensive engine damage that this presents, do not be tempted to 'economise' at this point.

4   The gearbox ball and roller bearings should be cleaned in a high flash-point solvent, or petrol (gasoline) if care is taken to avoid the obvious fire risk, and then checked for play or roughness when the bearing is rotated. Renew all bearings that show signs of damage or old age, noting that a worn bearing can cause accelerated wear of the gearbox components and may lead to poor gear selection.

5   If the general examination described above has indicated a likelihood of general wear, the gearbox shafts should be dismantled for further examination. Always deal with one shaft at a time to avoid confusion, and ensure that each component is kept scrupulously clean. The photographic sequence which accompanies this text shows the step-by-step reassembly order. The shafts are dismantled in the reverse order of this. See the accompanying figure for an exploded view of the gearbox assembly.

6   Check that each pinion moves freely on its shaft, but without undue free play. Check for blueing of the shaft or the gearbox pinions as this can indicate overheating due to inadequate lubrication. The dogs on each pinion should be checked for damage or rounded edges. Such damage can lead to poor gear engagement and will require renewal if extensively damaged. Look for signs of hairline cracks around the pinion bosses and dogs.

7   Set the shaft up on V-blocks and measure the runout at the shaft centre using a dial gauge. If this exceeds 0.08 mm (0.0031 in) the shaft should be renewed. Check the shaft surface for scuffing, scoring or cracks.

8   When rebuilding the gearbox shaft assemblies, check that all washers and circlips are fitted in the correct positions and renew any that appear weakened or bent. Follow the sequence illustrated in the accompanying photographic sequence, ensuring that the assembly is kept clean and is well lubricated.

9   The separate middle gear assembly can be dealt with in much the same way as has been described above. In view of the robustness of these latter components, attention is unlikely to be required.

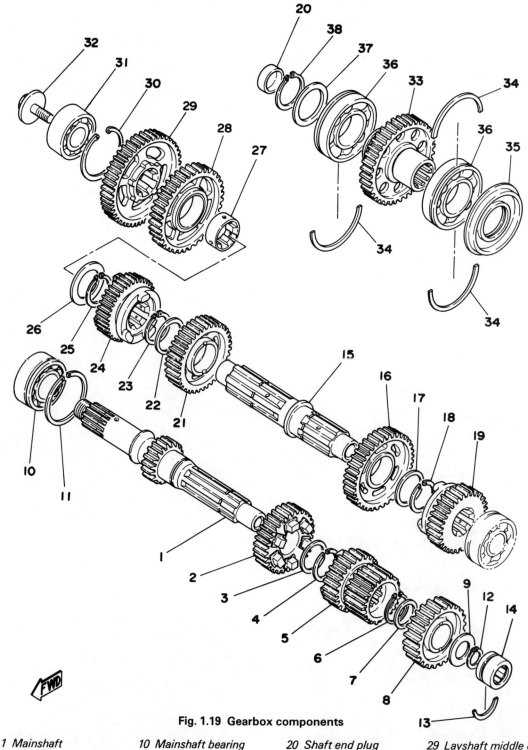

Fig. 1.19 Gearbox components

1 Mainshaft
2 Mainshaft 4th gear pinion
3 Washer
4 Circlip
5 Mainshaft 2nd and 3rd gear pinion
6 Circlip
7 Washer
8 Mainshaft 5th gear pinion
9 Shim
10 Mainshaft bearing
11 Circlip
12 Circlip
13 Bearing locating ring
14 Mainshaft bearing
15 Layshaft
16 Layshaft 2nd gear pinion
17 Washer
18 Circlip
19 Layshaft 5th gear pinion
20 Shaft end plug
21 Layshaft 3rd gear pinion
22 Washer
23 Circlip
24 Layshaft 4th gear pinion
25 Circlip
26 Washer
27 Bush
28 Layshaft 1st gear pinion
29 Layshaft middle drive gear
30 Circlip
31 Layshaft bearing
32 Bolt
33 Middle gear
34 Bearing locating ring – 3 off
35 Oil seal
36 Bearing – 2 off
37 Washer
38 Circlip

30.4 Check gearbox bearings for wear, renew as required

30.6 Check pinion bushes for wear, examine teeth

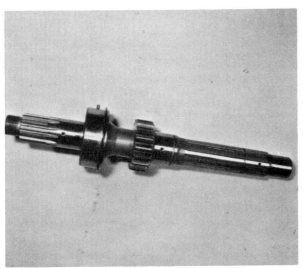

30.8a The gearbox mainshaft and drive side bearing

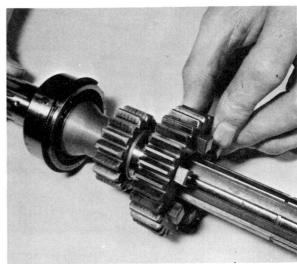

30.8b Fit the 4th gear pinion, noting direction of dogs …

30.8c … and retain with washer and circlip

30.8d Slide on the 2nd/3rd gear pinion as shown

30.8e Fit circlip and washer

30.8f Fit 5th gear pinion ...

30.8g ... and secure with plain washer and circlip

30.8h Fit bearing to shaft end

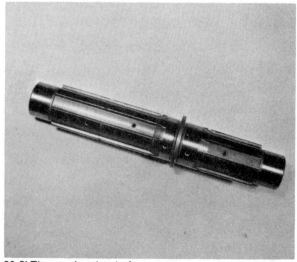

30.8i The gearbox layshaft

30.8j Fit the layshaft 2nd gear pinion ...

30.8k ... and secure with washer and circlip

30.8l 5th gear pinion is fitted with dogs facing inward

30.8m Working from other end of shaft, fit 3rd gear pinion ...

30.8n ... plain washer and circlip

30.8o Fit 4th gear pinion, selector groove inwards

30.8p Position circlip and washer as shown

30.8q Fit inner bearing over splines ...

30.8r ... followed by 1st gear pinion

30.8s Middle drive pinion is last to be fitted

31 Examination and renovation: gear selector mechanism

1   Examine the selector forks carefully, noting any signs of wear on the fork ends where they engage with the groove in the gear pinion. It is important that the forked end is not bent in any way. Check the fit of the forks on the support shaft. These should be a light sliding fit with no appreciable free play. Any movement at the bore will be greatly magnified at the fork end, leading to imprecise gear selection.
2   Check the support shaft for wear or scoring, renewing it if obviously damaged. Check for straightness by rolling it across a surface plate or a sheet of plate glass. If the shaft is even slightly bent, it must be renewed.
3   Examine the tracks in the selector drum in conjunction with the selector fork pins which run in them. In practice, the tracks will not wear appreciably, even over high mileages, but the small pins on the selector forks may show signs of flattening, in which case they should be renewed to reduce play. Note that the pins are integral with the fork, and thus the entire fork will have to be renewed if the pins are worn.
4   Examine the remainder of the selector components, looking for wear or damage, which should be self-evident. Renew any of the springs which appear weakened or are broken. Check the selector drum pins and claw for wear. The large locating pin is unlikely to warrant attention, as is the detent plunger assembly.

32 Examination and renovation: middle gear case unit

1   The middle gear case is a self-contained unit which is bolted to the rear of the main crankcase unit. Its purpose is to take the final drive from the middle gear assembly, turning it through 90° so that it can be fed to the final drive shaft. The case supports a pair of spiral bevel pinions by means of heavy ball bearings. The unit is similar to that fitted to the XS750 and 850 models, and is thus well proven. In practice, the unit should last the life of the machine, given that oil changes are performed at the specified intervals.
2   It should be noted that the unit must not be dismantled at home, because some of the equipment required will not be available to the home mechanic. Furthermore, the complicated shimming procedure necessary to ensure long life and quiet operation is the subject of an involved training programme available only to Yamaha Service Technicians. For this reason, all overhaul and adjustment work must be entrusted to an authorised Yamaha dealer.
3   Home maintenance is therefore confined to external checking only. If the unit has been leaking oil or if it feels rough or noisy in operation, take the complete unit to a Yamaha dealer for a full, professional examination. It is important to check the appearance of the oil at each oil change. Lubricant that is obviously contaminated with metallic particles will indicate the need for prompt attention if an expensive and inconvenient breakdown is to be avoided.

33 Examination and renovation: kickstart shaft assembly and engagement assembly

1   Due to the reliability of the electric start system it is unlikely that the kickstart will be used sufficiently to induce wear. Breakage of the kickstart return spring, which is perhaps the most common fault, can be rectified easily by direct replacement of the damaged spring. The old spring may be pulled off the kickstart shaft, after removal of the two

circlips, the backing plate and the spring guide. When fitting a new spring, ensure that the inner turned end is located correctly in the radically drilled hole in the shaft.

2   The integral gear on the kickstart shaft drives a double idler gear which incorporates the kickstart ratchet mechanism. This unit is built around a light alloy support block which forms the means of retention to the crankcase. The various components are retained to the idler shaft by two circlips, the disposition of each component being shown in the accompanying figure.

3   Check the various pinion teeth for wear or damage, renewing any part that is obviously defective. Examine the ratchet faces, rejecting either or both components if the ratchet teeth are rounded or badly worn. Check that the friction clip, which guides the ratchet into engagement, has not weakened. If in any doubt, the clip should be renewed.

34   Examination and renovation: electric starter drive

1   The starter motor turns the crankshaft via a roller clutch mounted on the primary shaft. The clutch comprises a body containing three spring-loaded rollers which move along an inclined plane to the driven gear boss. When the starter is operated the rollers are pressed hard against the boss, thus locking the drive and conveying movement to the crankshaft. As soon as the engine fires, the primary shaft, and thus the clutch body, moves faster than the driven gear. The rollers move back against spring pressure and the unit freewheels.

2   This type of starter clutch is almost foolproof in operation and does not suffer from rapid wear. If necessary, the driven gear can be pulled clear of the body for examination, noting that the rollers will become displaced as this is done. Check the surface of the driven gear boss for signs of indentation, renewing the gear if it is worn or damaged. The clutch rollers should also be checked for wear, renewing them if they appear marked or flattened at any point. If the three springs are bent or broken, or if there has been any evidence of slipping in the past, they should be renewed.

3   Check the three Allen bolts for security. If any of the bolts are loose, they should be removed and discarded. Fit new bolts, having coated their threads with Locktite, tightening to 2.8 – 3.2 kgf m (20 – 23 lbf ft). Yamaha also advise that the bolt ends are staked over for additional security.

31.2 Fit the idler pinion to the end of the selector fork shaft

32.1 Middle gear case must not be dismantled

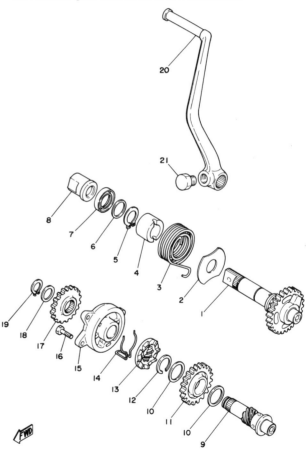

Fig. 1.20 Kickstarter

1 Kickstarter shaft	12 Circlip
2 Spring seating plate	13 Ratchet
3 Return spring	14 Clip
4 Spacer	15 Ratchet housing
5 Circlip	16 Bolt – 3 off
6 Washer	17 Idler gear
7 Oil seal	18 Shim
8 Shaft end cover	19 Circlip
9 Ratchet assembly shaft	20 Kickstarter lever
10 Washer	21 Bolt
11 Idler gear	

33.2a Check shaft and quick thread for wear

33.2b Position washer and pinion as shown

33.2c Retain with plain washer and circlip

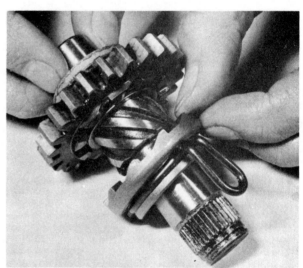

33.2d Refit ratchet block and friction clip

33.2e Fit support block, noting recess for clip location

33.2f Refit pinion to shaft end as shown

34.2a Examine pinion boss for indentation or scoring

34.2d Check that plungers and springs operate smoothly

34.2b Check condition of internal bush

34.2c Rollers should be unmarked

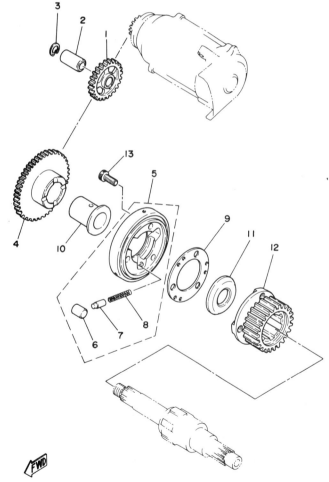

Fig. 1.21 Starter clutch

1 Starter idler gear
2 Spindle
3 Circlip
4 Starter driven gear
5 Starter clutch assembly
6 Roller − 3 off
7 Plunger − 3 off
8 Spring − 3 off
9 End plate
10 Bush
11 Spacer
12 Primary driven sprocket
13 Allen screw − 3 off

35 Engine reassembly: general

1   Before reassembly of the engine/gearbox unit is commenced, the various component parts should be cleaned thoroughly and placed on a sheet of clean paper, close to the working area.
2   Make sure all traces of old gaskets have been removed and that the mating surfaces are clean and undamaged.
   One of the best ways to remove old gasket cement is to apply a rag soaked in methylated spirit. This acts as a solvent and will ensure that the cement is removed without resort to scraping and the consequent risk of damage.
3   Gather together all of the necessary tools and have available an oil can filled with clean engine oil. Make sure all new gaskets and oil seals are to hand, also all replacement parts required. Nothing is more frustrating than having to stop in the middle of a reassembly sequence because a vital gasket or replacement has been overlooked.
4   Make sure that the reassembly area is clean and that there is adequate working space. Refer to the torque and clearance settings wherever they are given. Many of the smaller bolts are easily sheared if over-tightened. Always use the correct size screwdriver bit for the crosshead screws and never an ordinary screwdriver or punch. If the existing screws show evidence of maltreatment in the past, it is advisable to renew them as a complete set.

36 Engine reassembly: installing the lower crankcase components

1   The assembled kickstart idler and ratchet mechanism can be fitted into the casing, securing its support block with three hexagon-headed bolts. Check that the oil deflector plate, which diverts oil to the mechanism, is in position and that its single retaining bolt is secured.
2   Check that the journal ball bearing which supports the right-hand end of the gearbox layshaft is fitted correctly and that the locating circlip is firmly in position. Manoeuvre the assembled gearbox layshaft into the casing, the large aperture at the left-hand end providing the necessary clearance for this purpose. Fit the special flanged bolt which secures the left-hand end of the layshaft. In the absence of the factory holding tool (part number **90890-04009**) which

supports and locks the right-hand end of the shaft, the final tightening of the flanged bolt should be undertaken after the support block has been fitted, using a strap wrench to hold the shaft. Tighten the flanged bolt to 7.0 kgf m (51 lbf ft).
3   Fit the circular support block to the right-hand end of the layshaft. The support block is retained by the three special Torx countersunk screws, the tightening of which will require the use of the special tool used during dismantling. Prior to fitting the screws, coat their threads with Loctite to prevent loosening in service. Check that the layshaft rotates smoothly, and lubricate the gears and bearing surfaces with engine oil.
4   Slide the selector drum half way into position, then place the detent plate (stopper plate) over the end. Check that the plate locates on the small dowel pin in the drum end, then fit the retaining circlip. Drop the guide pin into its bore and secure it with its retainer and single holding bolt. At the opposite end of the drum, fit the detent assembly, tightening it to 2.0 kgf m (14.0 lbf ft) and then locking it by bending up the tabs of the lockwasher. Note that the detent is fitted from the underside of the casing.
5   Fit the oil pump idler gear to the end of the selector fork shaft, ensuring that the circlip on each side of the pinion locates correctly. Check that the small locating dowel is in position immediately inboard of the idler gear. Slide the shaft part way into the casing, then place each of the selector forks into their respective positions. Note that each of the selector forks is different in shape and must be fitted in its proper location. This can best be seen in Fig. 1.22. The two outer forks face downwards and engage in grooves in the layshaft 4th and 5th gears, whilst the centre fork faces upwards to engage with the mainshaft 2nd/3rd gear when the crankcase halves are joined. As the support shaft is slid fully home ensure that the small dowel pin on the oil pump idler gear end engages with the corresponding locating slot in the casing.
6   Moving to the other end of the support shaft, fit a circlip to the innermost groove to secure the shaft. The selector segment/claw assembly can now be fitted to the shaft end, lifting the claw into position at the end of the selector drum. Fit the remaining circlip to retain the segment on the shaft end.
7   Fit the main bearing shells to the lower crankcase, ensuring that each is fitted correctly, that the locating tang is positioned in its recess and that the oilways are unobstructed. Lubricate each shell with engine oil. The lower crankcase half can now be set aside until the upper half has been assembled.

36.1a Refit oil deflector and secure with bolt (arrowed)

36.1b Refit kickstart mechanism as shown ...

36.1c ... and retain with three bolts (arrowed)

36.1d Ensure that friction clip is located correctly (arrowed)

36.2a Manoeuvre the layshaft into position

36.2b Note position of kickstart pinion

36.3a Check that bearing is correctly seated in support block

36.3b Fit support block as shown ...

36.3c … and retain with three Torx screws

36.3d Fit and secure flanged bolt at opposite end

36.4a Slide selector drum half way into position

36.4b Fit detent plate, noting locating pin (arrowed) …

36.4c … and secure with circlip

36.4d Drop guide pin into casing hole …

36.4e … and fit locating plate, lockwasher and bolt

36.4f Fit detent plunger assembly as shown

36.5a Slide shaft into place through selector forks

36.5b Note small locating pin (arrowed) …

36.5c … which engages in slot in casing (arrowed)

36.5d Selector forks should be positioned as shown

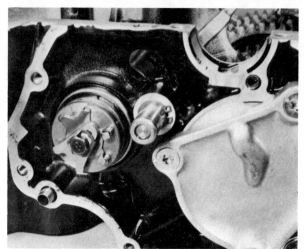

36.6a Retain shaft end with circlip

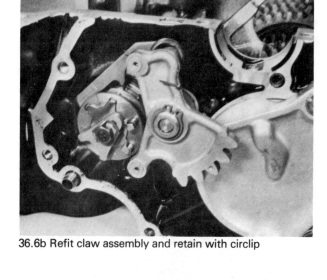

36.6b Refit claw assembly and retain with circlip

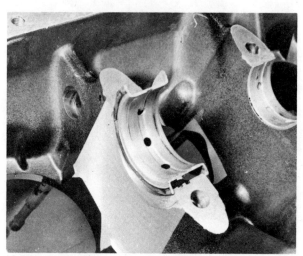

36.7 Note special thrust faces on main bearing shell

primary shaft housing and lubricate them and the bearing before fitting the housing into position. The housing is secured by three Allen screws. Installation of the primary drive pinion is easier if left until later.

3   Check that the circlip which locates the clutch end gearbox mainshaft bearing is fitted securely in its groove and that the half rings are located in the casing grooves. Place the assembled gearbox mainshaft in position, ensuring that the circlip and half-rings locate properly.

4   Fit a new oil seal to the end of the middle gear shaft, having first lubricated the seal face with grease. The shaft is located by half rings at each end, the oil seal end having a single half ring whilst the other end is fitted with two. Check that these are correctly located and place the assembled shaft in its casing recess.

5   Fit a new O-ring to the dowel at the centre of the casing, adjacent to the primary drive chain. This dowel forms the connection for the main oil gallery, and it is essential that an oil-tight seal is formed. For this reason, **never** re-use an old O-ring at this joint as lost oil pressure could have very expensive consequences.

37 Engine reassembly: installing the upper crankcase components

1   Place the inverted upper crankcase half on the workbench, arranging blocks under the rear of the casing so that it is supported level by the blocks and the cylinder head studs. Arrange the primary chain and cam chain over their respective crankshaft sprockets. If the original primary chain is to be re-used ensure that it is fitted to run in the same direction as it ran previously. Fit the upper crankcase main bearing shells in the same way as was described in the preceding section, not forgetting to lubricate each one with a little engine oil. Lower the crankshaft into place, guiding the connecting rods and the cam chain through the appropriate apertures. Make sure that the crankshaft oil seals seat correctly and that their locating lips engage in the casing grooves. Note that new seals should always be used, and should be lubricated with grease prior to fitting.

2   Loop the primary chain around the combined starter clutch/primary shaft sprocket and lower the unit into its recess in the casing. Slide the primary shaft into position from the left-hand side of the casing, guiding it through the centre of the starter clutch unit. Fit new O-rings to the

38 Engine reassembly: joining the crankcase halves

1   Check that the mating surfaces of each crankcase half are clean and dry, giving each one a final wipe with solvent to remove any residual grease or oil. Apply Yamabond No 4 or a silicone rubber jointing compound to the gasket faces, taking care to coat the surface evenly and completely. **Do not** allow the compound to come within 2 – 3 mm of the main bearing shells and do not apply it to the area around the central oil feed dowel.

2   Using an oil can filled with clean engine oil, lubricate the crankshaft big-end and main bearings and the gearbox bearings and pinions. Bear in mind that when the rebuilt engine is first started there will be a delay of several seconds before the oil begins to circulate, so careful oiling of vulnerable areas is essential.

3   At this stage it is invaluable to have an assistant to help during the joining operation. Check that the inverted upper crankcase is securely supported, then carefully lower the lower casing half into position. As the two halves meet, make sure that the central selector fork engages with the groove in the 2nd/3rd gear pinion. If this is not the case, it will be impossible to close the joint fully.

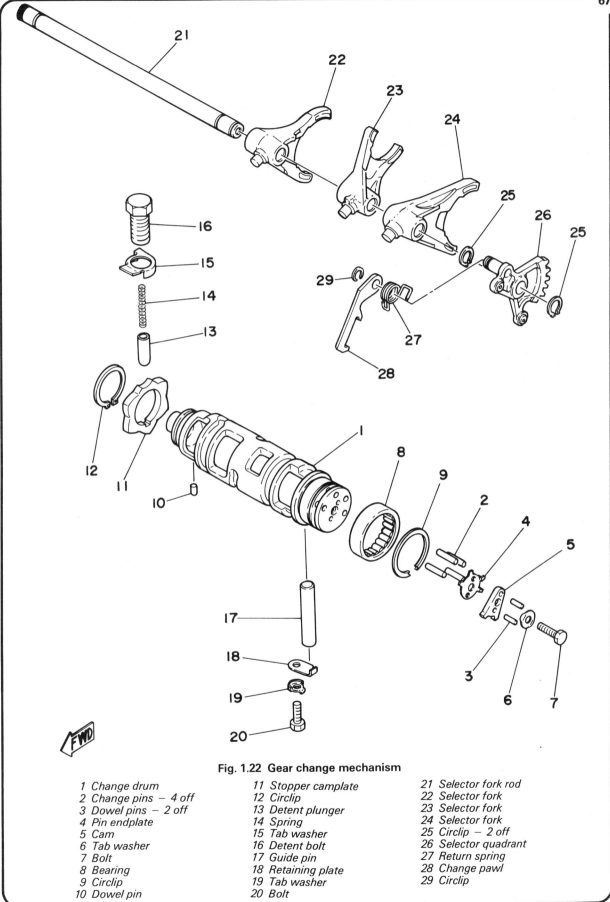

Fig. 1.22 Gear change mechanism

1 Change drum	11 Stopper camplate	21 Selector fork rod
2 Change pins − 4 off	12 Circlip	22 Selector fork
3 Dowel pins − 2 off	13 Detent plunger	23 Selector fork
4 Pin endplate	14 Spring	24 Selector fork
5 Cam	15 Tab washer	25 Circlip − 2 off
6 Tab washer	16 Detent bolt	26 Selector quadrant
7 Bolt	17 Guide pin	27 Return spring
8 Bearing	18 Retaining plate	28 Change pawl
9 Circlip	19 Tab washer	29 Circlip
10 Dowel pin	20 Bolt	

4   Having checked the selector fork position, the crankcase halves can be closed. Check around the unit to ensure that the various oil seals do not become displaced. It may prove helpful to tap around the crankcase to close the last few millimetres of gap. Use a soft-faced mallet, but avoid excessive force.

5   Drop the eleven 8 mm and twelve 6 mm crankcase bolts into place, following the accompanying illustration. Note that the two 8 mm bolts which fit inside the oil filter housing area do not have plain washers fitted beneath their heads, whilst the remainder do. Note that three of the bolts (Nos 18, 19 and 22) are fitted inside the sump area.

6   Tighten the bolts in the correct sequence to **half** the recommended torque value, then go over each one a second time to bring it up to the full torque figure. The appropriate torque values are as follows:

Crankcase bolt torque settings

6 mm   1.2 kgf m (8.7 lbf ft)
8 mm   2.4 kgf m (17.4 lbf ft)

7   Turn the unit over and fit the remaining eight 6 mm and four 8 mm bolts. Using the method described above, tighten each one to the correct torque figure, in the sequence shown in the tightening diagram. Note that one of the 6 mm bolts fits inside the oil separator housing.

8   Once all of the crankcase bolts are secure, check that the crankshaft, primary shaft and gearbox shafts are free to rotate. It should be noted that the crankshaft may feel stiff in operation due to its plain bearings, particularly if these have been renewed, but there should be no specific tight spots which might indicate misalignment.

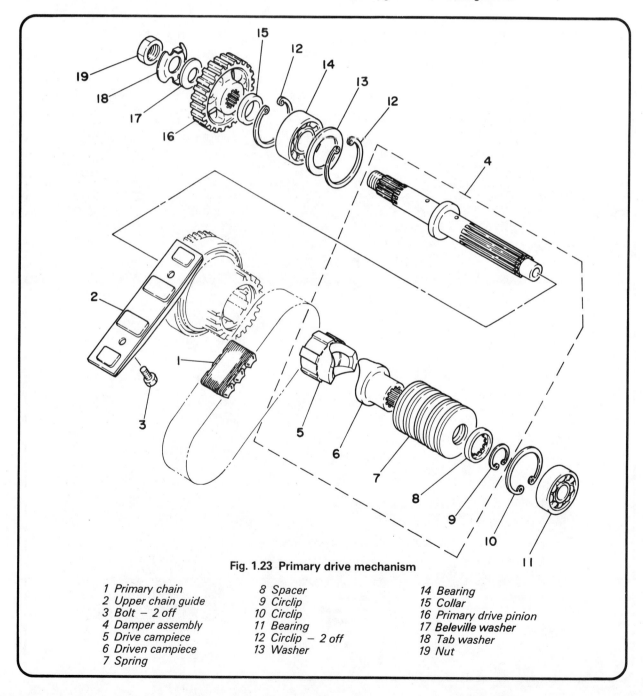

Fig. 1.23 Primary drive mechanism

1 Primary chain	8 Spacer	14 Bearing
2 Upper chain guide	9 Circlip	15 Collar
3 Bolt – 2 off	10 Circlip	16 Primary drive pinion
4 Damper assembly	11 Bearing	17 Beleville washer
5 Drive campiece	12 Circlip – 2 off	18 Tab washer
6 Driven campiece	13 Washer	19 Nut
7 Spring		

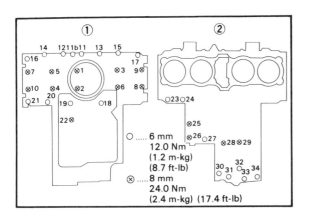

Fig. 1.24 Crankcase bolt tightening sequence

1 Lower crankcase half   2 Upper crankcase half

○ ..... 6 mm
12.0 Nm
(1.2 m-kg)
(8.7 ft-lb)
⊗ ..... 8 mm
24.0 Nm
(2.4 m-kg) (17.4 ft-lb)

37.1 Lower crankshaft into inverted upper crankcase

37.2a Fit starter clutch/sprocket unit as shown ...

37.2b ... then insert primary shaft

37.2c Fit bearing to support block as shown ...

37.2d ... and retain with circlip

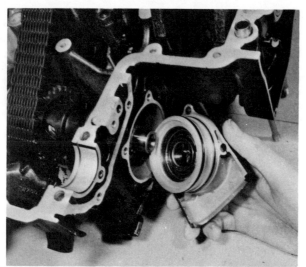

37.2e Support block can now be fitted to crankcase

37.3a Fit half-ring into groove in mainshaft recess (arrowed)

37.3b Place mainshaft into casing

37.3c Note half-ring and small locating pin

37.4a Fit half-ring as shown above ...

37.4b ... and place middle gear assembly in casing

37.5 Fit a new O-ring to central dowel (arrowed)

38.1 The assembled upper crankcase half

38.5 Note bolts inside filter housing (no washers fitted)

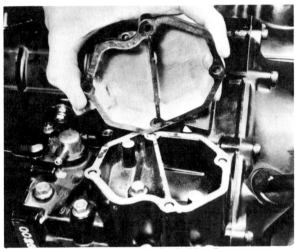

38.7 One upper crankcase bolt fits inside oil separator

39 Engine reassembly: refitting the sump components

1   The oil pump should be checked for wear prior to refitting it to the rebuilt engine. the appropriate procedure is given in Chapter 2 Section 12. It is important that the oil pump is primed at this stage, otherwise there is a risk of lubrication failure in service. Priming can be carried out by pouring oil into the inverted oil strainer whilst rotating the pump pinion by hand to distribute the oil through the pump.

2   Fit a new O-ring to the oil pump outlet and lower the pump into the inverted crankcase. Fit the three Allen screws which retain it and tighten them securely. If possible, use a torque wrench on the screws to obtain a setting of 1.0 kgf m (7.2 lbf ft).

3   Check that all three baffle plates are securely in position in the sump plate, and that the gasket faces of both the sump and the crankcase are clean and dry. Fit the sump using a new gasket and fit the fourteen retaining bolts finger tight. Do not omit the two wiring clips which are retained by the two rearmost retaining bolts. Tighten the bolts gradually in a criss-cross pattern to avoid any risk of distortion. The final torque figure is 1.0 kgf m (7.2 lbf ft).

39.3a Refit oil pump, then replace sump with new gasket

39.3b Note wiring guides on rear screws

40   Engine reassembly: fitting the selector mechanism

1   The selector claw and quadrant will normally have been fitted at this stage, prior to the crankcase halves being joined. If this operation was overlooked, the assembly should be located over the protruding end of the selector fork support shaft and its retaining circlip fitted. Note that a circlip is fitted to each side of the quadrant.

2   Slide the selector shaft and segment into position, ensuring that the index marks on the segment and quadrant align. Check that the two ends of the centring spring engage on either side of the eccentric locating screw.

3   Select second gear and check that the alignment marks on the selector drum end and the claw coincide. If necessary, make any adjustment by moving the eccentric screw, having first released its locknut. When the marks coincide exactly, hold the screw position and tighten the locknut. Fit the selector mechanism cover using a new gasket. Note the three wiring clips which should be fitted along the bottom edge of the cover.

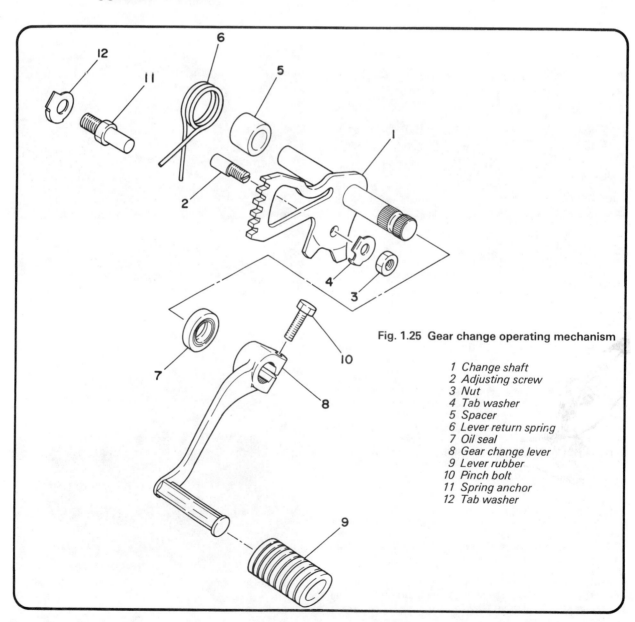

Fig. 1.25 Gear change operating mechanism

1 Change shaft
2 Adjusting screw
3 Nut
4 Tab washer
5 Spacer
6 Lever return spring
7 Oil seal
8 Gear change lever
9 Lever rubber
10 Pinch bolt
11 Spring anchor
12 Tab washer

40.1 Refit oil feed plate. Use new O-ring

40.2a Check that alignment marks coincide ...

40.2b ... and that centring spring locates properly

40.3a Check that selector claw is correctly adjusted (arrowed) ...

40.3b ... then refit outer cover

40.3c Refit screws, noting wiring clips on lower edge

41 Engine reassembly: refitting the clutch and starter assembly

1   If not already in place, fit the primary drive pinion to the end of the primary shaft. Fit the Belville washer with the concave face towards the pinion. Fit a new lockwasher and fit the retaining nut finger tight. Lock the pinion by inserting a screwdriver blade between the pinion teeth and the casing recess, and tighten it to 7.0 kgf m (50.6 lbf ft). Do not omit to bend over the locking tab.

2   Fit the kickstart idler gear in position on its shaft and retain it with its plain washer and circlip. Note that the above-mentioned components, plus the gearbox layshaft flanged bolt **must** be in position and secured before the clutch assembly is fitted, because they are not accessible with the clutch in position.

3   Place the kickstart shaft assembly in its casing recess and hook the free end of the return spring over the projection in the casing. Using the kickstart lever or a self-locking wrench or similar, turn the kickstart shaft anti-clockwise until the kickstart gear and idler gear engage, after about 180° movement. Carefully release the kickstart shaft which will now be under return spring tension.

4   Fit the thicker (2 mm) of the two plain thrust washers over the protruding end of the gearbox mainshaft. Lubricate and fit the clutch outer drum bearing, followed by the outer drum itself and the second plain washer.

5   The remaining clutch components should be fitted as an assembly, building them around the clutch centre. Fit the plain and friction plates in an alternating sequence, ensuring that the projecting tangs of the friction plates are kept in line. Fit the pressure plate and secure the assembly by fitting two or three of the clutch springs and bolts.

6   Fit the clutch centre assembly over the mainshaft end, followed by the Belville washer, a new lockwasher and the retaining nut. Lock the mainshaft by the same means as was employed during removal, and tighten the securing nut to 7.0 kgf m (50.6 lbf ft). Do not omit to secure the lockwasher. Remove the bolts and springs which were used during the assembly and tightening of the clutch, and fit the outer pressure plate (release plate) over all six clutch springs. Fit the retaining bolts, tightening them evenly and diagonally to 1.0 kgf m (7.2 lbf ft).

7   Check that the mushroom-headed clutch pushrod is in place in the release bearing, then fit the clutch outer casing using a new gasket. Take care not to damage the kickstart shaft oil seal as the cover is fitted. To this end, the splines on the shaft end can be wrapped with pvc tape until the cover is in place. Check that the two wiring clips are fitted behind the appropriate screw heads.

41.1a Place spacer over primary shaft end

41.1b Fit primary drive pinion ...

41.1c ... followed by Belville washer ...

41.1d ... and lock washer and retaining nut

41.2 Check that kickstart idler pinion is in place

41.3 Refit kickstart, turning shaft to engage mechanism

41.4a Fit thicker thrustwasher and clutch bearing

41.4b Place clutch outer drum into position ...

41.4c ... and fit remaining thrustwasher

41.6a Reassemble and fit the clutch centre and plates

41.6b Fit centre nut and lock washer …

41.6c … and tighten to specified torque

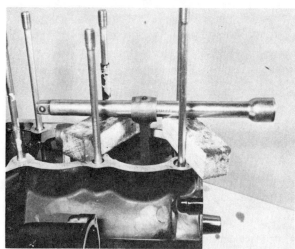

41.6d Use bar and wooden blocks to lock crankshaft

41.6e Refit the outer pressure plate …

41.6f … and tighten the six securing bolts

42 Engine reassembly: refitting the alternator

1   Check that the crankshaft taper is clean and dry, then offer up the alternator rotor, retaining it with its spring washer, plain washer and retaining bolt. Hold the crankshaft by whatever means was employed during the dismantling sequence, and tighten the rotor retaining bolt to 6.5 kgf m (47 lbf ft). Before fitting the cover and stator, check that the slip ring faces on the rotor are free from oil or grease. Place the cover assembly in position, using a new gasket, and secure it with its five retaining screws.

43 Engine reassembly: refitting the pistons and cylinder block

1   Before starting this stage of reassembly it should be noted that it will be necessary to arrange the cam chain so that it passes through its tunnel as the cylinder block is lowered into position. This can be accomplished after the cam chain tensioner and guide assembly has been fitted. Check that the baseplate of the tensioner locates squarely and engages the two dowel pins, then fit its four retaining

bolts. The cam chain runs between the two guide surfaces, and can be arranged so as not to impede the fitting of the cylinder block or head by holding the tensioner and guide together. The loop of chain which protrudes can be positioned to hang over one side and secured with an elastic band.

2   Pad the crankcase mouths with clean rag to prevent the ingress of foreign matter during piston and cylinder barrel replacement. It is only too easy to drop a circlip while it is being inserted into the piston boss, which will necessitate a further strip down for its retrieval.

3   Fit the piston rings in their correct relative positions, taking great care to avoid breakage. With a little practice the ring ends can be eased apart with the thumbs and the ring lowered into position. Alternatively, a piston ring expander can be used. This is a plier-like tool that does much the same thing as described above. One of the safest (and cheapest) methods is to use three thin steel strips such as old feeler gauges to ease the ring into place. Arrange the various ring end gaps as shown in the accompanying figure.

4   Fit the pistons onto their original connecting rods, with the arrow embossed on each piston crown facing forwards. If the gudgeon pins are a tight fit in the piston bosses, warm each piston first to expand the metal. Do not forget to lubricate the gudgeon pin, small-end eye and the piston bosses before reassembly.

5   Use new circlips. **never** re-use old circlips. Check that each circlip has located correctly in its groove. A displaced circlip will cause severe engine damage. Note that the circlips should be fitted with the gap facing down towards the piston skirt.

6   Fit a new cylinder base gasket, having checked that the crankcase and cylinder block gasket faces are clean and free from oil. Make sure that the two locating dowels are in position around the rear outer cylinder studs.

7   Rotate the engine so that cylinders No 2 and 3 are at TDC. Refitting of the cylinder block can be facilitated by the use of a piston ring clamp placed on each piston. This is by no means essential because the cylinder bore spigots have a good lead-in and the rings may therefore be hand-fed into the bores. Whichever method is adopted, an assistant should be available to guide the pistons.

8   Position a new sealing ring around each cylinder bore spigot and lubricate the bores thoroughly with clean engine oil. Carefully slide the cylinder block down the holding down studs until the pistons enter the cylinder bores; keeping the pistons square to the bores ease the block down until the piston clamps are displaced. Lower the cylinder block slightly further and remove the piston ring clamps (where used). Rotate the crankshaft slightly until the two outer pistons (1 and 4) approach their respective bores. These should be fitted as described above. Remove the piston ring clamps and the rag padding from the crankcase mouths and push the cylinder block down onto the base gasket.

9   Once all four pistons are securely in position, slide the cylinder block firmly onto the cylinder base gasket. Check that the cam chain is secured by passing a bar through the protruding loop, resting the ends across the gasket face.

44 Engine reassembly: refitting the cylinder head

1   Before the cylinder head can be refitted the valves, springs and cam followers must be replaced by reversing the dismantling procedure. Place a new valve guide seal onto each guide top. Lubricate the valve stems thoroughly. When fitting the springs do not omit the lower seating washer. Note that each spring has variable pitch coils. The springs **must** be fitted so that the more widely spaced coils are at the top. After fitting the valve collets and releasing the spring

compressor strike smartly the top of each valve stem with a hammer. This will ensure that the collets are seated correctly. Lubricate the cam followers and install them, ensuring that each is returned to its original location. Fit also the adjuster pads in their original locations.

2   Fit a new cylinder head gasket to the top of the cylinder and check that the two locating dowels are in position around the outer rear holding studs. Fit the cam chain tunnel seal with its locating tabs facing downwards to engage with the head gasket.

3   Lower the cylinder head into position over the holding down studs, ensuring that it locates over the two dowels. Fit the cylinder head nuts and washers finger tight. The nuts should be tightened in the sequence shown in the accompanying illustration, first to half the torque value, and then to the full torque value. This will ensure that the head is pulled down evenly with no risk of distortion. The final torque figure is 3.5 kgf m (25.3 lbf ft). Fit the smaller nuts to the downward-facing studs at the cylinder head/block joint at the front and rear of the cylinder block. These should be tightened to 2.0 kgf m (14.5 lbf ft).

42.1 Refit the alternator rotor, followed by stator

43.1a Check that tensioner locating dowels are in place

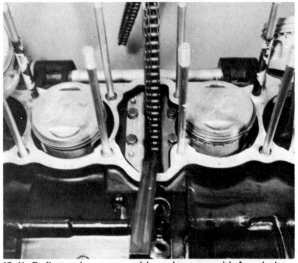

43.1b Refit tensioner assembly and secure with four bolts

43.4a Arrow mark on pistons must face exhaust port

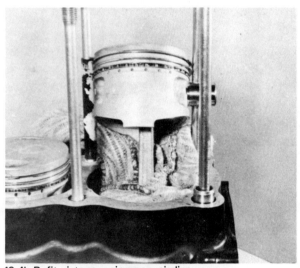

43.4b Refit pistons, using new circlips

43.7 Cylinder block can now be fitted

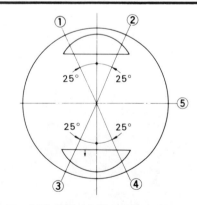

Fig. 1.26 Piston ring gap positions

1 Top ring
2 Oil scraper ring lower rail
3 Oil scraper ring upper rail
4 Second ring
5 Expander ring

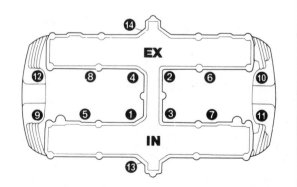

Fig. 1.27 Cylinder head nut tightening sequence

44.2 Fit new head gasket and tunnel seal

44.3a Place cylinder head in position over studs

44.3b Tighten cylinder head nuts in correct sequence

45.2 Refit ignition pickup assembly, noting hose routing

45 Engine reassembly: refitting the ignition pickup assembly

1   Check that the timing pointer is securely in position on the crankcase. Note that if the pointer was removed, it will be necessary to use a dial gauge to reset it, as described later in this Section.

2   Place the automatic timing unit (ATU) over the end of the crankshaft, noting that there is an offset location pin which ensures that the unit cannot be refitted incorrectly. Fit the pickup stator assembly, making use of the slot in the internal bore to clear the projecting lip of the reluctor. Fit the stator retaining screws, finger-tight at this stage. As mentioned in paragraph 5 the ignition timing must be checked; following this the screws can be tightened.

3   Offer up the timing plate. This is fitted to the end of the ATU, and is located by an offset slot. This makes it impossible to fit 180° out. Fit the long central retaining bolt and secure to 2.0 kgf m (14.5 lbf ft).

4   If it is desired to check the correct positioning of the timing pointer it will be necessary to use a dial gauge to establish the exact point at which cylinders 1 and 4 reach TDC. Using a suitable gauge with a spark plug adaptor, rock the crankshaft back and forth until the TDC 'dead spot' is located. Check the relationship of the timing plate and the pointer. If the latter is correctly positioned, it should coincide exactly with the T mark on the timing plate. If necessary, slacken the retaining screw and reposition the pointer.

5   On completion of engine reassembly, and soon after the engine is first started the ignition timing must be checked, and if necessary adjusted. The procedure for accomplishing this is given in Chapter 3, Sections 7 and 8.

46 Engine reassembly: refitting the camshafts and setting the valve timing

1   It is recommended that the timing pointer position is checked as described in Section 44.4, especially where a full overhaul has taken place. Although this will require a dial gauge and spark plug adaptor it is a worthwhile precaution, even though it is unlikely to require adjustment if it has remained undisturbed. Bear in mind that a small inaccuracy in the pointer position will create inaccuracies in both valve and ignition timing settings.

2   Using the large flat on the end of the timing plate, rotate the crankshaft until the T mark aligns with the timing pointer. It should be noted that, as the XS1100 models use an electronic tachometer, the cast-in gear which is normally found on exhaust camshafts is omitted and thus cannot be

used as a quick method of identifying the camshafts. Each camshaft is therefore marked IN or EX as appropriate, immediately to the right of the sprocket boss. Place the camshaft sprockets in position on the appropriate camshaft, but do not fit the retaining bolts. Fit the inlet camshaft in position, looping the cam chain around the sprocket. Position the exhaust camshaft in a similar manner, noting that extra clearance may be gained by displacing the sprockets to the right until they drop clear of the shouldered portion of the camshaft which normally serves to support and locate them.

3   The camshafts each carry an alignment mark which takes the form of a punch mark on the locating flange adjacent to the centre bearing journal. To minimise the amount of movement required at the timing stage, the marks should be arranged so that they face directly upwards.

4   At this stage the camshaft journals and bearing caps should be lubricated with copious quantities of engine oil. Bear in mind that when the engine is first started there will be a few seconds delay before oil pressure builds sufficiently to provide a steady supply to these bearing surfaces. It follows that lubrication during assembly is of the utmost importance during those first few seconds.

5   Place the camshaft bearing caps in position starting with the centre, dowelled, caps followed by the outer caps. Each cap is identified to indicate its position, the extreme left-hand inlet camshaft cap being I-1 and its exhaust counterpart E-1 and so on, the coding running from I-1 to I-5 and E-1 to E-5. Fit the nuts and washers finger tight. When tightening the retaining nuts, it is essential that the camshafts are pulled down evenly and squarely to avoid damage to the shafts, cylinder head and valve gear. Go over each nut in a diagonal sequence, turning it by about a half turn until the camshafts are fully located but without applying any torque loading to the caps. Set the torque wrench to 0.5 kgf m (3.62 lbf ft) and tighten each nut in a diagonal pattern. The torque wrench should now be set to the final torque figure of 1.0 kgf m (7.2 lbf ft) and the nuts tightened fully.

6   Check that the crankshaft is still in the correct position with the T mark aligned with the timing pointer. The index mark on each camshaft should coincide with the fixed mark on each of the centre bearing caps. If necessary, make any **small** adjustments by turning the camshaft(s) via the hexagon provided for this purpose. Be careful not to damage the cylinder head casting by inadvertently levering between it and the camshaft with the spanner. If for any reason an excessive amount of camshaft rotation is required, it is safest to remove the camshaft concerned and refit it with the timing mark in approximate alignment as described earlier. **Warning:** if the camshaft is rotated excessively when secured but independent of the crankshaft, it is likely to cause the valves to contact the pistons at TDC, thus bending the valve stems. If any resistance other than valve spring pressure is felt, it is vital that rotation of the camshaft be stopped promptly.

7   With all three timing marks correctly aligned it will be necessary to arrange the sprockets so that their fixing holes match those in the camshaft flanges. To this end it may prove necessary to disengage the sprocket(s) from the cam chain so that they can be positioned correctly. Make sure that no chain slack exists between the crankshaft and the inlet camshaft.

8   Lift both sprockets onto their respective shoulders and secure each with one of the two retaining bolts (finger tight only). It is important that only the correct hardened and shouldered bolts are used, as the consequences of one of these parts failing in service could prove disasterous. It may prove necessary to move the sprockets by a minute amount to align the fixing holes, but not to the extent that the crankshaft must be moved.

9   Place the upper chain guide in position, then turn the crankshaft through about 45° until the C mark aligns with the pointer. Take the tensioner plunger assembly and lock it in the retracted position by depressing the plunger and tightening the bolt. Fit the plunger assembly using a new gasket and tighten the two retaining bolts to 1.0 kgf m (7.2 lbf lb). The cam chain can now be correctly tensioned by releasing the locking bolt to allow the plunger to act on the tensioner blade. Secure the plunger by tightening the locking bolt to 0.6 kgf m (4.3 lbf ft) and the locknut to 0.9 kgf m (6.5 lbf ft).

10   Check the valve timing at this stage by turning the crankshaft through about two revolutions and then re-aligning the T mark. Check that the two camshaft index marks coincide exactly with their fixed reference marks on the bearing caps. If this is not the case it will be necessary to repeat the timing operation from paragraph 6 onwards.

11   Once the timing has been set up correctly turn the crankshaft until the remaining fixing hole is visible and fit the second retaining bolt to each camshaft sprocket. It is vital to ensure that the sprocket bolts are tightened securely to the recommended torque setting of 2.0 kgf m (14.5 lbf ft) to preclude any chance of loosening in service. To this end, the application of a non-hardening thread locking compound would be beneficial. Note that the valve clearances should now be checked and reset as described in Routine Maintenance.

46.2a Set crankshaft to valve timing position

46.2b Refit inlet camshaft first ...

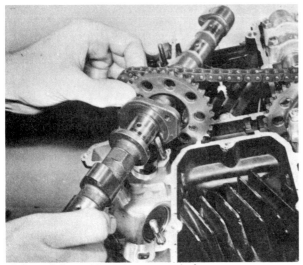

46.2c ... followed by exhaust camshaft

46.4 Lubricate camshafts and refit bearing caps

46.5 Tighten cap nuts in stages to prevent distortion

46.6 Camshaft timing marks align as shown

46.8 Refit cam chain sprocket bolts (arrowed)

46.9a Place cam chain guide bridge in position ...

46.9b ... and reset cam chain tension

46.9c Note crankshaft position during tensioning operation

47 Engine reassembly: refitting the cylinder head cover, oil feed pipe and timing cover

1   After the valve clearances have been set, the cylinder head cover can be fitted using a new gasket. Tighten the retaining screws evenly and progressively so that there is no chance that the light alloy cover will become warped.
2   Assemble the oil feed pipe which takes the feed from the crankcase to the camshafts. To ensure an oil-tight joint a new sealing washer should be fitted on each side of each of the banjo unions. Fit the union bolts finger tight, noting that the larger of the two secures the upper union. The upper bolt is identified by its dished head. When tightening the union bolt, use a spanner on the flats provided on the union to prevent it from turning and straining the pipe. The correct torque figure is 2.0 kgf m (14.5 lbf ft).
3   Place the timing cover in position and fit the retaining screws finger tight only. Note that the ignition timing must be checked when the engine is started for the first time.

47.1 Refit end seals and replace cylinder head cover

48 Engine reassembly: refitting the starter motor, separator cover and middle gear case

1   Fit a new O-ring to the nose of the starter motor casing, then slide it into position, ensuring that it engages correctly. Place the starter motor cover in position and fit the two retaining bolts to secure it and the motor.
2   If it is not already in position, fit the oil separator cover at the rear of the crankcase. The gasket may be re-used if it is intact. Tighten the four securing bolts evenly to prevent warpage.
3   Offer up the middle gear case having fitted a new gasket. If necessary, turn the output flange until the splines locate properly. Fit the securing bolts, tightening them to 2.4 kgf m (17.4 lbf ft).

49 Engine reassembly: refitting the engine/gearbox unit

1   Refitting the engine unit is a relatively straightforward operation, but the unit's considerable bulk and weight must be borne in mind. It is not feasible to install the unit unaided

47.2 Refit the cylinder head oil feed pipe

because it will be necessary to manoeuvre the crankcase mounting points into position, an operation which will require at least two pairs of hands. It was found in practice that two reasonably strong persons could just manage the refitting operation between them if the lifting phase was taken in stages.

2   Make sure that the area around the machine is clear, and that all cables and leads are lodged in a position which will not impede the engine fitting operation. Arrange the engine unit on a wooden crate or blocks on the right hand side of the frame. Find a position where both persons can lift the unit safely, then place it halfway into the frame cradle. One person should steady the unit whilst the other moves round to the left-hand side. The engine can now be manoeuvred into its final position.

3   Assemble the front engine plates, fitting the retaining bolts finger tight. The large mounting bolt should be slid into position before any of the bolts are tightened. Slide the lower front mounting bolts into place, noting that it may be necessary to lift the engine unit slightly to align the mounting holes. Slide the rear mounting bolt into position. The various bolts should be fitted with new self-locking nuts and tightened to the torque values shown below:

Engine mounting bolt torque settings
Front upper mounting bolt   6.7 kgf m (48.5 lbf ft)
Front lower mounting bolts   6.7 kgf m (48.5 lbf ft)
Rear mounting bolt   10.0 kgf m (72.5 lbf ft)
Front engine plate bolts   3.4 kgf m (24.5 lbf ft)

4   Turn the rear wheel until the marks on the edges of the drive shaft flange and middle gear case output flange align. Although this is not strictly essential it will ensure that there is no likelihood of driveshaft vibration due to any imbalance in the drive train. Position the flanges so that one of the four retaining bolts can be fitted, repeating the procedure with the remaining bolts. Tighten the bolts to 4.4 kgf m (40.0 lbf ft). Slide the gaiter back over the flanges and joint, and secure it with the spring retainer at each end.

5   Reassemble the footrest/silencer mounting plates by reversing the removal sequence. Note that it will be necessary to guide the rear master cylinder pushrod into position as the right-hand plate is fitted. Connect the engine earth strap between the frame brace tube and the rearmost screw of the middle gearcase. Reconnect the starter motor cable, routing it below the oil separator outlet and through the adjacent cable guide. The oil pressure switch lead is similarly routed and can also be connected at this stage.

6   Trace the alternator and ignition cables, routing them through their respective guide clips. Join the connector blocks which reside inboard of the fuse box backing plate. If it is not already in place, connect the starter motor lead to the solenoid terminal and slide down the protective plastic boot.

7   Reassemble the two halves of the air cleaner casing, not forgetting to fit the element as the lower half is offered up. Leave the securing bolts slack at this stage to allow movement when the carburettors are fitted.

8   Reconnect the throttle cable and manoeuvre the carburettor bank into position. This is a fairly awkward operation in view of the restricted space available and is much easier if an assistant is able to deal with one pair of instruments. Make sure that all four carburettors engage with the intake adaptors, then retain them by tightening the securing clamps. The air cleaner hoses are secured in a similar manner. Once the carburettors are in place the air filter casing can be secured.

9   Connect the vacuum advance hose to the stub provided

on the engine side of the No 2 cylinder carburettor, noting that it passes through a guide clip close to the stub. Check that the various hoses are connected to the air cleaner casing and that the carburettor drain hoses are routed clear of the rear of the crankcase.

10   Position the clutch cable and connect the nipple to the actuating lever. Bend over the small security tang which prevents the cable from working free in service. If the cable has been disconnected from the handlebar lever it should be refitted and the adjuster set to give 2 – 3 mm (0.08 – 0.12 in) free play between the lever and lever stock. **Do not** operate the clutch until the release mechanism has been adjusted as described below.

11   Slacken the clutch release adjuster locknut and turn the adjuster screw clockwise until it just contacts the pressure plate. Make sure that the normal resistance caused by the adjuster O-ring is not mistaken for contact. Back off the adjuster screw by ¼ turn and secure the locknut. Clutch adjustment is now complete and the inspection cover may be refitted.

12   UK and later G(US) versions are equipped with an engine oil cooler, which should be refitted at this stage. Make sure that the union faces are clean and dry and fit a new O-ring to each. Offer up the pipes and secure each union with its two retaining bolts. The oil cooler itself is secured to the frame by four bolts, the connecting hoses being retained by a total of four clips.

13   Assemble the oil filter bowl and its combined union bolt and relief valve, ensuring that the O-ring which seals the bolt head is in place. Fit the spring and plain washer over the end of the bolt on the inside of the filter bowl. Check that the large O-ring seal is fitted around the edge of the bowl. Place the new filter element in position and prime the filter bowl with 0.5 litres (0.9/1.0 Imp/US pint) of engine oil before fitting the assembly to the underside of the crankcase. The oil filter union bolt should be tightened to 3.2 kgf m (23.1 lbf ft).

14   Place a new exhaust port gasket in each exhaust port. These may be retained by a small dab of grease on each one until the exhaust system has been fitted. The system should be fitted in two halves by reversing the dismantling sequence. Fit the mounting and clamp bolts finger tight initially, and when all are in position tighten from the exhaust port backwards.

15   Reassemble the gearchange pedal assembly, checking that it is correctly aligned in relation to the footrest. Refit the horn(s) and ignition ballast resistor to the underside of the top frame tube. Refit the sparking plug caps to their respective plugs, noting that the leads are marked 1 to 4 from left to right. Reconnect the neutral switch lead, then install and connect the battery. The electrical system can now be checked.

16   Refit the fuel tank, remembering to connect the breather hose and the fuel gauge sender leads at the rear of the tank. Refit the side covers and the dual seat. Connect the fuel feed and vacuum pipes to the fuel cocks.

17   Top up the crankcase with 4.0 litres (7.04/8.45 Imp/US pints) of engine oil. If necessary, refer to Recommended Lubricants at the beginning of the book for details of oil grades. For normal applications, an SAE 10W/40 SE type oil will be suitable. The middle gear case should be filled with 0.36 litres (0.63/0.76 Imp/US pints) of SAE 80 or 90 hypoid gear oil. Use the dipstick provided in the tool kit to check the oil level. Note that for US models, a GL-4 rated gear oil is recommended. A GL-5 or GL-6 rated oil may also be used.

49.2 Place engine unit in frame cradle

49.3 Fit engine plates and bolts

49.4 Reconnect drive flange and fit gaiter

49.5a Refit left-hand footrest plate ...

49.5b ... followed by right-hand plate and brake pedal

49.5c Reconnect oil pressure switch lead ...

49.5d ... noting correct routing of wiring

49.8a Refit carburettors and various hoses

49.8b Slide air cleaner forward and secure top bolt (arrowed)

49.9 Refit vacuum pipe (arrowed) to No. 2 carburettor

49.10a Fit clutch cable, bending over tang to secure

49.10b Reset clutch adjustment as shown

49.12 Assemble oil cooler (where fitted)

49.13 Prime and refit oil filter assembly

49.14 Refit exhaust system, using new gaskets

49.15a Fit gearchange pedal and washer …

49.15b … and secure with circlip

49.15c Adjust to obtain correct pedal height

49.15d Check brake pedal adjustment and lubricate

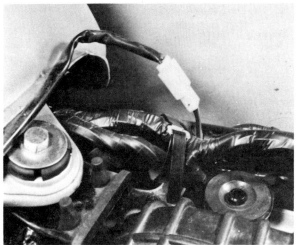

49.16a Refit tank and connect sender cable

49.16b Fit battery clamp strip and battery

49.17 Top up crankcase oil. Re-check after first run

50 Starting and running the rebuilt engine

1   Turn the fuel taps to the 'Prime' position and wait a few seconds whilst the carburettor float bowls fill. Return the fuel taps to the 'On' position once the engine is running. Check that the engine kill switch is set to the 'On' position. Start the engine using either the kickstart or the electric starter. Raise the chokes as soon as the engine will run evenly and keep it running at a low speed for a few minutes to allow oil pressure to build up and the oil to circulate. If the red oil pressure indicator lamp is not extinguished, stop the engine immediately and investigate the lack of oil pressure.

2   The engine may tend to smoke through the exhaust initially, due to the amount of oil used when assembling the various components. The excess of oil should gradually burn away as the engine settles down.

3   Check the exterior of the machine for oil leaks or blowing gaskets. Make sure that each gear engages correctly and that all the controls function effectively, particularly the brakes. This is an essential last check before taking the machine on the road.

51 Taking the rebuilt machine on the road

1   Any rebuilt machine will need time to settle down, even

if parts have been replaced in their original order. For this reason it is highly advisable to treat the machine gently for the first few miles to ensure oil has circulated throughout the lubrication system and that any new parts fitted have begun to bed down.

2   Even greater care is necessary if the engine has been rebored or if a new crankshaft has been fitted. In the case of a rebore, the engine will have to be run-in again, as if the machine were new. This means greater use of the gearbox and a restraining hand on the throttle until at least 500 miles have been covered. There is no point in keeping to any set speed limit; the main requirement is to keep a light loading on the engine and to gradually work up performance until the 500 mile mark is reached. These recommendations can be lessened to an extent when only a new crankshaft is fitted. Experience is the best guide since it is easy to tell when an engine is running freely.

3   If at any time a lubrication failure is suspected, stop the engine immediately, and investigate the cause. If an engine is run without oil, even for a short period, irrepairable engine damage is inevitable.

4   When the engine has cooled down completely after the initial run, recheck the various settings, especially the valve clearances. During the run most of the engine components will have settled into their normal working locations. Check the various oil levels, particularly that of the engine as it may have dropped slightly now that the various passages and recesses have filled.

52 Fault diagnosis: engine

Symptom	Cause	Remedy
Engine will not start	Defective sparking plugs	Remove the plugs and lay them on cylinder heads. Check whether spark occurs when ignition is switched on and engine rotated.
	Ignition fault	Recheck connections and/or timing. If necessary, refer to Chapter 3.
Engine runs unevenly	Ignition and/or fuel system fault	Check each system independently, as though engine will not start.
	Blowing cylinder head gasket	Leak should be evident from oil leakage where gas escapes.
	Incorrect ignition timing	Check accuracy and if necessary reset.
Lack of power	Fault in fuel system or incorrect ignition timing	See above.
Heavy oil consumption	Cylinder block in need of rebore	Check for bore wear, rebore and fit oversize pistons if required.
	Damaged oil seals	Check engine for oil leaks.
Excessive mechanical noise	Worn cylinder bores (piston slap) Worn camshaft drive chain (rattle) Worn big-end bearings (knock) Worn main bearings (rumble)	Rebore and fit oversize pistons. Adjust tensioner or replace chain. Renew. See text. Renew. See text.
Engine overheats and fades	Lubrication failure	Stop engine and check whether internal parts are receiving oil. Check oil level in crankcase.

53 Fault diagnosis: clutch

Symptom	Cause	Remedy
Engine speed increases as shown by tachometer but machine does not respond	Clutch slip	Check clutch adjustment for free play at handlebar lever. Check thickness of inserted plates.
Difficulty in engaging gears. Gear changes jerky and machine creeps forward when clutch is withdrawn. Difficulty in selecting neutral.	Clutch drag	Check clutch adjustment for too much free play. Check clutch drums for indentations in slots and clutch plates for burrs on tongues. Dress with file if damage not too great.
Clutch operation stiff	Damaged, trapped or frayed control cable	Check cable and renew if necessary. Make sure cable is lubricated and has no sharp bends.

54 Fault diagnosis: gearbox

Symptom	Cause	Remedy
Difficulty in engaging gears	Selector forks bent Gear clusters not assembled correctly	Renew. Check gear cluster arrangement and position of thrust washers.
Machine jumps out of gear	Worn dogs on ends of gear pinions Detent mechanism worn	Renew worn pinions. Renew as required.
Gearchange lever does not return to original position	Broken return spring	Renew spring.
Kickstarter does not return when engine is turned over or started.	Broken or poorly tensioned return spring	Renew spring or retension.

Chapter 2 Fuel system and lubrication

Contents

Specifications

Petrol tank capacity

E, F and G models	20 lit (4.40/5.28 Imp/US gal)
SF and SG models	15 lit (3.30/3.96 Imp/US gal)

Carburettors

	E and G models (UK)	E, F and SF models (US)	G model (US)	SG model (US)
Type	BS34-II 2H9-0	BS34-II 2H7-00 (E) BS34-II 2H7-10 (F) BS34-II 3H3-00 (SF)	BS34-III 3H5-00	BS34-III 3J6-00
Main jet	132.5	137.5	115 (Cyl 1 and 4) 120 (Cyl 2 and 3)	110
Needle jet	X-2	X-2	X-2	X-2
Jet needle	5Z1	5GZ6	5IZ7	5GL16
Clip position	3rd groove	3rd groove	Fixed	Fixed
Pilot jet	42.5	42.5	42.5	42.5
Starter jet	32.5	40 (E), 32.5 (F, SF)	25	25
Main air jet	140	140	140	140
Pilot air jet	180	180	185	185
Throttle valve	135	135	135	135
Pilot screw (turns out)	1 ¼	1 ¼	Preset	Preset
Float height	25.7 ± 1 mm (1.012 ± 0.04 in)	25.7 ± 1 mm (1.012 ± 0.04 in)	23.0 mm (0.906 ± 0.02 in)	23.0 mm (0.906 ± 0.02 in)
Idle speed	1050 – 1150 rpm	1050 – 1150 rpm	1100 rpm	1100 rpm

Oil capacity

Dry:
US models*	4.0 lit (8.46 US pint)
UK models	4.2 lit (7.39 Imp pint)

At oil change:
US models*	3.0 lit (6.34 US pint)
UK models	3.2 lit (5.63 Imp pint)

At oil and filter change:
US models*	3.5 lit (7.40 US pint)
UK models	3.7 lit (6.51 Imp pint)

*US models fitted with an oil cooler have UK model capacity

Oil pump

Type	Trochoid
Outer rotor/housing clearance	0.09 – 0.15 mm (0.0035 – 0.0059 in)
Inner rotor/outer rotor clearance	0.12 mm (0.0047 in)

1 General description

The fuel system comprises a petrol tank from which petrol is fed by gravity to the four CD (constant depression) carburettors, via two vacuum-controlled fuel cocks. In the normal 'On' position the fuel flow from the tap is regulated by a diaphragm and plunger. The diaphragm chamber is connected by a small rubber pipe to the inlet tract, and thus will only open the plunger valve when the engine is running. Thus for normal running the fuel cock lever is set to the 'On' position at all times, although the fuel supply is turned off as soon as the engine stops. The 'Reserve' lever position provides a small emergency supply of fuel in the event that the fuel gauge is ignored, whilst the 'Prime' setting is provided to fill the carburettor float bowls should these have been dismantled for any reason or if the machine has run completely dry.

The throttle twistgrip is connected by cable to the four throttle butterfly valves. These can be opened or closed to control the overall air flow through the instruments, and thus the engine speed. Each carburettor contains a diaphragm-type throttle valve which moves in response to changes in manifold depression and in this manner automatically controls the volume and strength of the mixture entering the combustion chamber. Because the carburettors react automatically the engine runs at the optimum setting at any given throttle twistgrip setting and engine load condition, and with compensation for variations in atmospheric pressure due to changes in altitude.

The CD carburettor is ideally suited to provide an accurately controlled mixture which conforms with the increasingly stringent emission laws in the US and Europe. This allows the overall mixture to be proportionally weaker than that of a conventional slide-type instrument, and in turn should give better fuel economy.

A more sophisticated two-stage cold start device is included to offset the normally weak mixture. When fully-on the fuel-rich mixture allows starting from cold, the control being moved to the half-on position during engine warm up. The half-on setting allows the engine to run smoothly during this transition period and eliminates many of the problems that the usual on-off arrangement tends to cause.

Engine lubrication is by a wet sump arrangement which is shared by the primary transmission and gearbox components. Oil from the sump is picked up by an engine-driven trochoid oil pump and delivered under pressure to the working surfaces of the engine and gearbox components. The accompanying line drawing shows the layout of the lubrication system.

The middle gear case is a separate unit and has its own lubrication system consisting of an oil bath. The loadings on the bevel gears are such that a high-pressure hypoid type gear oil is necessary to avoid rapid wear of the gear teeth, the light multigrade engine oil being inadequate for this application.

2 Petrol tank: removal and replacement

1   The fuel tank is retained at the forward end by two rubber buffers fitted either side of the under side of the tank which fit into cups on the frame top tube. The rear of the tank sits on a small rubber saddle placed across the frame top tube and is retained by a single bolt passing through rubber buffers either side of the tank lug.
2   To remove the tank, pull off the fuel lines at the petrol tap unions where they are held by spring clips. Detach also the vacuum pipes leading to the taps. Raise the seat and remove the rear bolt. Pull the tank up at the rear and back, off the buffers. As the rear of the tank is lifted, separate the connector in the fuel gauge sender leads. The tank can now be lifted clear of the frame and placed to one side.

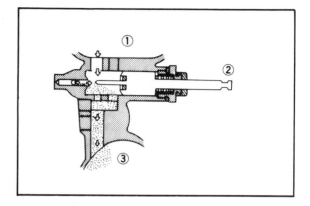

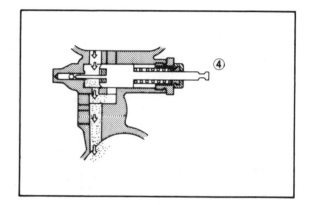

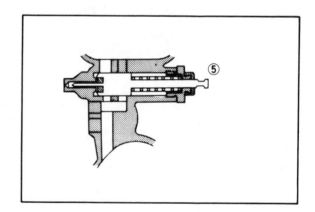

Fig. 2.1 Cold start plunger positions

1 Lower diaphragm chamber   *4 Half open position*
2 Fully open position   *5 Fully closed position*
3 Venturi

3 Petrol taps: removal, filter cleaning and replacement

1   Before either petrol tap is removed for filter cleaning or for attention to the lever, the petrol tank must be drained. Detach the petrol feed pipes and substitute a longer length of suitable piping through which to drain the fuel. Turn the tap to the 'Prime' position to allow the petrol to flow freely.
2   To remove either tap, loosen the two screws which pass through the flange into the petrol tank and withdraw the tap, complete with filter tower. The filter is a push fit on the hollow T-piece which projects from the top of the tap.

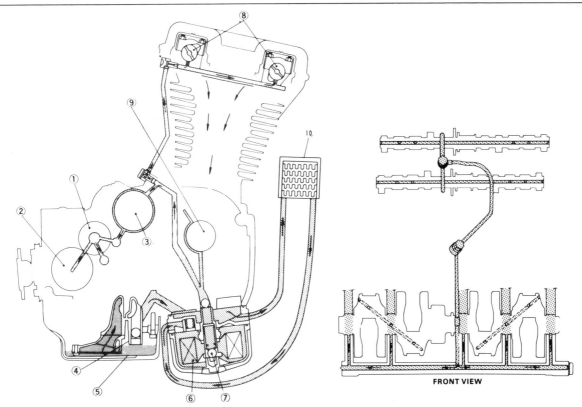

Fig. 2.2 Lubrication system

1 Mainshaft	5 Sump	8 Camshafts
2 Layshaft	6 Oil filter	9 Crankshaft
3 Primary shaft	7 Oil filter bypass valve	10 Oil cooler
4 Oil pump		

3   The filter should be cleaned at regular intervals to remove any entrapped matter. Use clean petrol and a soft brush.

4   It is seldom necessary to remove the lever which operates the petrol tap, although occasions may occur when a leakage develops at the joint. Although the tank must be drained before the lever assembly can be removed, there is no need to disturb the body of the tap.

5   To dismantle the lever assembly, remove the two cross-head screws passing through the plate on which the operating positions are inscribed. The plate can then be lifted away, followed by a spring, the lever itself and the seal behind the lever. The seal will have to be renewed if leakage has occurred. Reassemble the tap in the reverse order. Gasket cement or any other sealing medium is **not** necessary to secure a petrol tight seal. It is important to note that the popular silicone rubber or RTV instant gasket compounds must never be used on any part of the fuel system. The compound is attacked by fuel and will break-up allowing small rubber-like particles to obstruct the fuel filter or carburettor jets.

6   On E, F and G models the fuel flow control diaphragm and plunger assembly is housed behind a square cover on the inboard face of the tap body. In the event of the diaphragm becoming holed or split the plunger valve will close, blocking the fuel supply. As a temporary expedient, the machine can be ridden by selecting the prime position. Repair presents something of a problem because Yamaha do not list the diaphragm as a separate part, indicating that the entire fuel cock assembly must be renewed. On SF and SG models the diaphragm is omitted from the fuel taps and placed in a separate diaphragm housing connected to the taps, and carburettors by hoses. Access to the diaphragm can be gained by removing the housing cover. The foregoing remarks relating to condition and renewal apply.

7   Reassembly and installation are a straightforward reversal of the removal sequence, bearing in mind the above-mentioned caution against the use of jointing compounds. Petrol has a remarkable ability to locate and exploit the smallest leaks, so it is best to renew all O-rings and seals as a precaution. Apart from environmental considerations, the resultant fuel vapour would create a very dangerous fire hazard. Note that there is an O-ring seal between the petrol tap body and the petrol tank, which must be renewed if it is damaged or if petrol leakage has occurred.

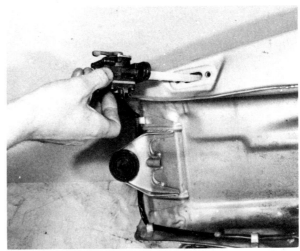

3.2 Fuel tap is retained by two bolts

3.4a Remove cover to release switch lever

3.4b Check seal around lever boss for damage

3.4c Check that internal seal faces are undamaged

3.6a Remove diaphragm cover and spring ...

3.6b ... to release diaphragm assembly

3.7 Check condition of fuel pipe union gasket

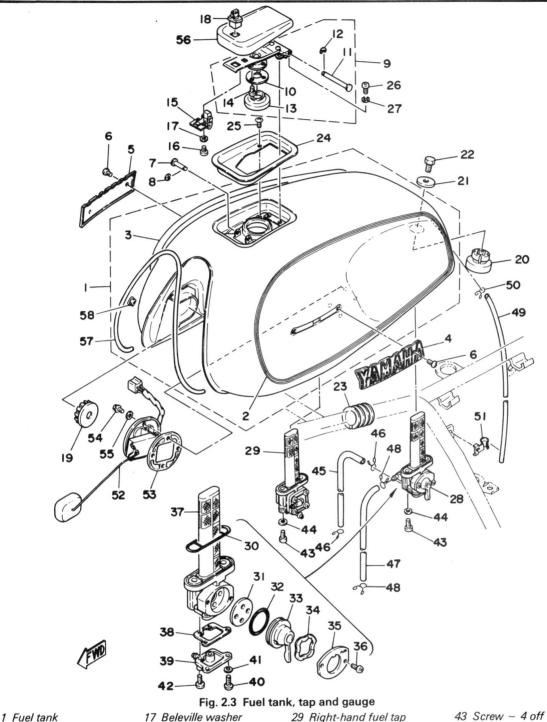

Fig. 2.3 Fuel tank, tap and gauge

1 Fuel tank	17 Beleville washer	29 Right-hand fuel tap	43 Screw – 4 off
2 Left-hand transfer	– 2 off	30 O-ring – 2 off	44 Washer – 4 off
3 Right-hand transfer	18 Filler cap key	31 Seal – 2 off	45 Fuel hose – 2 off
4 Left-hand emblem	19 Front mounting	32 Sealing ring – 2 off	46 Hose clip – 4 off
5 Right-hand emblem	damper – 2 off	33 Tap lever – 2 off	47 Vacuum hose – 2 off
6 Screw – 4 off	20 Rear mounting	34 Wave washer – 2 off	48 Hose clip – 4 off
7 Clevis pin	damper	35 Retaining plate	49 Hose
8 E-clip	21 Washer	– 2 off	50 Hose clip
9 Filler cap assembly	22 Bolt	36 Screw – 4 off	51 Hose clamp
10 Gasket	23 Top tube damping	37 Filter gauze – 2 off	52 Fuel gauge
11 Clevis pin	block – 2 off	38 Filter bowl gasket	53 Gasket
12 E-clip	24 Filler cover seal	– 2 off	54 Bolt – 4 off
13 Seal	25 Screw – 4 off	39 Filter bowl – 2 off	55 Washer – 4 off
14 Screw – 3 off	26 Screw – 2 off	40 Screw – 4 off	56 Filler cap cover
15 Releasing mechanism	27 Spring washer – 2 off	41 Spring washer – 4 off	57 Trim
16 Screw – 2 off	28 Left-hand fuel tap	42 Screw – 4 off	58 Clip – 4 off

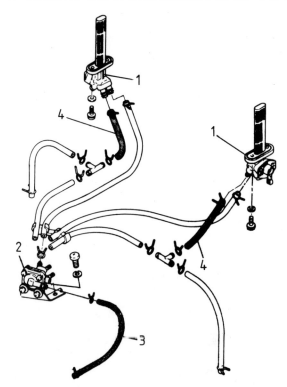

Fig. 2.4 Fuel tap and diaphragm chamber – SF and SG models

1 Fuel tap – 2 off	3 Vacuum fuel pipe
2 Diaphragm chamber	4 Fuel pipes

4 Petrol feed pipes: examination

1   Synthetic rubber feed pipes are used to convey the flow of petrol from the petrol tap to the float chamber of each of the four carburettors. Each pipe is retained by a wire clip, which must hold the pipe firmly in position. Check periodically to ensure the pipes have not begun to split or crack and that the wire clips have not worn through the surface.

2   **Do not** replace a broken pipe with one of natural rubber, even temporarily. Petrol causes natural rubber to swell very rapidly and disintegrate, with the result that minute particles of rubber would easily pass into the carburettors and cause blockages of the internal passageways. Plastic pipe of the correct bore size can be used as a temporary substitute but it should be replaced with the correct type of tubing as soon as possible since it will not have the same degree of flexibility.

5 Carburettors: removal

1   Carburettor removal will be necessary if any serious dismantling or overhaul work is necessary. Although it is possible to effect adjustment and a small amount of dismantling with the assembly in situ, the cramped location makes this an awkward proposition. It is almost invariably best to start by removing the entire bank of instruments from the machine.

2   Start by removing both side panels and the dual seat to give access to the air cleaner casing and its mounting points. The casing is retained by a total of three bolts; a single central bolt at the top and one to the rear of each side. These should be removed to free the casing, but the screws which secure the brackets to the plastic casing should be left undisturbed.

3   Slacken the clips which retain the air cleaner and intake adaptors to either end of the carburettors. The carburettor bank can now be pulled rearward to free the intake adaptors, the elasticity of the rubber and the free movement of the air cleaner casing providing just enough clearance. The instruments can now be twisted clear of the air cleaner adaptors and moved to one side. Disconnect the various pipes, the clutch cable guide clip and the throttle cable to allow the assembly to be lifted clear of the machine.

4   The assembly is refitted in the reverse order of the above, remembering to connect the cables and pipes **before** the instruments are in their final positions. Due to the limited space for manoeuvring, the aid of an assistant would prove invaluable, particularly during reassembly.

6 Carburettors: dismantling and reassembly

1   Most of the dismantling work that is likely to be required can be undertaken without the need for separating the instruments. This is a rather laborious task which is best avoided if at all possible. Should the need arise, however, details are given later in this section.

2   To gain access to the float chamber components, namely the float assembly and jets, the float bowl concerned is removed after its four retaining screws have been released. It is recommended that one instrument at a time should be dealt with to preclude any possibility of parts becoming interchanged. Note that it is not necessary to remove the connecting bracket.

3   Using a small piece of wire or a pair of pointed-nose pliers displace the headed pivot pin which locates the twin float assembly and lift the float from position. This will expose the float needle. The needle is very small and should be put away in a safe place so that it is not misplaced. Make sure that the float chamber gasket is in good condition. Do not disturb the gasket unless leakage has occurred or it appears damaged.

4   Check that the twin floats are in good condition and not punctured. Because they are made of brass it is possible to solder a damaged float. This form of repair should only be made in an emergency, when a set of new floats is not available. Soldering will affect the weight of the float assembly and result in a different petrol level. Great care must be exercised when attempting to solder a float because the combination of heat and residual fuel which may be inside the float can have unpleasant consequences. There is also a tendency for the entire assembly to fall apart as the various soldered joints liquefy. The application of a two-part epoxy adhesive is often a better choice.

5   The float needle seating is screwed into the carburettor body and may be removed for renewal if badly worn. The pilot jet is located in the smaller of the two projections in the centre of the carburettor body and is surmounted by a blanking screw. Remove the screw and use a small electrical screwdriver to extract the pilot jet, taking care not to damage the slot. The main jet is located at the end of the remaining projection and is simply unscrewed. It will be noted that it doubles as a retainer for the needle jet which is also located by a small peg in its bore. The needle jet can be removed after the diaphragm assembly has been removed, as described later in this section.

6   Examine the float needle and seat for wear, which will be evident as a ridge around the seating face of the needle. Wear in these components will allow flooding to take place and will make normal running impossible. Symptoms will be most noticeable at idle speed where the excessively rich mixture may cause the engine to stall. A magnifying glass is useful for checking these and other small carburettor parts. Note that the float needle valve seat incorporates a small fuel filter screen. This should be cleaned noting any debris which may have produced the problems which initiated the overhaul.

7 Examine the main and pilot jet bores, looking for debris or water droplets which may have obstructed them. Such obstructions can be removed by blowing the jets through with compressed air, or as a last resort, by clearing them with a fine **nylon** bristle. On no account should wire be used to clear a jet because it can enlarge or score the orifice, either of which will upset its fuel metering rate.

8 Remove the four screws which retain the diaphragm cover, noting the position of any guide clips which may be disturbed. Lift away the cover to expose the diaphragm and piston (valve) assembly. Carefully free the edges of the diaphragm then tip the assembly out of the carburettor. The needle jet may drop free at this stage but if required can be dislodged from the underside.

9 The jet needle is retained by a small internal circlip which locates a white plastic retainer in the centre of the piston. It is essential to have a pair of internal circlip pliers to effect its removal. Once the retainer has been freed the needle assembly can be displaced. Below the needle position clip are a plain washer and a small coil spring. Take care not to lose these, or the small collar which is fitted between the needle position clip and the retainer.

10 Examine the diaphragm for splits or any other damage, noting that any air leakage past the diaphragm will prevent the carburettor from functioning at all but idle speed. If damage is discovered it will be necessary to renew the diaphragm and piston as an assembly; the two components are not available separately.

11 Examine the jet needle for straightness by rolling it on a sheet of plate glass or a surface plate. Check for wear on the needle, looking for scuffing or discolouration, using a magnifying glass where possible. Any defect in the needle surface will indicate the need for its renewal together with the needle jet which will probably be correspondingly worn. It is rather difficult to measure wear in the needle jet directly, but after high mileages the jet orifice will become elongated, fuel economy and performance worsening as a result.

12 As mentioned earlier in this Section, there are few occasions where it is advantageous to separate the individual instruments. Should this prove necessary however, proceed as follows. Start by freeing the cold start lever on the left-hand carburettor by releasing the circlip on the end of the cold start shaft. Slacken the locating screws which secure the various cold start operating links. The shaft can now be withdrawn, noting that the detent balls and springs will be released, and provision must be made to catch them. Remember to refit them during reassembly, because they control the three plunger positions in use.

13 Note the positions of the various parts in the throttle connecting links, in particular, how the plain tang of one carburettor is fitted between the synchronising screw and the small sprung pin below it. The connecting links do not impede separation, but they must be reassembled correctly. The carburettors may be separated after the three brackets between the adjacent carburettor tops and the single lower bracket have been removed.

14 Reassembly of the carburettors is a straight-forward reversal of the dismantling sequence, bearing in mind the following points. As the cold start shaft is fitted, position the detent balls and springs, holding them in place with a piece of stiff wire as the shaft enters its bore. Check that the connecting links are correctly arranged, noting that it will be necessary to check the carburettor synchronisation as described in Section 7 of this Chapter.

15 When fitting the diaphragm/piston assembly, ensure that the needle is fitted correctly with its position clip in the correct (middle) groove. It will be noted that the diaphragm has a small locating tab which should fit in the corresponding recess in the carburettor body. Take care not to omit the needle jet which must be fitted before the diaphragm assembly. When fitting the various jets take great care not to overtighten them as the carburettor threads and the jets themselves are easily damaged. Before the float chamber is fitted the float height must be checked as described in Section 8.

16 When all four instruments have been assembled check that the throttle butterfly valves are mechanically synchronised, making any necessary adjustments by turning the synchronising screws by an appropriate amount. All four must operate in unison if smooth running is to be obtained.

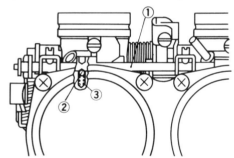

Fig. 2.5 Cold starting shaft assembly

1 Cold starting shaft
2 Ball bearing
3 Spring

5.3 Intake and air cleaner adaptors are secured by clips

6.2 Float chamber is retained by four screws

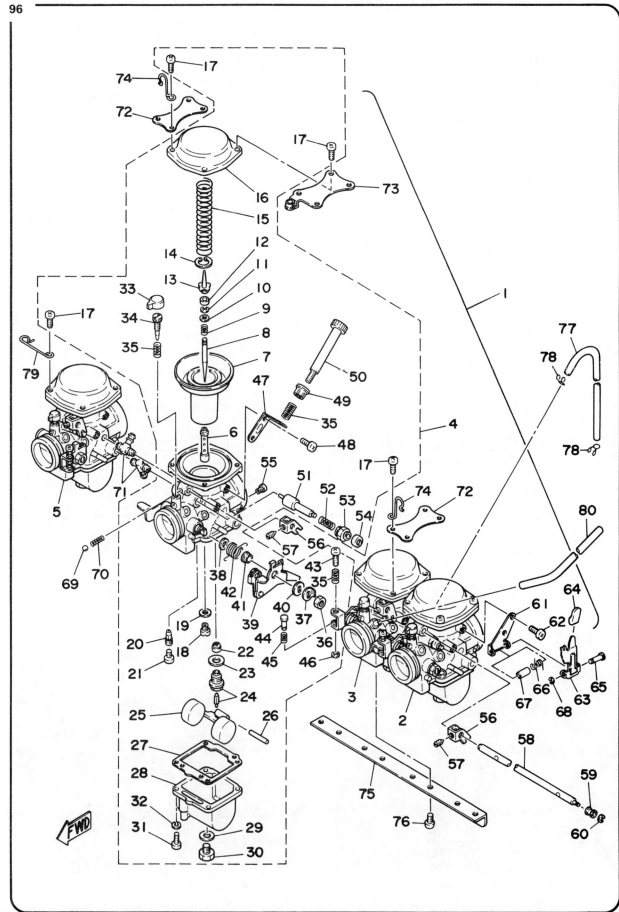

Fig. 2.6 Carburettor

1 Carburettor assembly
2 No. 1 carburettor
3 No. 2 carburettor
4 No. 3 carburettor
5 No. 4 carburettor
6 Needle jet — 4 off
7 Diaphragm — 4 off
8 Jet needle — 4 off
9 Spring — 4 off
10 Washer — 4 off
11 Needle clip — 4 off
12 Ring — 4 off
13 Needle retainer — 4 off
14 Circlip — 4 off
15 Diaphragm spring
   — 4 off
16 Carburettor top — 4 off
17 Screw — 16 off
18 Main jet — 4 off
19 Washer — 4 off
20 Pilot jet — 4 off
21 Plug
22 Filter
23 Sealing washer — 4 off
24 Float valve and seat
   — 4 off
25 Float — 4 off
26 Pivot pin — 4 off
27 Float chamber gasket
   — 4 off
28 Float chamber — 4 off
29 Sealing washer — 4 off
30 Drain plug — 4 off
31 Screw — 16 off
32 Spring washer — 16 off
33 Pilot air screw cap
   — 4 off
34 Pilot air screw — 4 off
35 Spring — 4 off
36 Nut — 4 off
37 Washer — 4 off
38 Seal — 4 off
39 Throttle lever
40 Collar — 2 off

41 Lever insert
42 Lever spring
43 Throttle stop screw
   — 3 off
44 Push piece — 3 off
45 Spring — 3 off
46 Clip — 3 off
47 Bracket
48 Screw — 2 off
49 Bush
50 Main throttle stop
   adjuster
51 Choke plunger — 4 off
52 Plunger spring — 4 off
53 Housing — 4 off
54 Cover — 4 off
55 Pilot air jet — 4 off
56 Choke link arm — 3 off
57 Screw — 4 off
58 Choke shaft
59 Bush
60 E-clip
61 Bracket
62 Screw — 2 off
63 Choke lever
64 Choke lever cap
65 Clevis pin
66 Spring
67 Spacer
68 E-clip
69 Ball bearing — 2 off
70 Spring — 2 off
71 Fuel transfer pipe
   — 4 off
72 Bracket — 2 off
73 Bracket/cable anchor
74 Hose guide — 2 off
75 Mounting bar
76 Screw — 8 off
77 Hose — 2 off
78 Hose clip — 4 off
79 Hose clip
80 Hose

6.3a Displace pivot pin (arrowed) and lift float assembly clear

6.3b Float needle can now be removed

6.5a Float valve seat unscrews — note gauze strainer

6.5b Remove blanking plug and washer ...

6.5c … to expose pilot jet

6.5d Main jet can be unscrewed for inspection (arrowed)

6.5e Note locating pin for needle jet (arrowed)

6.7a Pilot air jet can be unscrewed for cleaning

6.7b Main air jet is pressed into carburettor body (arrowed)

6.8a Release connecting bracket and retaining screws …

6.8b ... and remove the cover, spring and diaphragm

6.8c Needle jet/main nozzle can be displaced upwards (arrowed)

6.9 Needle assembly is secured by circlip

6.12a Release circlip to free cold start lever from shaft (arrowed)

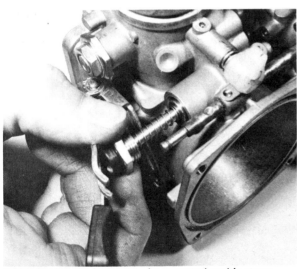

6.12b Cold start plunger can be removed at this stage

6.12c Note grub screws which locate operating links

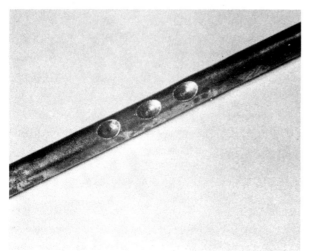

6.12d Depressions in shaft provide the detent positions

6.15 Note locating tab on edge of diaphragm (arrowed)

6.16 Screw and spring plunger provide synchronisation adjustment

7 Carburettors: synchronisation

1   On any multi-carburettor engine the accurate synchronisation of the carburettors is essential if smooth running and good performance and fuel economy are to be obtained. This is especially true of four cylinder engines, and in cases of extreme mal-adjustment the engine will refuse to idle reliably and may even produce expensive-sounding noises due to backlash in the primary transmission. It will be appreciated that if one or more of the carburettors is out of adjustment, the related cylinder will have to be 'carried' by the remaining cylinders, thus the engine will be attempting to run at two different speeds for any given throttle setting.

2   Synchronisation poses something of a problem in that there is no way in which it can be carried out accurately without the use of a vacuum gauge set. This may be of the manometer (mercury column) type or may have one or more clock-type gauges. Yamaha can supply a single clock type gauge with a four way selector switch; its part number is 90890-03094. Alternatively a number of mail order suppliers can supply vacuum gauge sets of various types. They all have something in common in that they are rather expensive,

so a decision must be made as to whether it is worth spending money on the equipment or if it is best to entrust this operation to a Yamaha dealer. If gauges are available, proceed as described below.

3   Remove the seat, and prop the rear of the fuel tank so that access to the vacuum take-off points and synchronising screws is possible. Remove the vacuum take-off caps from the No 1 and 4 manifolds. Remove the fuel tap vacuum pipes from the No 3 and 2 manifolds. Note that the fuel taps should be set to 'Pri' during the test sequence. Connect the vacuum gauge hoses to the appropriate vacuum take-off points.

4   Start the engine and set up the vacuum gauge(s) to the manufacturers recommendations. This normally entails setting a small damping valve or valves so that the gauge(s) respond quickly as the throttle is opened, but do not oscillate too wildly with each engine revolution. Allow the engine to idle until it reaches its normal operating temperature, then set the large throttle stop control to give an idle speed of about 1000 rpm.

5   Start by synchronising carburettors No 1 and 2 by turning the synchronising screw located between the two instruments. No specific vacuum reading is given by the manufacturer, but it is essential that the two carburettors give the same reading. Now synchronise carburettors No 3 and 4 in the same way, using the right-hand screw.

6   The two pairs of carburettors must now be synchronised to each other. This is done by turning the centre synchronising screw until No 1 and 2 carburettors give the same reading as No 3. It is likely that the engine speed will have increased by now, and this should be checked and reset at 1000 rpm. If the adjustment sequence was carried out accurately, the four carburettors should show a similar reading. If this is not the case, repeat the procedure until the correct balance is obtained. After synchronisation has been carried out, set the idle speed to within the prescribed limits of 950 – 1050 rpm using the central throttle stop control.

Important note: On no account should the pilot mixture screws be moved. See Section 8 for details.

8 Carburettor settings

1   Some of the carburettor settings, such as the sizes of the needle jets, main jets and needle positions, etc are pre-determined by the manufacturer. Under normal circum-

stances it is unlikely that these settings will require modification, even though there is provision made. If a change appears necessary, it can often be attributed to a developing engine fault.

2   Some alterations to the mid-range mixture characteristics may be made by raising or lowering the jet needle (all models except G(US) and SG). This is accomplished by changing the position of the needle clip. Raising the needle will richen the mixture and lowering the needle will weaken the mixture. Reference to Chapter 3 will show how the condition of the spark plugs can be interpreted with some experience as a reliable guide to carburettor mixture strength. Flat spots in the carburation can usually be traced to a defective timing advancer. If the advancer action is suspect, it can be detected by checking the ignition timing with a stroboscope.

3   If problems are encountered with fuel overflowing from the float chambers, which cannot be traced to the float/needle assembly, or if consistent fuel starvation is encountered, the fault will probably lie in maladjustment of the float level. It will be necessary to remove the float chamber bowl from each carburettor to check the float level, the carburettor bank being removed from the machine and inverted during this check.

4   If the float level is correct the distance between the uppermost edge of the floats and the flange of the mixing chamber body will be as shown in the specifications at the front of this Chapter.

   Adjustments are made by bending the float assembly tang (tongue), which engages with the float, in the direction required (see accompanying diagram).

5   It should be noted that no mention has been made concerning pilot mixture adjustment. This is because the screw settings are 'pre-set' by the factory and no adjustment is recommended. Even dealers are advised not to attempt adjustment, so it is impossible to give advice on this point. Yamaha have chosen to take this precaution to avoid possible infringement of the exhaust emission regulations in certain US states. If incorrect mixture settings are suspected, it will be necessary to solicit the aid of a competent motorcycle dealer with full exhaust analysis facilities. Using this equipment it is possible to set the pilot mixture screws accurately and within the required legal limits. Those living in areas where stringent anti-pollution laws are in operation should check whether **any** proposed carburettor adjustment or modification is permitted.

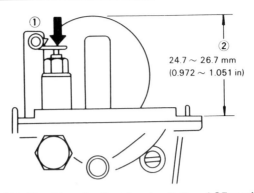

Fig. 2.7 Checking the float level – E, F and SF models

1 Float tang   *2 Float height*

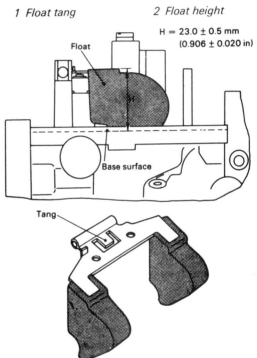

Fig. 2.8 Checking the float level – G(US) and SG models

---

9   Exhaust system

---

1   Unlike a two-stroke, the exhaust system does not require frequent attention because the exhaust gases are usually of a less oily nature.

2   Do not run the machine with the exhaust baffles removed, or with a quite different type of silencer fitted. The standard production silencers have been designed to give the best possible performance, whilst subduing the exhaust note to an acceptable level.

3   Whilst there are a number of good quality after-market exhaust systems available, there are others which may be of poor construction and fit, and which may reduce performance rather than improve it. When purchasing such systems it is helpful to obtain recommendations from other owners who have had time to evaluate the system under consideration. Do not forget that there are noise limits which will be met by the more reputable manufacturers. It is not advised that a non-standard system is fitted during the warranty period, because this could result in subsequent claims being refuted.

8.5 The plastic-capped mixture screw (arrowed) *Do not disturb*

10 Air cleaner: operation and maintenance

1   The air cleaner assembly forms part of a rather complicated induction system which serves to clean the incoming air whilst providing intake silencing. The carburettors are attached to four synthetic rubber pipes which project into the plenum chamber area above the filter casing. Air is drawn from the rear of the assembly by way of a rectangular duct which guides it to the centre of the filter element. After passing through the element the air moves upwards in the large chamber formed by the casing and enters the intake pipes near the top of the casing.

2   The lower section of the casing can be released after unscrewing the four wing bolts which retain it. As it is lifted away the element will come with it and can be removed for cleaning. The filter element is of composite structure and operates dry, unlike the more common oiled foam types. Cleaning is restricted to tapping the element to remove loose dust, after which it can be cleaned further by blowing compressed air through from the inner surface. Cleaning should be carried out every 1600 km (1000 miles) or more frequently where the machine is used in particularly dusty conditions. If any damage is discovered the element must be renewed promptly.

3   If the element is damp or oily it must be renewed. A damp or oily element will have a restrictive effect on the breathing of the carburettor and will almost certainly affect the engine performance.

4   On no account run the engine without the air cleaners attached, or with the element missing. The jetting of the carburettors takes into account the presence of the air cleaners and engine performance will be seriously affected if this balance is upset.

5   To replace the element, reverse the dismantling procedure. Give a visual check to ensure that the inlet hoses are correctly located and not kinked, split or otherwise damaged. Check that the air cleaner boxes are free from splits or cracks.

11 Engine lubrication

1   The engine lubrication system, which is also shared by the gearbox and primary drive, is of the wet sump type, where the oil reservoir is contained in the sump. The sump has a capacity of 3.5 litres (7.4/6.1 US/Imp pints) including the oil filter which holds approximately 0.5 litres (0.9/1.1 US/Imp pints).

2   A trochoid oil pump driven via an idler pinion from the clutch housing gear delivers oil from the sump to the rest of the engine. The pump components are retained in a casting which also houses a pressure release valve. Oil is picked up from the sump through a wire gauze strainer, which protects the oil pump from any large particles of foreign matter. The delivery section of the pump feeds oil at a preset pressure via a pressure release valve, which by-passes oil to the sump if the pressure exceeds the preset limit. As a result, it is possible to maintain a constant pressure in the lubrication system.

3   Since the oil flow will not, under normal circumstances, actuate the pressure release valve, it passes directly through the full flow filter which has a replaceable element, to filter out any impurities which may otherwise pass to the working parts of the engine. The oil filter unit has its own by-pass valve to prevent the cut-off of the oil supply if the filter element has become clogged.

4   Oil from the filter is fed direct to the crankshaft and big-end bearings with a separate pressure feed to the camshaft and valve assemblies. Oil is also fed directly to the mainshaft and layshaft in the gearbox and thence to the pinion bushes. Surplus oil drains to the sump where it is picked up again and the cycle is repeated.

5   An oil pressure warning light is included in the lubrication circuit to give visual warning by means of an indicator light if the pressure should fall to a low level.

10.1 Rubber intake adaptors project into plenum chamber

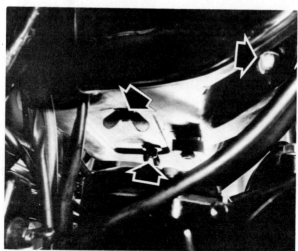

10.2a Air cleaner casing is retained by wing-bolts (arrowed)

10.2b Lift casing away to gain access to filter element

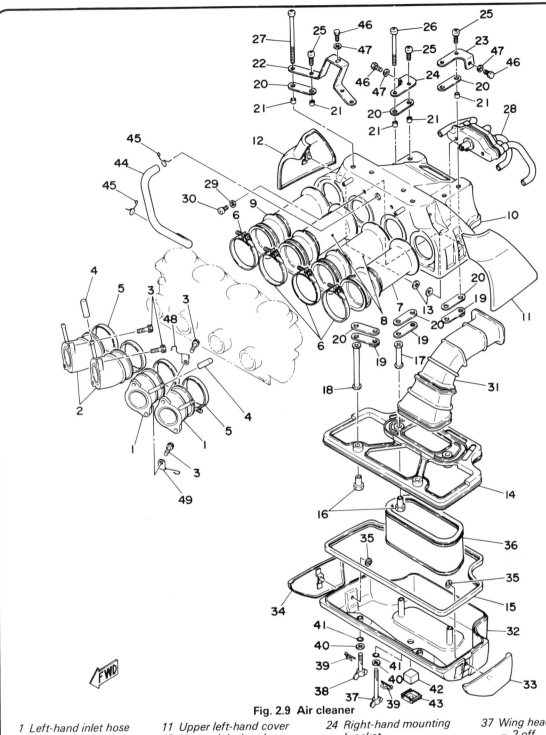

Fig. 2.9 Air cleaner

1 Left-hand inlet hose – 2 off
2 Right-hand inlet hose – 2 off
3 Allen screw – 8 off
4 Gauge adaptor cover – 2 off
5 Hose clamp – 4 off
6 Hose clamp – 4 off
7 Left-hand transfer hose
8 Centre transfer hose – 2 off
9 Right-hand transfer hose
10 Upper half filter case

11 Upper left-hand cover
12 Upper right-hand cover
13 Spring nut – 2 off
14 Case partition
15 Case seal
16 Nut – 4 off
17 Collar – 2 off
18 Collar – 2 off
19 Backing plate – 4 off
20 Gasket – 8 off
21 Spacer – 8 off
22 Front case mounting bracket
23 Left-hand mounting bracket

24 Right-hand mounting bracket
25 Screw – 4 off
26 Screw – 2 off
27 Screw – 2 off
28 Oil separator
29 Washer – 2 off
30 Screw – 2 off
31 Main inlet hose
32 Lower filter case half
33 Lower left-hand cover
34 Lower right-hand cover
35 Retaining clip – 2 off
36 Air cleaner element

37 Wing headed bolt – 2 off
38 Wing headed bolt – 2 off
39 R-pin – 4 off
40 Washer – 4 off
41 O-ring – 4 off
42 Plug
43 Plug cover
44 Breather pipe
45 Pipe clip – 2 off
46 Bolt – 3 off
47 Washer – 3 off
48 Clamp
49 Clamp

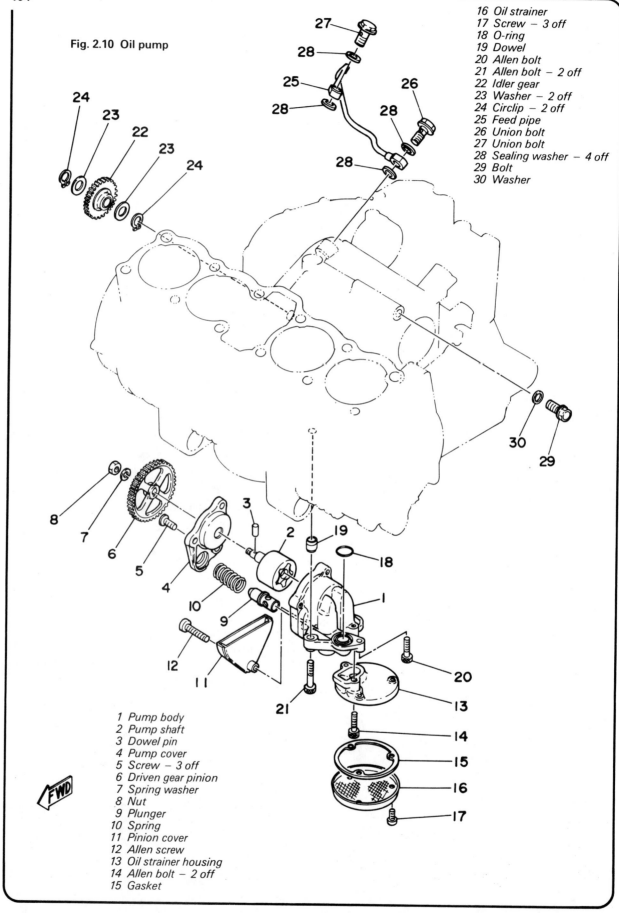

Fig. 2.10 Oil pump

16 Oil strainer
17 Screw – 3 off
18 O-ring
19 Dowel
20 Allen bolt
21 Allen bolt – 2 off
22 Idler gear
23 Washer – 2 off
24 Circlip – 2 off
25 Feed pipe
26 Union bolt
27 Union bolt
28 Sealing washer – 4 off
29 Bolt
30 Washer

1 Pump body
2 Pump shaft
3 Dowel pin
4 Pump cover
5 Screw – 3 off
6 Driven gear pinion
7 Spring washer
8 Nut
9 Plunger
10 Spring
11 Pinion cover
12 Allen screw
13 Oil strainer housing
14 Allen bolt – 2 off
15 Gasket

FWD

12 Oil pump: dismantling, examination and reassembly

1 The oil pump can be removed from the engine while the engine is still in the frame. However, it will be necessary to detach the sump after draining the engine oil.
2 The pump is retained by three Allen screws to the underside of the crankcase. Note that it is located by two hollow dowel pins. Start dismantling by removing the circular oil pickup screen by removing its three retaining screws. The housing to which the screen is attached is itself retained by two screws. Remove the single long screw which secures the oil pump pinion cover and lift the cover away.
3 Remove the nut and spring washer which secure the oil pump pinion, lifting the pinion clear of the pump spindle and driving pin. Access to the oil pump and cover is now possible. The cover is retained by three Torx screws, requiring the use of a T-30 Torx wrench, or a home-made equivalent, to release them. It was found that judicious modification of an Allen key, using a hacksaw to cut slots in its flat sides, would produce an acceptable alternative to the prescribed tool. Refer to Fig. 1.6, page 39.
4 Lift the small driving pin clear of the pump spindle, then remove the pump cover and gasket. As the cover is removed, the pressure relief valve spring will be freed and can be lifted away, as can the valve plunger. Tip the pump body to displace the inner and outer pump rotors.
5 Wash all the pump components with petrol and allow them to dry before carrying out an examination. Before partially reassembling the pump for various measurements to be carried out, check the casting for breakage or fracture, or scoring on the inside perimeter.
6 Reassemble the pump rotors and measure the clearance between the outer rotor and the pump body, using a feeler gauge. If the measurement exceeds the service limit of 0.15 mm (0.0059 in), the rotor or the body must be renewed, whichever is worn. Measure the clearance between the outer rotor and the inner rotor, using a feeler gauge. If the clearance exceeds 0.12 mm (0.0047 in) the rotors must be renewed as a set.
7 Examine the rotors and the pump body for signs of scoring, chipping or other surface damage which will occur if metallic particles find their way into the oil pump assembly. Renewal of the affected parts is the only remedy under these circumstances, bearing in mind that the rotors must always be replaced as a matched pair. Reassemble the pump

components by reversing the dismantling procedure. The component parts must be **absolutely** clean or damage to the pump will result. Replace the rotors and lubricate them thoroughly before refitting the cover.
8 Before refitting the pump, it should be filled with oil by holding it inlet side upwards and pouring clean engine oil in through the inlet orifice, whilst simultaneously rotating the drive pinion in an anti-clockwise direction. When oil can be seen to escape from the feed aperture, the pump is sufficiently primed for replacement. Check that the sealing O-ring is in good condition, to prevent oil pressure loss at the mating surfaces.
9 If damage occurs to the pump pinion, the latter may be removed after loosening and detaching the centre nut. The pinion is located by a cross-pin which is a push fit in the shaft and provides the drive medium.

13 Oil filter: renewing the element

1 The oil filter is contained within a detachable chamber fitted to the base of the sump. Access to the element is made by unscrewing the filter chamber centre bolt which will bring with it the chamber and also the element. Before removing the chamber place a receptacle beneath the engine to catch the engine oil contained in the filter chamber.
2 When renewing the filter element it is wise to renew the filter cover O-ring at the same time. This will obviate the possibility of any oil leaks. Do not overtighten the centre bolt on replacement; the correct torque setting is 3.2 kgf m (23 lbf ft).
3 The filter by-pass valve, comprising a plunger and spring, is situated in the bore of the filter cover centre bolt. It is recommended that the by-pass valve be checked for free movement during every filter change. The spring and plunger are retained by a pin across the centre bolt. Knocking the pin out will allow the spring and plunger to be removed for cleaning.
4 Never run the engine without the filter element or increase the period between the recommended oil changes or oil filter changes. Engine oil should be changed every 3000 miles and the element changed every 6000 miles. Use only the recommended viscosity. Note that the filter chamber should be primed whenever a new filter is fitted. This is accomplished by adding about ½ a pint of engine oil prior to fitting the filter assembly to the underside of the crankcase.

12.2a Remove retaining screws (arrowed) and lift away filter gauze

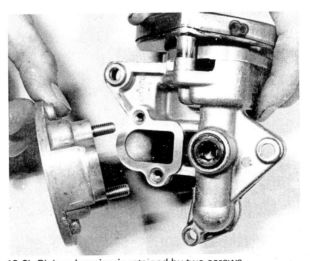

12.2b Pickup housing is retained by two screws

12.2c Release single screw and remove shroud

12.3a Remove drive pinion and locating pin

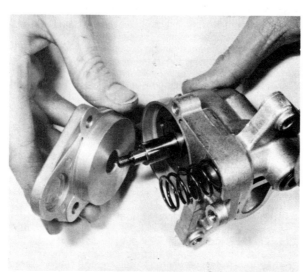

12.3b Release pump cover to expose pump rotors

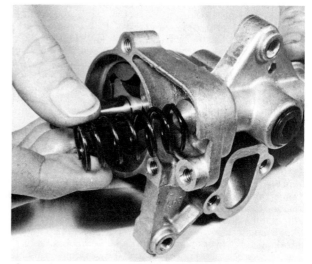

12.4a Lift away pressure relief valve spring …

12.4b … and valve plunger

12.5a Inner rotor and drive spindle can be withdrawn …

12.5b ... as can the outer rotor, to permit examination

12.6a Checking the outer rotor to body clearance

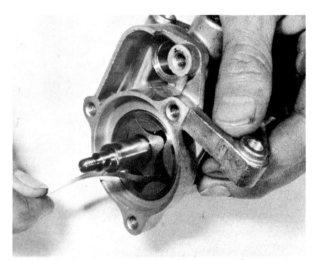

12.6b Checking the outer rotor to inner rotor clearance

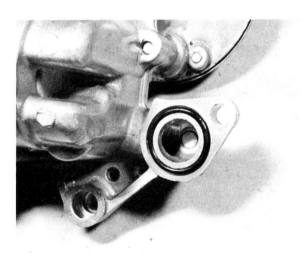

12.8 Renew all O-rings during reassembly

14 Oil cooler: description

1 An oil cooler is fitted to UK models as standard and also to some US models either as original or optional equipment. The oil cooler matrix is mounted on the frame front downtubes to gain the best possible benefit from the cooling airflow. The feed and return pipes are interconnected at their lower ends with a distributor block interposed between the oil filter chamber and sump.
2 To maintain peak efficiency the matrix should be kept clear of any debris, preferably using an air jet directed from behind to blow out the air channels. Avoid using sharp instruments to dislodge any foreign matter; this may easily lead to damaged vanes. Should leakage of the matrix occur renewal of the complete component will probably be the only satisfactory solution. Repair is unlikely to be successful.
3 Leakage at the hose unions will result from deteriorating O-rings. These can be renewed without difficulty.

14.2 Oil pressure switch is located to rear of cylinder block

15 Oil pressure warning lamp

1   An oil pressure warning lamp is incorporated in the lubrication system to give immediate warning of excessively low oil pressure.

2   The oil pressure switch is screwed into the crankcase, immediately to the rear of the cylinder block. The switch is interconnected to a warning light on the lighting panel on the handlebars. The light should come on when the ignition is first switched on but will usually go out at about 1500 rpm.

3   If the oil warning lamp comes on whilst the machine is being ridden the engine should be switched off immediately, otherwise there is a risk of severe engine damage due to lubrication failure. The fault must be located and rectified before the engine is restarted and run, even for a brief moment. Machines fitted with plain shell bearings rely on high oil pressure to maintain a thin oil film between the bearing surfaces. Failure of the oil pressure will cause the working surfaces to come into direct contact, causing overheating and eventual seizure.

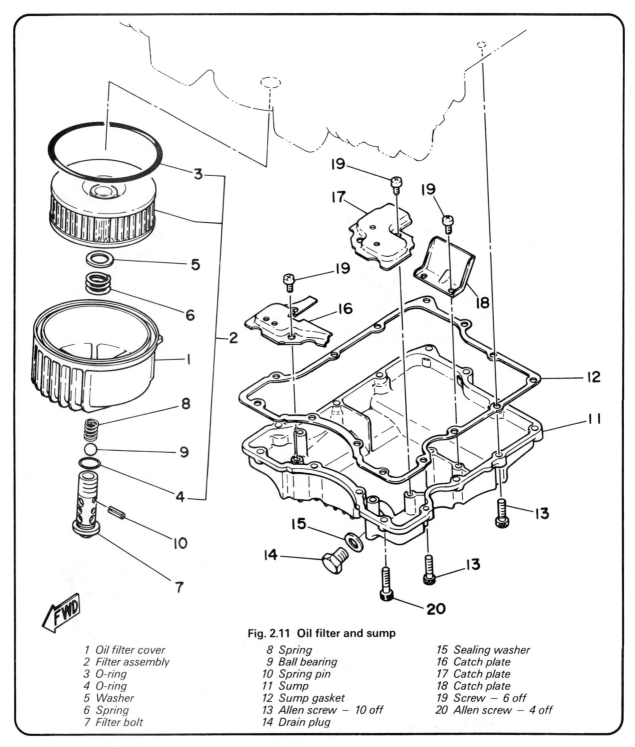

Fig. 2.11 Oil filter and sump

1 Oil filter cover	8 Spring	15 Sealing washer
2 Filter assembly	9 Ball bearing	16 Catch plate
3 O-ring	10 Spring pin	17 Catch plate
4 O-ring	11 Sump	18 Catch plate
5 Washer	12 Sump gasket	19 Screw − 6 off
6 Spring	13 Allen screw − 10 off	20 Allen screw − 4 off
7 Filter bolt	14 Drain plug	

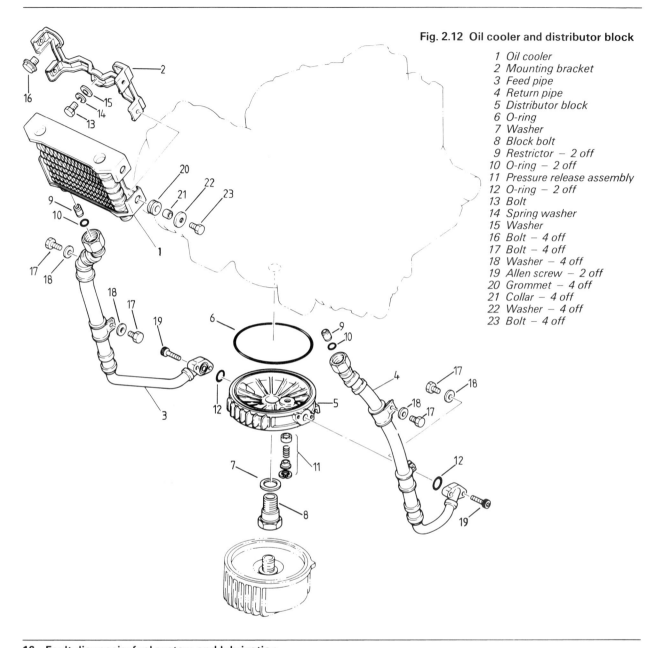

Fig. 2.12 Oil cooler and distributor block

1 Oil cooler
2 Mounting bracket
3 Feed pipe
4 Return pipe
5 Distributor block
6 O-ring
7 Washer
8 Block bolt
9 Restrictor − 2 off
10 O-ring − 2 off
11 Pressure release assembly
12 O-ring − 2 off
13 Bolt
14 Spring washer
15 Washer
16 Bolt − 4 off
17 Bolt − 4 off
18 Washer − 4 off
19 Allen screw − 2 off
20 Grommet − 4 off
21 Collar − 4 off
22 Washer − 4 off
23 Bolt − 4 off

16 Fault diagnosis: fuel system and lubrication

Symptom	Cause	Remedy
Engine gradually fades and stops	Fuel starvation	Check vent hole in filler cap. Sediment in float chamber. Dismantle and clean.
Engine runs badly. Black smoke from exhausts	Carburettor flooding	Dismantle and clean carburettor. Check for punctured float or sticking float needle.
Engine lacks response and overheats	Weak mixture Air cleaner disconnected or hose split Modified silencer has upset carburation	Check for partial block in carburettors. Reconnect or renew hose. Replace with original design.
Oil pressure warning light comes on	Lubrication system failure	Stop engine immediately. Trace and rectify fault before re-starting.
Engine gets noisy	Failure to change engine oil when recommended	Drain off old oil and refill with new oil of correct grade. Renew oil filter element.

Chapter 3 Ignition system

Contents

Specifications

Ignition system
Type .... TCI, fully electronic

Ignition timing

	UK models	US models
Retarded:		
E model	5° @ 1100 rpm	10° @ 1000 rpm
F and SF models	−	10° @ 1050 − 1150 rpm
G and SG models	5° @ 1100 rpm	5° @ 1100 rpm
Centrifugal advance:		
SF model	−	31° @ 5400 rpm
All others	36° @ 5400 rpm	36° @ 5200 rpm
Vacuum advance	16° @ 150 mm Hg	16° @ 150 mm Hg

Sparking plugs
Make	NGK or Champion
Type	BP8ES or N-8Y
Gap	0.7 − 0.8 mm (0.028 − 0.032 in)

Ballast resistor
Resistance .... 1.6 ohms ± 10% at 20°C (68°F)

Pick-up coil
Resistance .... 720 ohms ± 20% at 20°C (68°F)

Ignition coil
Type	Hitachi CM12-08
Spark gap	6 mm (0.24 in) + at 500 rpm
Primary resistance	1.5 ohms ± 10% at 20°C (68°F)
Secondary resistance	15 K ohms ± 20% at 20°C (68°F)

Torque wrench settings
Component	kgf m	lbf ft
Automatic advance unit	2.0	14.5
Baseplate	0.8	5.8

1 General description

The Yamaha XS1100 models employ a fully transistorised electronic ignition system, described by the manufacturer as TCI. The system is controlled by the TCI unit, a large rectangular 'black box' mounted at the rear of the machine beneath the dual seat. The system is triggered, electronically rather than mechanically, by a pickup assembly mounted on the crankshaft end. Two pickup coils are fitted, one triggering the spark for cylinders 1 and 4 and the other controlling cylinders 2 and 3. It should be noted that each pickup provides a spark simultaneously at **both** of its related spark plugs. However, only one of the cylinders concerned will be near TDC on the compression stroke, and thus ignition will only take place in this cylinder, the remaining spark being wasted. This principle is normal on most four cylinder motorcycle engines and is known as the spare spark system.

The pickups consist of small electromagnetic coils mounted on opposite sides of a moving reluctor. As the raised tang of the reluctor passes the coil poles, a small signal current is induced and passed to the TCI unit. The unit senses the signal from the pickup and switches off the current to the primary windings of the relevant pair of coils. This induces a high tension pulse in the secondary winding which is fed via the HT leads to the appropriate sparking plugs.

At the moment that the unit initiates the spark in one set of coils, it switches the current on to the remaining pair, thus setting them up for the same cycle once the reluctor reaches the next pickup coil. This cycle takes place once in each crankshaft revolution.

The TCI unit incorporates a bypass circuit which works in conjunction with a ballast resistor to provide a heavy spark during starting. Once the engine is running the ballast resistor reduces the power to the coils, lowering their power consumption and extending coil life. The TCI unit also incorporates a coil protection circuit which switches off the supply to the coils should the ignition be left switched on without the engine running for more than a few seconds. When the starter button is next operated, the supply to the coils is restored after the crankshaft has turned through 180°.

The ignition system retains two mechanical components, namely the automatic timing unit (ATU) or centrifugal advance, and the vacuum advance unit. The former responds to changes in engine speed, advancing the ignition in relation to the crankshaft in response to the centrifugal force acting upon the unit's bobweights. The latter device is rather unusual on a motorcycle engine, despite having been a standard fitment on car engines for several decades. Its function is to provide additional advance control in response to engine vacuum and thus load, and working in conjunction with the ATU to provide a better controlled and more responsive spark.

2 Testing the ignition system: general information

An electronic ignition system does not require maintenance in the generally accepted sense. With the exception of the advance mechanisms there are no mechanical parts, thus wear does not take place and the need for compensation by adjustment does not arise. Ignition problems in this type of system can be broken down as follows.
1   Loose, broken or corroded connections
2   Damaged or broken wiring
3   Wear or damage of the advance mechanism(s)
4   Faulty or inoperative electronic components.

The above are arranged in the order in which they are most likely to be found, and with the exception of number 4 should provide no undue problem in the event of fault finding or rectification. Where part of the electronic side of the system fails, however, diagnosis becomes rather more difficult. The following sections provide details of the necessary test procedures, but it must be remembered that basic test equipment will be required. Most of the tests can be carried out with an inexpensive pocket multimeter. Many home mechanics will already have one and be conversant with its use. Failing this, they are easily obtainable from mail order companies or from electronics specialists, or can be ordered through a Yamaha dealer.

When carrying out tests on the electronic ignition system, bear in mind that wrong connections could easily damage the component being tested. Adhere strictly to the test sequence described and be particularly careful to avoid reversed battery connections. Note that the system must **not** operate with one or more HT leads isolated, as the very high secondary winding voltage may destroy the ignition coil. Beware of shocks from the high tension leads or connections. Although not inherently dangerous, they can be rather unpleasant.

3 Ignition system faults: tracing defective area

1   Ignition problems must be tackled in a methodical fashion if time is not to be wasted in jumping to incorrect conclusions. The flow chart which follows shows the correct sequence for investigating a failure or partial failure of the system. Note that apart from the TCI unit there are two distinct sub-systems controlling cylinders 1 and 4 and cylinders 2 and 3 respectively. It follows that the appropriate sub-system should be investigated in the event of a malfunction of one pair of spark plugs.

4 Testing the TCI unit and pickup coils

1   If a check of the ignition system has indicated a possible fault in the TCI unit or pickup coils, they should be tested as described below. A 0 – 20 volt (dc) voltmeter and a 0 – 1000 ohm ohmmeter, or a multimeter having the appropriate test ranges will be required. In the absence of the appropriate equipment or if the operator feels unsure of the tests described, it is safest to refer the problem to a qualified Yamaha Service Agent who will possess the correct equipment and experience to carry out the tests.
2   Separate the **4-pin** connector from the TCI unit and check the resistances between the terminals indicated below. Refer to Fig. 3.3 for details of terminal locations.

Pickup coil resistance test

Coil No.	Terminal colours	Reading
1	White/red to White/green	720 ohms ± 20%
2	Yellow/green to Yellow/red	720 ohms ± 20%

If the reading is markedly lower than 576 ohms or greater than 864 ohms, the pickup coil concerned is outside its service limit and should be renewed.
3   The TCI unit can be tested for voltage readings at the unit terminals. The ignition system components must all be in place and connected during the test, which is conducted with the ignition switched on, and at the **6-pin** connector.

TCI unit terminal voltage tests

	Terminal colours	*Reading*
1	*Grey to earth (ground)*	*12 volts*
2	*White/red to earth (ground)*	*12 volts*
3	*Black/white to earth (ground)*	*6 volts*
4	*Orange to earth (ground)*	*12 volts*
5	*Red/white to earth (ground)*	*12 volts*

If any of the above tests produce readings which differ radically from those shown above, the TCI unit is probably defective and may require renewal. Before condemning the unit, however, check that the unit is correctly earthed by measuring the resistance between the black terminal and a convenient sound earth point. A zero resistance reading should be obtained.

4   It is possible that the unit can show the required test readings but still be defective, in which case renewal will be required in spite of the test indications. To avoid unnecessary expense, carry out the remaining checks on the ignition system first. If the unit is still suspect, have its condition verified by a Yamaha service agent before purchasing a replacement. Note that the TCI unit has a removable cover. This does not indicate that it is in any way adjustable or that it can be repaired at home. There is no advantage to be gained by removing the cover.

4.1 TCI unit is mounted on rear mudguard

4.4 Cover houses TCI circuitry — **Do not** remove

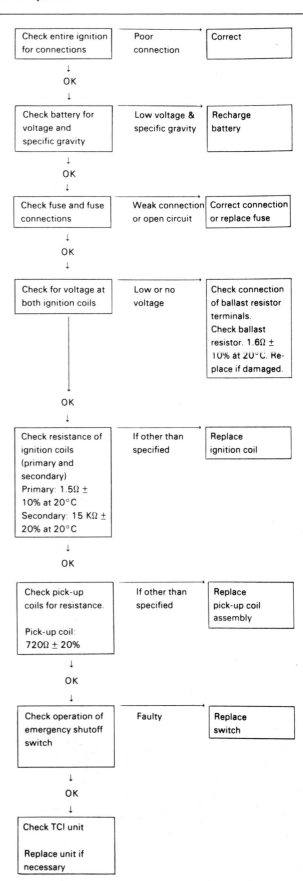

Fig. 3.1 Ignition system test flow-chart

Fig. 3.2 Transistorized ignition system wiring circuit

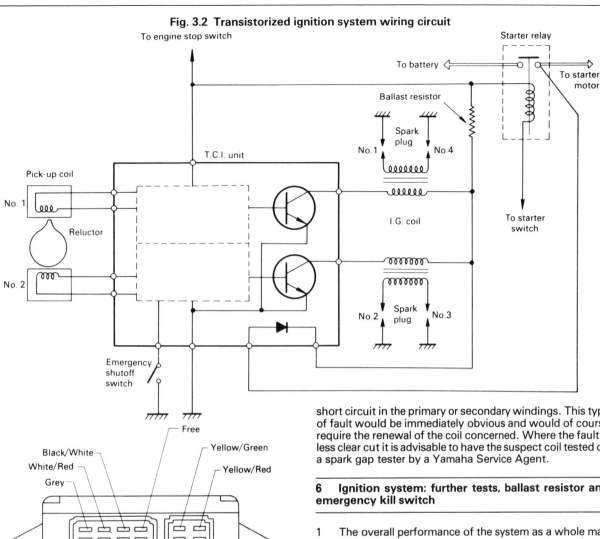

Fig. 3.3 Wire colour positions on TCI unit block connector

5   Ignition coils: resistance tests

1   If one of the ignition coils is suspected of partial or complete failure, its internal resistance and insulation can be checked by measuring the primary and secondary winding resistances. Note that it is very unlikely that both coils would fail simultaneously, and if this appears to be the case, be prepared to look elsewhere for the problem.

2   Set the multimeter to the ohms scale, and connect one probe lead to each of the thin low tension wires. Note that it does not matter which probe is connected to which lead. A reading of 1.5 ohms ± 10% at 20°C should be obtained (1.35 – 1.65 ohms) if the primary windings are in good order.

3   Repeat the test for the high tension leads, this time with the meter set on the KY ohms scale. A resistance of 15k ohms ± 20% (12 – 18 k ohms) at 20°C should be indicated.

4   If the coil has failed it is likely to have either an open or

short circuit in the primary or secondary windings. This type of fault would be immediately obvious and would of course require the renewal of the coil concerned. Where the fault is less clear cut it is advisable to have the suspect coil tested on a spark gap tester by a Yamaha Service Agent.

6   Ignition system: further tests, ballast resistor and emergency kill switch

1   The overall performance of the system as a whole may be checked using a spark gap tester, running the engine at various speeds and with various spark gaps to provoke misfiring at the weakest combination of the two. As this involves the use of special workshop equipment it is outside the scope of this book, but it may be worth having the work done to identify a persistent partial failure or misfiring problem. The ignition system should be capable of producing a reliable spark at all engine speeds across a minimum spark gap of 6 mm (0.24 in).

2   Failure of the ballast resistor can result in poor starting or can overload the coils, depending upon whether it has failed open or short circuit. It is mounted beneath the top frame tubes adjacent to the left-hand coil and is retained by a single screw. Check the ballast resistor by connecting an ohmmeter across its terminals. The specified resistance is 1.6 ohms ± 10% (1.44 – 1.76 ohms) at 20°C (68°F).

3   A further, but unlikely, culprit in the event of total ignition failure could be the emergency ignition cutout which is located beneath the fuel tank. This takes the form of an ignition earth switch which automatically cuts the ignition if the machine is leant by 60° or more from the vertical. In practice it is more likely that the switch will fail to operate, than operate inadvertently, but in the event that water finds its way inside or there is a short circuit of the switch leads or terminals it would cut the ignition circuit. Check the switch by removing it and testing its operation horizontally and at more than 60° using a multimeter set on the resistance scale. The switch should show contact when tilted beyond the 60° angle. Make sure that the associated wiring is undamaged.

6.2 Ballast resistor (arrowed) is mounted under frame tubes

6.3 Emergency shut-off switch is located beneath tank

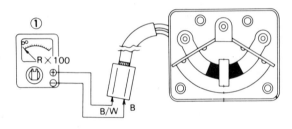

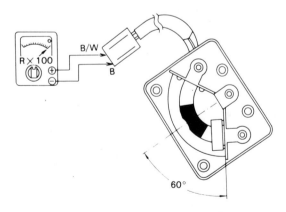

Fig. 3.4 Emergency shut off switch testing

1 Ohmmeter or Multimeter on the resistance scale

7   Ignition timing: checking and resetting — all models except G(US) and SG

1   The ignition timing should be checked at 4000 mile (6400 km) intervals, although it is unlikely to require adjustment unless the ignition pickup assembly has been removed in the course of overhaul. Before starting the timing check it should be noted that the fixed timing pointer is adjustable, and if it has been removed or bent, or if there is some doubt about its accuracy, check its position as described in Chapter 1, Section 44. For normal timing checks, this stage can be ignored.

2   A stroboscopic timing lamp, or 'strobe', will be required for the timing check, because the test must be carried out with the engine running. Two basic types of strobe are available, namely the neon and xenon tube types. Of the two, the neon type is much cheaper and will usually suffice if used in a shaded position, its light output being rather limited. The brighter but more expensive xenon types are preferable if funds permit, because they produce a much clearer image.

3   Connect the strobe to the left-hand (No 1 cylinder) high tension lead, following the makers instructions. If an external 12 volt power source is required it is best **not** to use the machine's battery as spurious impulses can be picked up from the electrical system. A separate 12 volt car or motorcycle battery is preferable. Remove the timing inspection plate, then start the engine. Check that it is within the prescribed idle speed limits, shown at the end of this section, making any necessary adjustments.

4   Direct the timing lamp towards the timing disc on the crankshaft end. The flashing light pulses will make the disc appear to freeze in relation to the pointer, and the 'F' mark should align precisely with this. If this is not the case, slacken the baseplate screws and move the pulser or pickup assembly until the marks align.

5   Once the left-hand (No 1) cylinder is timed correctly, it can be assumed that the remaining three cylinders are also set correctly. It is not possible to adjust one cylinder in relation to the remainder.

6   Before the inspection cover is refitted, check that the automatic timing unit (ATU) is functioning correctly. Pull off the vacuum advance pipe and temporarily block the end. Start the engine and increase its speed to the full advance figure shown below for a few seconds. The strobe should show an advance to the appropriate position on the timing disc. If the action of the unit is hesitant or inaccurate it should

Spark plug maintenance: Checking plug gap with feeler gauges

Altering the plug gap. Note use of correct tool

Spark plug conditions: A brown, tan or grey firing end is indicative of correct engine running conditions and the selection of the appropriate heat rating plug

White deposits have accumulated from excessive amounts of oil in the combustion chamber or through the use of low quality oil. Remove deposits or a hot spot may form

Black sooty deposits indicate an over-rich fuel/air mixture, or a malfunctioning ignition system. If no improvement is obtained, try one grade hotter plug

Wet, oily carbon deposits form an electrical leakage path along the insulator nose, resulting in a misfire. The cause may be a badly worn engine or a malfunctioning ignition system

A blistered white insulator or melted electrode indicates over-advanced ignition timing or a malfunctioning cooling system. If correction does not prove effective, try a colder grade plug

A worn spark plug not only wastes fuel but also overloads the whole ignition system because the increased gap requires higher voltage to initiate the spark. This condition can also affect air pollution

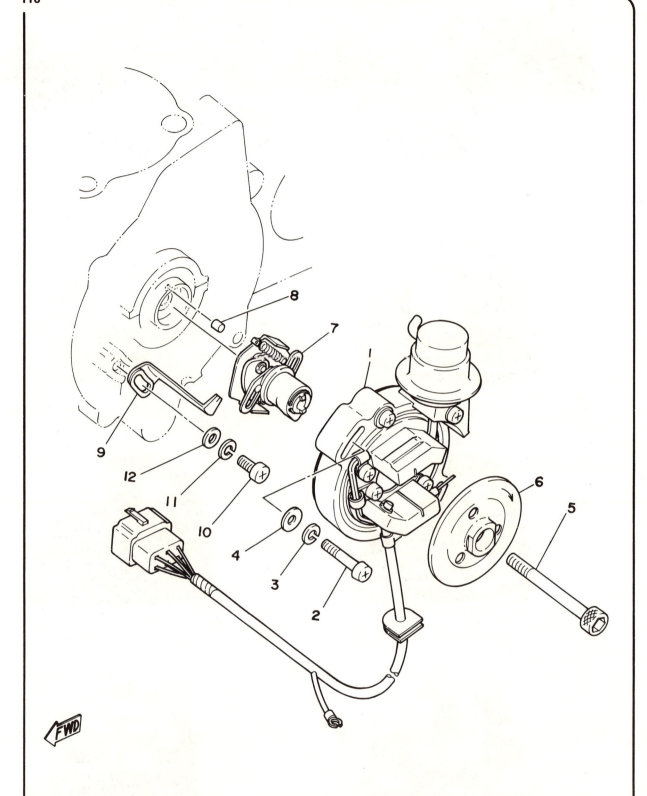

Fig. 3.5 CDI pick-up assembly

1 CDI unit
2 Screw – 2 off
3 Spring washer – 2 off
4 Washer – 2 off
5 Allen screw
6 Timing plate
7 Automatic timing unit
8 Dowel pin
9 Timing arm
10 Screw
11 Spring washer
12 Washer

be removed for examination and overhaul.

Ignition timing
Retarded:
XS1100 E(US)	*10° BTDC @ 1000 rpm*
XS1100 E(UK)	*5° BTDC @ 1100 rpm*
XS1100 F, SF(US)	*10° BTDC @ 1050 – 1150 rpm*
XS1100 F(UK)	*5° BTDC @ 1100 rpm*
XS1100 G(UK)	*5° BTDC @ 1100 rpm*

Centrifugal advance (vacuum pipe disconnected):
XS1100 E, F(US)	*36° BTDC @ 5200 rpm*
XS1100 E, F(UK)	*36° BTDC @ 5400 rpm*
XS1100 SF(US)	*31° BTDC @ 5400 rpm*
XS1100 G(UK)	*36° BTDC @ 5400 rpm*

8 Ignition timing: checking and resetting – G(US) and SG models

1   The procedure for checking and setting the ignition timing is similar for all models except the G(US) and SG versions, where the ignition pickup base plate is retained by 'anti-tamper' shear-head Torx bolts. The idea behind this move is to eliminate unwarranted changes in the ignition timing which could lead to higher exhaust emission levels. As the ignition timing should, in theory, require no adjustment, this modification will not normally cause any problem, the procedure for checking the timing being the same as for the earlier models.
2   Follow the checking procedure described in paragraphs 1 to 3 of Section 7, noting that adjustment is not normally possible on these models. In the case of the G(US) and SG, Yamaha recommend that, in the event of a discrepancy, the automatic timing unit, vacuum advance unit and the crankshaft bearings should be checked for damage.
3   If it becomes necessary to remove the pickup baseplate on the latter models, it will be necessary to obtain new securing screws and the appropriate Torx socket (Yamaha Part No 90890-01308-00) before work commences. Remove the centre bolt and lift away the timing disc to give unobstructed access to the bolts. Flatten the surface of the bolt heads with a suitable flat punch, then mark the exact centre of the bolts using a sharp centre punch. Drill a 3 mm hole to the depth of 10 mm, then use a proprietory screw extractor to remove the screws.
4   When refitting the baseplate, new shear-head Torx bolts are supposed to be used. Fit the new bolts and special washers, tightening them **lightly** to hold the baseplate in position. Carry out the timing procedure, and when it is set correctly, tighten the bolts until the heads break off. It should be noted that, apart from legal constraints, it would make far more sense to fit ordinary bolts to avoid this procedure becoming necessary in the future.

Ignition timing
Retarded:
XS1100 G and SG(US)	*5° @ 1100 rpm*

Centrifugal advance (vacuum pipe disconnected):
XS1100 G and SG(US)	*36° @ 5200 rpm*

9 Vacuum advance unit: examination and testing

1   As mentioned previously, the vacuum advance unit serves to modify the ignition advance in response to changes in engine load. It does this by means of a diaphragm connected by a small hose to the intake adaptor of No 2 cylinder. Changes in manifold depression act upon the diaphragm, which in turn moves the pickup baseplate through a small arc.
2   Little can be done by way of maintenance apart from ensuring the smooth operation of the unit and checking that there are no leaks in the hose or connections. To test the operation of the unit correctly, a vacuum pump and gauge are required to ensure that full advance is reached at 150 mm Hg (5.9 in Hg). This check can be carried out quickly and inexpensively by a Yamaha Service Agent.

10 Automatic timing unit: examination

1   The automatic timing mechanism rarely requires attention, although it is advisable to examine it periodically, when the ignition timing is receiving attention. It is retained by a small bolt and washer through the centre of the integral reluctor and can be pulled off the end of the crankshaft when the bolt is removed.
2   The unit comprises spring loaded balance weights, which move outward against the spring tension as centrifugal force increases. The balance weights must move freely on their pivots and be rust-free. The tension springs must also be in good condition. Keep the pivots lubricated and make sure the balance weights move easily, without binding. Most problems arise as a result of condensation, within the engine, which causes the unit to rust and balance weight movement to be restricted.
3   The automatic timing unit mechanism is fixed in relation to the crankshaft by means of a dowel. In consequence the mechanism cannot be replaced in anything other than the correct position. This ensures accuracy of ignition timing to within close limits, although a check should always be made when reassembly of the contact breaker is complete.
4   The correct functioning of the auto-advance unit can be checked when carrying out ignition timing checks using a stroboscope as described in Section 7.

11 Sparking plugs: checking and resetting the gaps

1   The standard sparking plug types recommended for the Yamaha XS1100 models are NGK BP6ES or Champion N-8Y. Certain operating conditions may require a change in sparking plug grade, but generally the type recommended by the manufacturer gives the best all round service.
2   Check the gap of the plug points every three monthly or 2,000 mile service. To reset the gap, bend the outer electrode to bring it closer to, or further away from the central electrode until a 0.7 mm (0.028 in) feeler gauge can be inserted. Never bend the centre electrode or the insulator will crack, causing engine damage if the particles fall into the cylinder whilst the engine is running.
3   With some experience, the condition of the sparking plug electrodes and insulator can be used as a reliable guide to engine operating conditions. See the accompanying photographs.
4   Always carry a spare pair of sparking plugs of the recommended grade. In the rare event of plug failure, they will enable the engine to be restarted.
5   Beware of over-tightening the sparking plugs, otherwise there is risk of stripping the threads from the aluminium alloy cylinder heads. The plugs should be sufficiently tight to seat firmly on their copper sealing washers, and no more. Use a spanner which is a good fit to prevent the spanner from slipping and breaking the insulator.
6   If the threads in the cylinder head strip as a result of overtightening the sparking plugs, it is possible to reclaim the head by the use of a Helicoil thread insert. This is a cheap and convenient method of replacing the threads; most motorcycle dealers operate a service of this nature at an economic price.
7   Make sure the plug insulating caps are a good fit and have their rubber seals. They should also be kept clean to prevent tracking. These caps contain the suppressors that eliminate both radio and TV interference.

7.4 A: Retarded timing position B: Advanced timing position

7.5 Elongated holes permit baseplate adjustment

10.1 Vacuum unit moves pickups in response to engine load

11.1 Remove centre bolt and timing disc to free ATU

11.2 Check timing unit for signs of wear or damage

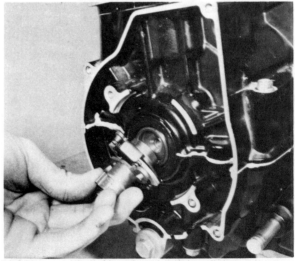

11.3 Note position of locating pin when refitting unit

12 Fault diagnosis: Ignition system

Symptom	Cause	Remedy
Engine will not start	Faulty ignition switch	Operate switch several times in case contacts are dirty. If lights and other electrics function, switch may need renewal.
	Starter motor not working	Discharged battery. Use kickstart until battery is recharged.
	Short circuit in wiring	Check whether fuse is intact. Eliminate fault before switching on again.
	Completely discharged battery	If lights do not work, remove battery and recharge.
Engine misfires	Faulty connection	Check all ignition connections. Check wiring for breaks.
	Coil failure	Remove and test (see text).
	Sparking plug failure	Renew.
	TCI system failure	Test to establish cause of problem.
	Incorrect grade of fuel	Drain and refill with correct grade.
	Faulty ATU or vacuum advance unit	Remove and check operation.
Engine lacks power and overheats	Retarded ignition timing	Check timing. Check whether auto-timing unit has jammed.
Engine 'fades' when under load	Pre-ignition	Check grade of plugs fitted; use recommended grades only.

Chapter 4 Frame and forks

Contents

Specifications

Front forks

	UK models	US models
Type:		
G(UK), E and F models	Oil damped, telescopic	Oil damped, telescopic
All others	–	Oil damped, air-assisted telescopic
Oil capacity (per leg):		
E and F models	212 cc	212 cc
SF model	–	225 cc
G model	212 cc	241 cc
SG model	–	210 cc
Oil grade	SAE 10W/30 motor oil	SAE 10 or ATF
Air pressure:		
Standard	–	5.7 psi (0.4 kg/cm²)
Range	–	0 – 36 psi (0 – 2.5 kg/cm²)
Travel	175 mm (6.89 in)	175 mm (6.89 in)
Spring free length:		
E and F models	503.5 mm (19.82 in)	503.5 mm (19.82 in)
SF model	–	612.2 mm (24.10 in)
G model	503.5 mm (19.82 in)	516.0 mm (20.31 in)
SG model	–	612.2 mm (24.10 in)

Rear suspension units

Type	Oil damped, telescopic	
Spring preload settings	5	
Damper settings:		
SF, G(US) and SG models	4	
All others	No facility	
Travel	80 mm (3.15 in)	
Spring free length:		
SF and SG models	243.5 mm (9.59 in)	
All others	237.0 mm (9.33 in)	

Torque wrench settings

Component	kgf m	lbf ft
Steering stem bolt	8.5	61.5
Stem pinch bolt	2.0	14.5

Upper yoke pinch bolts..	2.0	14.5
Lower yoke pinch bolts	1.7	12.3
Stanchion cap bolt...	2.3	16.5
Wheel spindle clamp nuts	2.0	14.5
Front wheel spindle nut	10.7	77.4
Rear wheel spindle nut	15.0	108.4
Swinging arm spindles	10.0	72.3
Caliper securing bolt:		
Front..	4.5	32.5
Rear...	2.6	18.8
Rear suspension unit (upper)	3.2	23.1
Rear suspension unit (lower):		
Right-hand	4.2	30.4
Left-hand	3.2	23.1

1 General description

The frame used on the Yamaha XS1100 models is of the full cradle type, in which the engine/gearbox unit is supported in duplex tubes running below the crankcase. The frame tubes run from the steering head lug above and below the engine unit, meeting at the swinging arm pivot point. An outrigger section provides support and location for the seat, rear suspension units and ancilliary components. The frame is extensively braced and gusseted to minimise flexing.

The front forks are of the oil-damped telescopic type and feature three-way spring preload adjustment, plus adjustable air pressure assistance on SF, G(US) and SG models. The fork legs are retained by a pair of fork yokes which pivot on tapered roller steering head bearings. Rear suspension is provided by a pivoted fork, or swinging arm, which is supported on tapered roller bearings located by adjustable stubs, and controlled by oil-damped coil spring suspension units. The latter are adjustable to give 5 variations in spring preload plus four damping settings on SF, G(US) and SG models. The left-hand longitudinal section of the swinging arm takes the form of a torque tube which contains the final drive shaft and to which the final drive housing is retained.

2 Front fork legs: removal and replacement

1 Place the machine securely on its centre stand, leaving plenty of working area at the front and sides. Arrange wooden blocks beneath the crankcase so that the front wheel is raised clear of the ground.
2 Release the speedometer drive cable at the front wheel and lodge it clear of the forks. Slacken and remove the two bolts, spring washers and plain washers which secure each of the front brake calipers to its fork leg. As the calipers are lifted clear position some small pieces of scrap wood between the pads so that they are not expelled if the brake lever is inadvertently operated whilst the calipers are removed. Tie the calipers to the frame so that their weight is not supported by the hydraulic hoses.
3 Remove the split pin from the castellated wheel spindle nut, then slacken and remove the nut. Slacken the clamp nuts on the bottom of the left-hand lower leg and withdraw the wheel spindle to release the front wheel. Lower the wheel clear of the forks and place it to one side.
4 Remove the front mudguard mounting bolts and disengage the mudguard from the fork legs. Slacken the single pinch bolt at the upper yoke and the two pinch bolts at the lower yoke to release the fork leg, which can then be twisted and pulled downwards to disengage it from the steering head assembly. Repeat this operation to remove the remaining fork leg.
5 Reassembly is a straightforward reversal of the removal sequence, noting that the tops of the fork stanchions should

be just flush with the top of the upper yoke. When tightening the forks and related components, start with the wheel spindle and work upwards. Tighten the wheel spindle nut to 10.7 kgf m (77.4 lbf ft), then fit the left-hand brake caliper, tightening its two mounting bolts to 4.5 kgf m (32.5 lbf ft). Check that the disc is central in relation to the caliper bracket, and if necessary pull or push the left-hand fork leg until the correct position is obtained. Tighten the front wheel spindle clamp nut to 2.0 kgf m (14.5 lbf ft), then secure the rear nut to the same figure, leaving a small gap between the rear of the clamp and the fork leg.
6 Continue reassembly, securing the right-hand caliper bolts to the same torque setting as was applied to the left-hand unit. The upper and lower yoke pinch bolts and the front mudguard mounting nuts should be tightened to 2.0 kgf m (14.5 lbf ft). Do not omit to check the fork oil level and, where appropriate, the fork air pressure.

3 Steering head assembly: removal and replacement

1 The steering head will rarely require attention unless it becomes necessary to renew the tapered roller bearing or if accident damage has been sustained. It is theoretically possible to remove the lower yoke together with the fork legs, but as this entails a considerable amount of unwieldy manoeuvring this approach is not recommended. A possible exception may arise if the fork stanchions have been damaged in an accident and are jammed in the lower yoke, and in this case a combination of this Section and Section 2 must be applied.
2 Remove the front wheel, brake calipers, front mudguard and fork legs as described in Section 2 of this Chapter. Cover the fuel tank with a blanket or similar to protect the paintwork from scratches or spilled hydraulic fluid. Note that hydraulic fluid will act as an efficient paint remover and will also damage plastic finishes.
3 The procedure from this point onwards must depend on individual circumstances. For obvious reasons, the full dismantling sequence is described here, but it is quite in order to avoid as much of the dismantling as possible by careful manoeuvring of the ancillary components. As an example, the handlebar assembly can be removed as a unit, and threaded around the yokes as these are released. The same applies to the headlamp unit and instrument panel. Obviously, much depends on a commonsense approach and a measure of ingenuity on the part of the owner.
4 Remove the screws which secure the headlamp lens and reflector assembly to the headlamp shell. Disconnect the headlamp bulb connector and the parking lamp bulb (UK and European models) and place the unit to one side. Trace the various multi-pin connectors which enter the headlamp shell, making a quick sketch to show their relative positions. Separate the connectors and push them out of the headlamp shell. Remove the headlamp shell mounting nuts and release the shell, noting the disposition of the various washers and spacers. On models equipped with round headlamps the indicators will be removed at this stage. In the case of the

remaining models fitted with the rectangular unit, disconnect the indicator leads at their single connectors and remove the lamps from the lower yoke after slackening the retaining clamps.

5   Disconnect the speedometer drive cable from the underside of the instrument panel. Slacken and remove the two mounting bolts which retain the panel assembly to the upper yoke, noting the position of the panel bracket in relation to the yoke. The electrical connector will have been separated when the headlamp was dismantled and the panel can now be lifted away and placed in a safe place.

6   Remove the cable retaining plate from the front of the lower yoke to expose the front brake hose union block. Without disturbing the banjo union bolts, release the single bolt which retains the union block to cable guide and lower yoke. Check that the master cylinder cap is secure and remove all clips and ties which secure the front brake hydraulic system to the frame. Release the two clamp bolts which retain the front brake master cylinder assembly, and remove it together with the hydraulic pipes and the brake calipers.

7   Slacken off the clutch cable adjuster and disconnect the cable at the handlebar end. Remove all remaining cable ties and clips from the handlebar area. It is now necessary to remove the clutch lever, throttle assembly and handlebar switch clusters. These are quite straightforward to deal with,

the method of retention being self-evident. Prise out the black plastic caps which cover the handlebar clamp bolts, slacken the Allen screws and remove the handlebars.

8   Slacken the upper yoke pinch bolt and remove the large steering stem bolt to free the upper yoke. The yoke should now lift away, but if reluctant to move can be dislodged by tapping its underside with a soft-faced mallet. Using the C-spanner supplied in the machine's toolkit, slacken and remove the steering stem locknut. Support the lower yoke and release the steering stem adjuster nut. The yoke and steering stem can now be lowered clear of the steering head lug.

9   Reassembly is a direct reversal of the foregoing, noting that the tapered roller steering head bearings should be well greased prior to assembly. When fitting the adjuster nut tighten it until any free play has **just** been removed. The steering stem must turn freely without the resistance that would result from overtight bearings. Although the bearings are designed to accept a degree of thrust loading, over-tightening should be avoided. If possible, use a torque wrench with a peg spanner socket to tighten the nut to $1.0 - 1.2$ kgf m ($7.2 - 8.7$ lbf ft). Secure the upper nut to lock the adjustment. The correct torque setting for the upper yoke pinch bolt is 2.0 kgf m (14.5 lbf ft) whilst the steering stem bolt should be tightened to 8.5 kgf m (61.5 lbf ft).

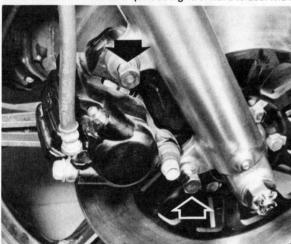

2.2 Release caliper mounting bolts (arrowed) and tie calipers clear of forks

2.3a Remove split pin and slacken wheel spindle nut

2.3b Slacken clamp nuts (arrowed) and withdraw spindle

2.4a Slacken the upper yoke pinch bolt ...

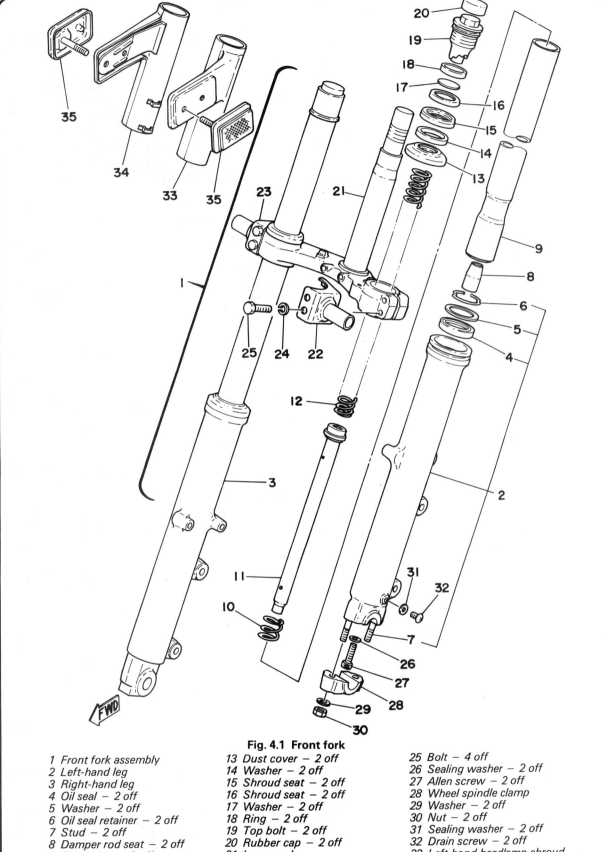

Fig. 4.1 Front fork

1 Front fork assembly
2 Left-hand leg
3 Right-hand leg
4 Oil seal – 2 off
5 Washer – 2 off
6 Oil seal retainer – 2 off
7 Stud – 2 off
8 Damper rod seat – 2 off
9 Stanchion – 2 off
10 Rebound spring – 2 off
11 Damper rod – 2 off
12 Main spring – 2 off

13 Dust cover – 2 off
14 Washer – 2 off
15 Shroud seat – 2 off
16 Shroud seat – 2 off
17 Washer – 2 off
18 Ring – 2 off
19 Top bolt – 2 off
20 Rubber cap – 2 off
21 Lower yoke
22 LH indicator bracket
23 RH indicator bracket
24 Spring washer – 4 off

25 Bolt – 4 off
26 Sealing washer – 2 off
27 Allen screw – 2 off
28 Wheel spindle clamp
29 Washer – 2 off
30 Nut – 2 off
31 Sealing washer – 2 off
32 Drain screw – 2 off
33 Left-hand headlamp shroud
34 Right-hand headlamp shroud
35 Reflector – 2 off

2.4b ... and double pinch bolt on lower yoke

2.5 Note slot in speedometer drive and its locating lug

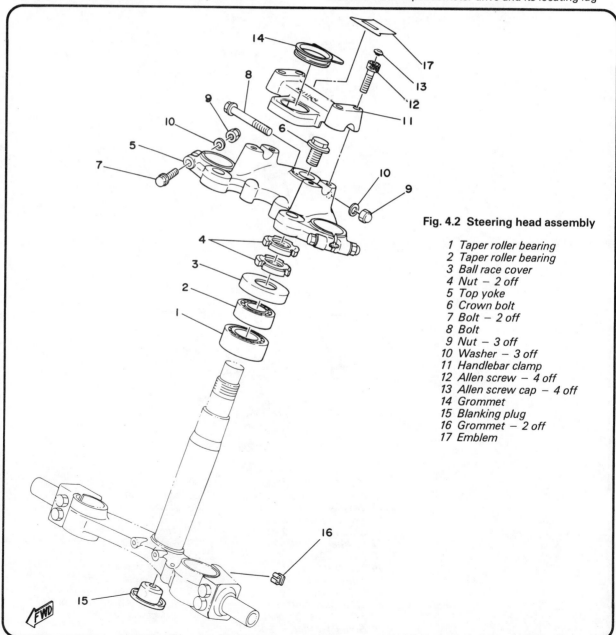

Fig. 4.2 Steering head assembly

1 Taper roller bearing
2 Taper roller bearing
3 Ball race cover
4 Nut – 2 off
5 Top yoke
6 Crown bolt
7 Bolt – 2 off
8 Bolt
9 Nut – 3 off
10 Washer – 3 off
11 Handlebar clamp
12 Allen screw – 4 off
13 Allen screw cap – 4 off
14 Grommet
15 Blanking plug
16 Grommet – 2 off
17 Emblem

4   Front forks: dismantling and reassembly

1   The front forks can be dismantled for examination and overhaul after the individual legs have been removed from the machine as described in Section 2. Alternatively, attention to all but the stanchions is possible by removing the springs and lower legs as described later in this Section, leaving the stanchions clamped in the yokes. Needless to say, it will first be necessary to remove the front wheel, brakes and mudguard.

2   Prise off the black plastic fork top bolt caps (XS1100 E, F and G(UK). In the case of the XS1100 SF, G(US) and SG models unscrew the fork air valve caps and release the air pressure by depressing the valve for one or two seconds.
      Slacken and remove the top bolts and withdraw the spring spacer, washer and fork spring from each leg. Remove the fork drain plugs from the bottom of the lower legs and pump the forks to expel the oil content.

3   Clamp the lower leg gently but securely in a vice, using soft jaws or rag to protect the soft alloy. Using an Allen key, slacken the damper retaining bolts which pass upwards from the underside of the lower leg. This will free the stanchion and damper assembly which can then be pulled out of the lower leg. If the damper unit turns as the bolt is slackened it can be held by making up a tool as shown in the accompanying photographs, using a section of tube with a bolt welded into one end. The hexagon head will engage in the damper recess. Note that during this and subsequent operations, work should be confined to one leg at a time to prevent parts from becoming interchanged.

4   If the oil seal is obviously damaged and is to be renewed, remove the wire retaining ring and plain washer, then remove the seal by levering it upwards with a screwdriver blade. Note that the seal will almost certainly be destroyed during removal, so it is essential that new seals are available **before** the old ones are levered out. Take great care not to damage the top edge of the lower leg.

5   Reassemble the forks by reversing the dismantling sequence. When fitting a new seal it should be carefully tapped into position with a flat wooden block and a hammer, making sure that it enters the bore squarely and seats fully. Grease the seal lip before the stanchion assembly is inserted. When fitting the fork springs note that the lower end of each has one small diameter coil, and that the tighter pitch coils face the top of the fork. It is convenient to put in the damping oil at this stage, having first fitted and tightened the drain screws. The correct quantity of oil for each fork leg for each model is given in the Specifications at the beginning of the chapter. After filling, pump the fork legs a few times to expel any air, then refit the fork top bolts, tightening them to 2.3 kgf m (16.6 lbf ft).

6   The air forks fitted to the later US models should be re-pressurised after final reassembly to the required setting, bearing in mind the permissible pressure range of 0 – 2.5 kg/cm² (0 – 36 psi). The normal pressure setting is 0.4 kg/cm² (5.7 psi) and each leg **must** be within 0.1 kg/cm² (1.4 psi) of the other. On no account must the maximum pressure level be exceeded, as seal damage will invariably result.

5   Front forks: examination and renovation

1   The parts most liable to wear over an extended period of service are the wearing surfaces of the fork stanchion and lower leg, the damper assembly within the fork tube and the oil seal at the sliding joint. Wear is normally accompanied by a tendency for the forks to judder when the front brake is applied and it should be possible to detect the increased amount of play by pulling and pushing on the handlebars when the front brake is applied fully. This type of wear should not be confused with slack steering head bearings, which can give identical results.

2   Renewal of the worn parts is quite straightforward. Particular care is necessary when renewing the oil seal, to ensure that the feather edge seal is not damaged during reassembly. Both the seal and the fork tube should be greased, to lessen the risk of damage. Note that oil seal condition is of particular significance on those forks which are air-assisted.

3   After an extended period of service, the fork springs may take a permanent set. If there is any doubt as to their condition check the free lengths against those of a new spring. If there is a noticeable difference, renew the springs as a complete set.

4   Check the outer surface of the fork tube for scratches or roughness. It is only too easy to damage the oil seal during reassembly, if these high spots are not eased down. The fork tubes are unlikely to bend unless the machine is damaged in an accident. Any significant bend will be detected by eye, but if there is any doubt about straightness, roll the tubes on a flat surface. If the tubes are bent, they must be renewed. Unless specialised repair equipment is available, it is rarely practicable to straighten them to the necessary standard.

5   The dust seals must be in good order if they are to fulfil their proper function. Replace any that are split or damaged.

6   Damping is effected by the damper units contained within each fork tube. The damping action can be controlled within certain limits by changing the viscosity of the oil used as the damping medium, although a change is unlikely to prove necessary except in extremes of climate.

7   Note that the forks are not fitted with renewable bushes. If wear develops, the stanchions and/or lower fork legs will have to be renewed.

6   Steering head bearings: examination and renovation

1   Before reassembling and refitting the front forks, the steering head bearings should be checked for wear. Clean the inner and outer races thoroughly in petrol before inspection. Check the rollers and the bearing tracks for indentation or pitting or in extreme cases for fracture of the outer races.

2   The bearing outer races are a tight drive fit in the head lug casting. If their condition dictates renewal, they may be driven from position using a long handled drift. The lower bearing inner race is a push fit on the steering stem and may be levered from place.

3   Before reassembling the fork yoke sub-assembly, grease the steering head bearings thoroughly with a multi-purpose grease. There is no provision for further lubrication after assembly.

4.2a Pull off black plastic cap (XS1100 E and F models)

4.2b Remove fork top bolt and spring seat ...

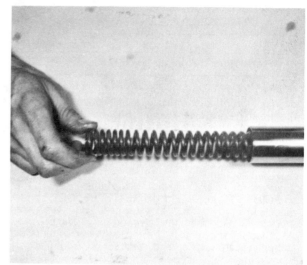

4.2c ... and withdraw the fork spring

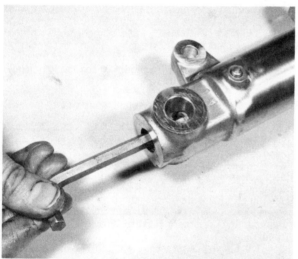

4.3a Using Allen key through base of lower leg ...

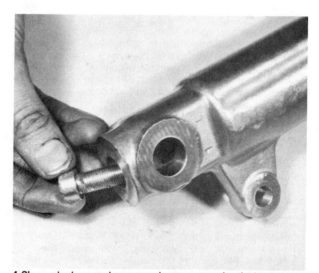

4.3b ... slacken and remove damper securing bolt

4.3c Home-made tool (left) can be used ...

4.3d ... to prevent damper body from rotating

4.3e Withdraw stanchion assembly from lower leg

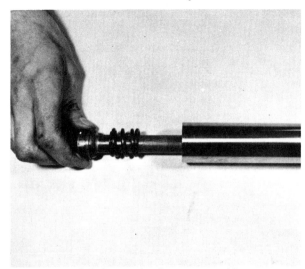

4.3f Invert and shake out the damper assembly

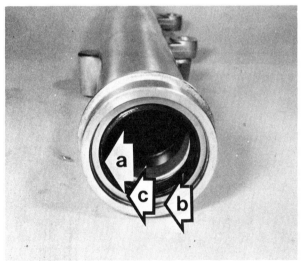

4.4 Oil seal (A) is retained by circlip (B) and plain washer (C)

4.5a Check that fork drain screw is secure ...

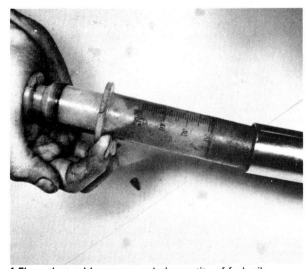

4.5b ... then add recommended quantity of fork oil

5.5 Check that dust seal is undamaged

7   Steering head locks

1   The steering head lock is attached to the left-hand side of the steering head. It is retained by a rivet. When in a locked position, the plunger extends and engages with a portion of the steering head stem, so that the handlebars are locked in position and cannot be turned.

2   If the lock malfunctions, it must be renewed. A repair is impracticable. When the lock is changed it follows that the key must be changed too, to correspond with the new lock.

3   All models other than those sold in Germany have a steering head lock incorporated in the ignition switch. In the event of a failure of the locking mechanism, renewal of the switch assembly will be required. In practice, it will be cheaper and easier to use the steering stem lock instead.

8   Frame: examination and renovation

1   The frame is unlikely to require attention unless accident damage has occurred. In some cases, replacement of the frame is the only satisfactory course of action if it is badly out of alignment. Only a few frame repair specialists have the jigs and mandrels necessary for resetting the frame to the required standard of accuracy and even then there is no easy means of assessing to what extent the frame may have been overstressed.

2   After the machine has covered a considerable mileage, it is advisable to examine the frame closely for signs of cracking or splitting at the welded joints. Rust can also cause weakness at these joints. Minor damage can be repaired by welding or brazing, depending on the extent and nature of the damage.

3   Remember that a frame which is out of alignment will cause handling problems and may even promote 'speed wobbles'. If misalignment is suspected, as the result of an accident, it will be necessary to strip the machine completely so that the frame can be checked and, if necessary, renewed.

9   Swinging arm bearings: checking and adjustment

1   The rear swinging arm fork pivots on two tapered roller bearings, which are supported on adjustable screw stubs fitted to the lugs either side of the frame. After a period of time the tapered roller bearings will wear slightly, allowing a small amount of lateral shake at the rear wheel. This condition, even in its early stages, will have a noticeable effect on handling.

2   To check the play accurately, and if necessary to make suitable adjustments, it will be necessary to remove the rear wheel and detach the rear suspension units.

3   The machine should be placed securely on its centre stand, leaving the rear wheel clear of the ground. It will be noted that on E, F and G models, the silencers are so

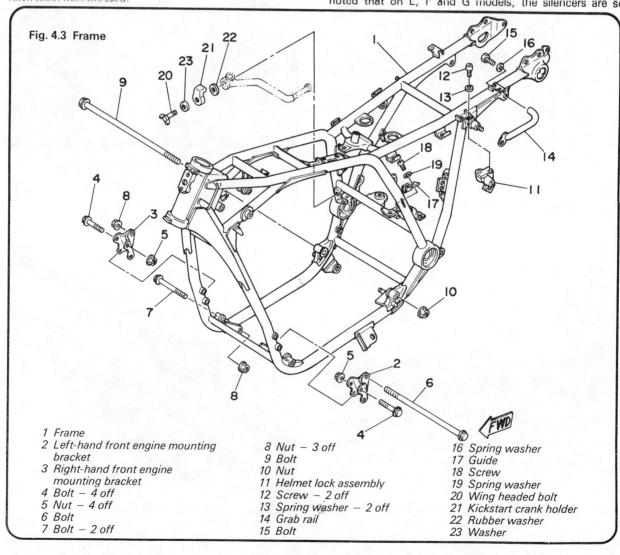

Fig. 4.3 Frame

1   Frame
2   Left-hand front engine mounting bracket
3   Right-hand front engine mounting bracket
4   Bolt – 4 off
5   Nut – 4 off
6   Bolt
7   Bolt – 2 off

8   Nut – 3 off
9   Bolt
10   Nut
11   Helmet lock assembly
12   Screw – 2 off
13   Spring washer – 2 off
14   Grab rail
15   Bolt

16   Spring washer
17   Guide
18   Screw
19   Spring washer
20   Wing headed bolt
21   Kickstart crank holder
22   Rubber washer
23   Washer

positioned that they prevent wheel spindle removal. To overcome this problem, the machines are supplied with a length of steel cable with four attachment loops. Using this and a special lever the suspension is compressed whilst the spindle is withdrawn. If further information is required on this procedure see Chapter 5 for details. The shorter silencers used on the SF and SG models avoid this complication.

4   Remove the rear wheel spindle nut, which is secured by a split pin. Slacken the clamp bolt from the end of the right-hand swinging arm member and withdraw the wheel spindle. Rotate the caliper unit upwards on its upper pivot bolt so that the pads clear the disc, and lift the caliper support bracket up so that it rests on the lug provided on the end of the swinging arm right-hand member. Note the spacer which is placed between the caliper and support bracket. Lift the wheel across to the right and off the final drive box splines. The rear mudguard is hinged at a point to the rear of the dualseat, which allows easy removal of the rear wheel. Unscrew the two hinge bolts, raise the hinged piece and push the bolts in again to support the raised mudguard flap.

5   Detach the rear suspension units at their lower ends by removing the pivot bolts.

6   The swinging arm fork can now be checked for play. Grasp the fork at the rear end and push and pull firmly in a lateral direction. Any play will be magnified by the leverage

effect. Move the swinging arm up and down as far as possible. Any roughness or a tightness at one point may indicate bearing damage. If this is suspected, the bearings should be inspected after removal of the swinging arm as described in the following Section.

7   If play is evident, remove the plastic cover plugs from the adjuster stubs either side of the frame and slacken off the adjuster locknuts. Using a vernier gauge, check that the distances between each end of the swnging arm cross-member and the adjacent part of the frame are within 1.6 mm (0.062 in) of each other. If the difference is greater than this, slacken the adjuster stub ½ of a turn on the side with the larger gap, and then tighten the opposite stub to 0.5 – 0.6 kg m (43 – 52 lbs in). Check the gap again and if necessary, readjust, using the same procedure. When using a torque wrench the load on the bearings is adjusted automatically so that all play is taken up. Where no torque wrench is available, centralise the swinging arm and then tighten the stubs an equal amount, about ⅛ of a turn at a time. Whilst tightening, move the swinging arm up and down until it can be felt that the bearings are beginning to drag. It is at this point that adjustment is correct.

8   After adjustment is completed, tighten the locknuts without allowing the stubs to rotate. Refit the plastic plugs.

9   Reassemble the rear wheel and suspension units by reversing the dismantling procedure.

9.4a Slacken the pinch bolt to free wheel spindle

9.4b Displace caliper assembly and remove spacer

9.4c Disengage wheel from splines and remove rearwards

9.7 Check that frame to swinging arm gap is equal on each side

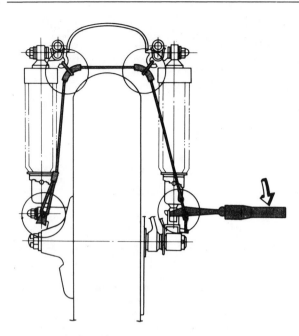

Fig. 4.4 Method of rear wheel removal

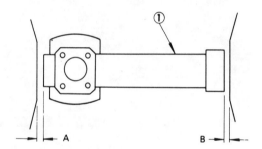

Fig. 4.5 Checking swinging arm centralisation

1 Swinging arm cross-member

Gaps A & B should be within 1.6 mm (0.062 in) of each other

10 Swinging arm: removal, renovation and replacement

1   If on inspection for play in the swinging arm bearings it is found that damage has occurred, or wear is excessive, the swinging arm fork should be removed. Commence by following paragraphs 3 – 5 of the preceding Section and then detach the swinging arm as follows.

2   Prise the final driveshaft rubber gaiter off the boss to the rear of the gearbox so that access to the final driveshaft flange is gained. Slacken evenly and remove the four flange bolts, turning the flange as necessary to reach the bolts.

3   The final drive box may be detached as a complete unit after removing the four flange nuts and washers. Support the weight of the casing as the nuts are removed. Drainage of the lubricating oils is not required, provided the casing is moved and stored in an upright position.

4   Remove the pivot nut washers which secure the rear of the caliper support bracket. The nut is secured by a split pin. The complete caliper/support bracket may be lifted towards the front of the machine and tied to a suitable portion of the frame.

5   Loosen the locknuts on the swinging arm adjuster stubs after detaching the plastic covers from either side of the frame. Unscrew the stubs completely and lift the swinging arm fork, complete with final driveshaft, from the machine.

6   To each end of the swinging arm cross-member is fitted a spacer, oil seal and tapered roller bearing. The spacer is a push fit in the oil seal. To inspect or remove the bearing on either side, the seal must be prised from position. Removal will almost certainly damage the seal and a new one will therefore be required. Lever out the seals with a screwdriver. Take out the bearing inner races and clean and inspect them. Clean the bearing outer races whilst they are still in place. Check the rollers for pitting and the outer race for pitting or indentation. If the bearings need renewing, the inner races may be levered from position.

7   When assembling, clean and lubricate the bearings. Use a waterproof grease of the type recommended for wheel bearings.

8   Refit the swinging arm by reversing the dismantling procedure. Adjust the bearings by referring to Section 9, paragraphs 7 and 8.

10.3 Final drive casing is retained by four studs and nuts

10.4 Disengage caliper assembly and torque plate (arrowed) from swinging arm

10.5a Slacken the adjuster stub locknuts ...

10.5b ... and unscrew the stubs completely

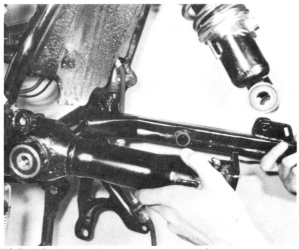

10.5c Lift the swinging arm unit rearwards

10.6a Each side is fitted with spacer and oil seal ...

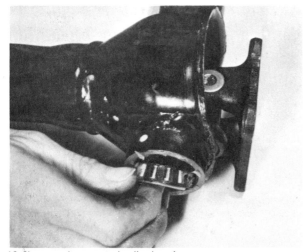

10.6b ... and a tapered roller bearing

11 Final driveshaft: examination and renewal

1   In due course the joint on the upper end of the driveshaft will wear. The joint is of the constant velocity type, sealed for life with its own lubrication reservoir and hence should have a long life expectancy. The final driveshaft and joint may be removed from the swinging arm unit, after the latter component has been removed from the machine.

2   Using two screwdrivers as levers with the lever ends placed behind the splined lower boss, withdraw the shaft from the swnging arm. The CV joint may be lifted from the forward end. Wear of the joint will be self-evident, giving a rough notchy feel when it is flexed.

3   Check the condition of the splines at both ends of the shaft. If damage is evident, the shaft should be renewed. Inspect the condition of the seal and renew it, if required.

4   When refitting the shaft, lubricate the splined ends with graphite grease.

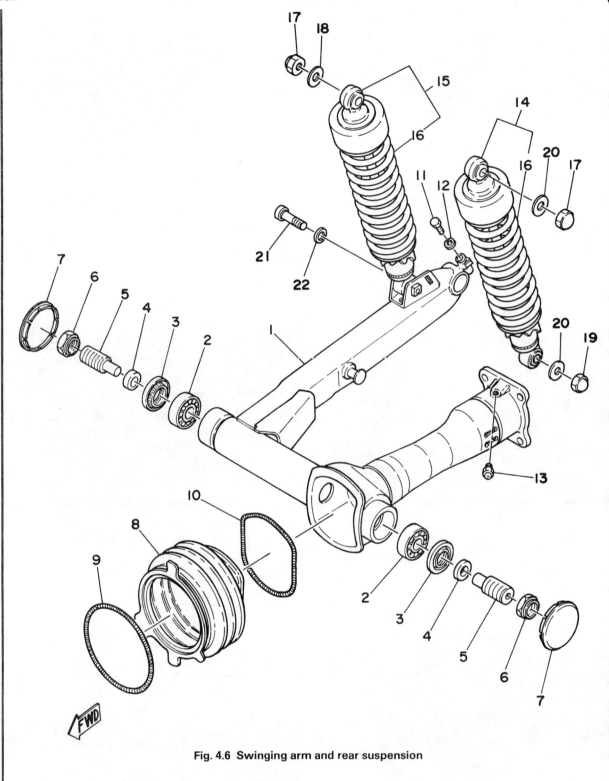

Fig. 4.6 Swinging arm and rear suspension

1 Swinging arm
2 Bearing – 2 off
3 Oil seal – 2 off
4 Collar – 2 off
5 Pivot shaft – 2 off
6 Nut – 2 off
7 Cover – 2 off
8 Rubber boot
9 Spring clip
10 Spring clip
11 Bolt
12 Spring washer
13 Grease nipple
14 Left-hand suspension unit
15 Right-hand suspension unit
16 Spring – 2 off
17 Nut – 2 off
18 Washer
19 Nut
20 Washer – 2 off
21 Bolt
22 Spring washer

11.2a Drive shaft and joint can be separated ...

11.2b ... noting that joint is located by wire clip

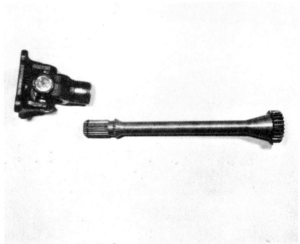

11.2c Drive shaft and universal joint removed from tube

11.2d Joint **can** be dismantled, but bearings are not supplied for overhaul

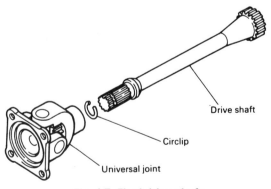

Fig. 4.7 Final drive shaft

Drive shaft

Circlip

Universal joint

12 Final drive bevel gear: examination and renovation

1   Dismantling the bevel drive is beyond the scope of this manual, and the majority of amateur mechanics. Wear or damage may be indicated by a high pitched whine. Backlash between the crownwheel and pinion may be assessed by holding the output splined boss and rotating the input shaft, first one way and then the other.

2   Failure of the seals either at the input shaft or output shaft will be self-evident by oil leakage.

3   Check the splines on the input shaft and output boss for wear or damage.

4   If attention to the final drive bevel box is required, the complete unit should be returned to a Yamaha Service Agent, who will have the necessary tools and experience to carry out inspection and overhaul.

13 Rear suspension units: examination

1   The rear suspension units fitted to the Yamaha XS1100 models are of the normal hydraulically damped type, adjustable to give 5 different spring settings. A screwdriver shaft or round metal rod should be used to turn the lower spring seat and so alter its position on the adjustment projection. When the spring seat is turned so that the effective length of the spring is shortened the suspension will become heavier.

2   If a suspension unit leaks, or if the damping efficiency is reduced in any other way the two units must be replaced as a pair. For precise roadholding it is imperative that both units react to movement in the same way. It follows that the units must always be set at the same spring loading.

3   The XS1100 SF, G(US) and SG models are equipped with slightly more sophisticated units having four damping adjustment settings. A knurled ring near the upper mounting provides the adjustment control and is marked from 1 (soft) to 4 (hard).

14   Centre stand: examination

1   The centre stand is attached to the machine by two bolts on the bottom of the frame. It is returned by a centre spring. The bolts and spring should be checked for tightness and tension respectively. A weak spring can cause the centre stand to 'ground' on corners and unseat the rider.

12.3a Check for signs of wear on internal splines ...

12.3b ... and corresponding splines on drive shaft

12.3c Check spline condition at wheel boss

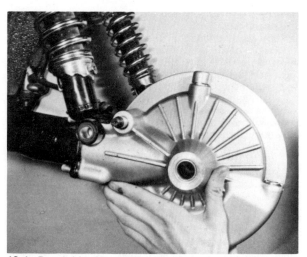

12.4a Bevel drive box can be detached after wheel and suspension units have been removed

12.4b Grease nipple permits lubrication of splined boss

15 Prop stand: examination

1   The prop stand is secured to a plate on the frame with a bolt and nut, and is retracted by a tension spring. Make sure the bolt is tight and the spring not overstretched, otherwise an accident can occur if the stand drops during cornering.

16 Footrests: examination and renovation

1   Each footrest is an individual unit retained by a single bolt to a suitable part of the frame.
2   Both pairs of footrests are pivoted on clevis pins and spring loaded in the down position. If an accident occurs, it is probable that the footrest peg will move against the spring loading and remain undamaged. A bent peg may be detached from the mounting, after removing the clevis pin securing split pin and the clevis pin itself. The damaged peg can be straightened in a vice, using a blowlamp flame to apply heat at the area where the bend occurs. The footrest rubber will, of course, have to be removed as the heat will render it unfit for service.

17 Rear brake pedal: examination and renovation

1   The rear brake pedal pivots on a shaft which passes through the frame right-hand intersection lug. The shaft carrying the brake arm is splined, to engage with splines of the rear brake pedal. The pedal is retained to the shaft by a simple pinch bolt arrangement.
2   If the brake pedal is bent or twisted in an accident, it should be removed by slackening the pinch bolt and straightened in a manner similar to that recommended for the footrests in the preceding Section.
3   Make sure the pinch bolt is tight. If the lever is a slack fit on the splines, they will wear rapidly and it will be difficult to keep the lever in position.

18 Dualseat: removal and replacement

1   The dualseat is secured by means of two extended nuts which retain studs projecting through keyhole plates on the frame. When the two nuts have been slackened, the seat can be pulled rearwards and disengaged from the front hooked mounting, and then can be lifted away. Replacement is a direct reversal of the removal sequence.

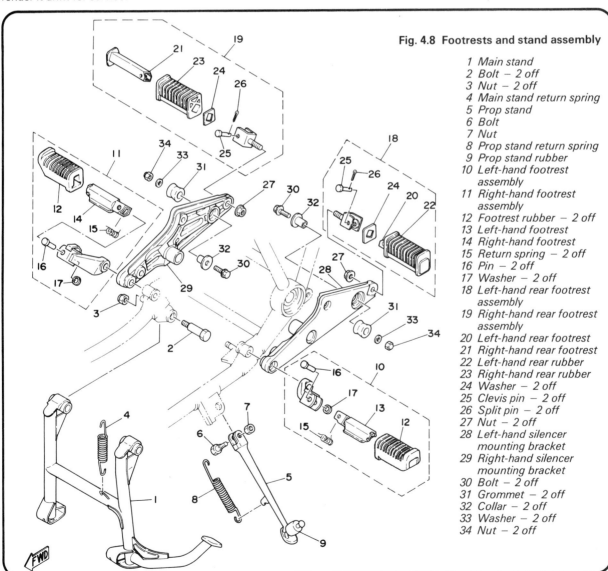

Fig. 4.8 Footrests and stand assembly

1 Main stand
2 Bolt − 2 off
3 Nut − 2 off
4 Main stand return spring
5 Prop stand
6 Bolt
7 Nut
8 Prop stand return spring
9 Prop stand rubber
10 Left-hand footrest assembly
11 Right-hand footrest assembly
12 Footrest rubber − 2 off
13 Left-hand footrest
14 Right-hand footrest
15 Return spring − 2 off
16 Pin − 2 off
17 Washer − 2 off
18 Left-hand rear footrest assembly
19 Right-hand rear footrest assembly
20 Left-hand rear footrest
21 Right-hand rear footrest
22 Left-hand rear rubber
23 Right-hand rear rubber
24 Washer − 2 off
25 Clevis pin − 2 off
26 Split pin − 2 off
27 Nut − 2 off
28 Left-hand silencer mounting bracket
29 Right-hand silencer mounting bracket
30 Bolt − 2 off
31 Grommet − 2 off
32 Collar − 2 off
33 Washer − 2 off
34 Nut − 2 off

19 Instrument panel: removal and dismantling

1   The instruments are contained in a panel assembly mounted on the upper fork yoke. In the case of E, F and G models, the instruments are rectangular and are themselves housed in a rectangular nacelle assembly. The SF and SG models feature conventional round instruments in chromium plated nacelles, but which are otherwise similar.

2   To remove the complete instrument panel it will be necessary to release the headlamp assembly so that the instrument wiring connectors can be separated. Disconnect the speedometer drive cable from the underside of the instrument head. Release the two panel mounting screws and lift the assembly clear of the fork yoke.

3   The instruments can be removed with the panel separated from the machine or in situ. In the latter case, it will be necessary to disconnect the speedometer cable, where appropriate and to trace back and release the necessary wiring connectors. Each instrument is retained by two domed nuts. Note that the retaining studs pass through anti-vibration grommets where they pass through the casing. A rubber seal supports the instrument head in its casing.

4   In the event of speedometer failure, check that the drive cable and gearbox are working before suspecting the instrument head itself. Note that if the odometer functions whilst the speedometer is inoperative or vice versa, the instrument can be considered defunct. The tachometer is of the electronic impulse type and is triggered by one of the alternator coils. If either unit malfunctions it will be necessary to purchase a new replacement. The instruments are sealed and repair is impractical.

5   Remember that a speedometer in correct working order is a statutory requirement in the UK and many other countries. Apart from this legal requirement, reference to the odometer reading is the best means of keeping in pace with the maintenance schedule.

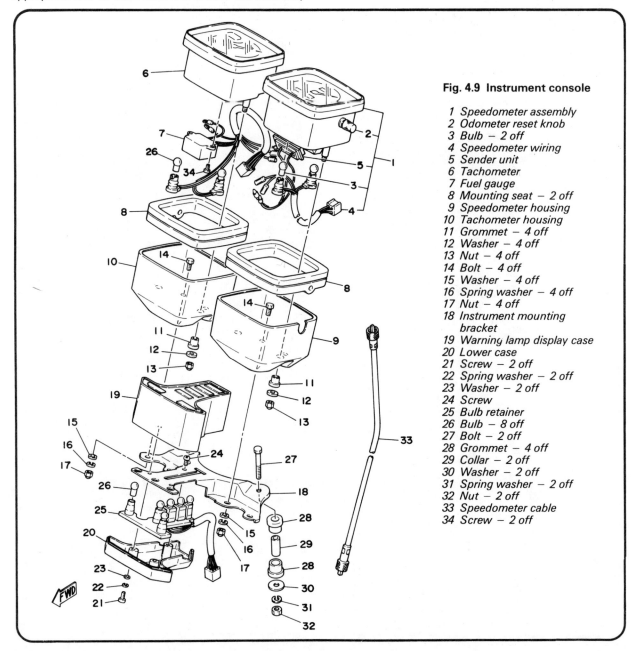

Fig. 4.9 Instrument console

1   Speedometer assembly
2   Odometer reset knob
3   Bulb – 2 off
4   Speedometer wiring
5   Sender unit
6   Tachometer
7   Fuel gauge
8   Mounting seat – 2 off
9   Speedometer housing
10 Tachometer housing
11 Grommet – 4 off
12 Washer – 4 off
13 Nut – 4 off
14 Bolt – 4 off
15 Washer – 4 off
16 Spring washer – 4 off
17 Nut – 4 off
18 Instrument mounting bracket
19 Warning lamp display case
20 Lower case
21 Screw – 2 off
22 Spring washer – 2 off
23 Washer – 2 off
24 Screw
25 Bulb retainer
26 Bulb – 8 off
27 Bolt – 2 off
28 Grommet – 4 off
29 Collar – 2 off
30 Washer – 2 off
31 Spring washer – 2 off
32 Nut – 2 off
33 Speedometer cable
34 Screw – 2 off

19.1 The XS1100 E and F instrument panel

19.3 Instrument heads are retained by two domed nuts

20 Speedometer drive gearbox and cable: examination

1   The speedometer drive gearbox is fitted on the front wheel spindle where it is driven internally by the left-hand side of the wheel hub.

2   The gearbox rarely gives trouble if it is lubricated with grease at regular intervals. This can only be done after the wheel has been removed and the gearbox has been detached since no external grease nipple is fitted. The gearbox can be pulled from position after wheel removal.

3   The drive cable can often give rise to speedometer faults, ranging from complete failure to jerky or erratic operation due to a kinked inner cable. In the event of malfunction a new cable must be fitted, repair or dismantling being impracticable.

21 Cleaning the machine

1   After removing all surface dirt with warm water and a rag or sponge, use a cleaning compound such as 'Gunk' or 'Jizer' for the oily parts. Apply the cleaner with a brush when the parts are dry so that it has an opportunity to soak into the film of oil or grease. Finish off by washing down liberally, taking care that water does not enter into the carburettors,

air cleaners or electrics. If desired, a polish such as Solvol Autosol can be applied to the alloy parts to give them full lustre. Application of a wax polish to cycle parts and a good chrome cleaner to the chrome parts will also give a good finish. Always wipe the machine down if used in the wet. There is less chance of water getting into control cables if they are regularly lubricated, which will prevent stiffness of action.

22 Suspension air pressure and damping adjustments: SF, G(US) and SG models

1   As mentioned earlier in the Chapter, the later models feature air-assisted front forks and rear suspension units which are adjustable for both spring preload and damping. These facilities permit a degree of fine tuning of the suspension to suit different terrain and rider preference. Experience will indicate the best combinations of settings, but always ensure that the two sides of the suspension are set to the same positions, thus avoiding any imbalance which might cause handling problems. Never exceed the maximum front fork air pressure setting of 2.5 kg cm² (36 psi). The combinations of front fork air pressure and rear suspension unit damping and spring settings recommended by Yamaha are given in the table.

	Front fork	Rear shock absorber		Loading condition		
	Air pressure	Spring seat	Damping adjuster	Solo rider	With passenger	With accessory equipments and/or passenger
1.	0.4~1.0 kg/cm² (5.7~14 psi)	A ~ E	1	O		
2.	0.4~1.0 kg/cm² (5.7~14 psi)	A ~ E	2	O	O	
3.	1.0~1.5 kg/cm² (14~21 psi)	C ~ E	3		O	O
4.	1.5 kg/cm² (21 psi)	E	4			O

Fig. 4.10 Rear suspension table

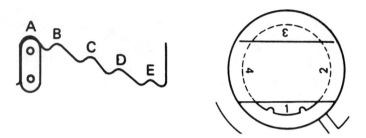

Fig. 4.11 Rear suspension adjuster positions

23 Fault diagnosis: Frame and forks

Symptom	Cause	Remedy
Machine veers to the left or right with hands off handlebars	Wheels out of alignment Forks twisted Frame bent	Check and realign. Strip and repair. Strip and repair or renew.
Machine tends to roll at low speeds	Steering head bearings not adjusted correctly or worn	Check adjustment and renew bearings if necessary.
Machine tends to wander	Worn swinging arm bearings	Check and renew bearings. Check adjustment and renew if necessary.
Forks judder when front brake applied	Steering head bearings slack Fork components worn	Adjust bearings. Strip forks, and renew all worn parts.
Forks bottom	Short of oil	Replenish with correct viscosity oil.
Fork action stiff	Fork legs out of alignment Bent shafts, or twisted ie. yokes	Slacken clamp bolts, front wheel spindle and top bolts. Pump forks several times and tighten from bottom upwards. Strip and renew parts, if damaged.
Machine pitches badly	Defective rear suspension units or ineffective fork damping	Check damping action. Check grade and quantity of oil in front forks.

Chapter 5 Wheels, brakes and tyres

Contents

Specifications

Tyres

Type:		
G(UK), E and F models	Tubed	
All others	Tubeless	
Size:	**Front**	**Rear**
E and F(US) models	3.25H19-4PR	4.50H17-4PR
E and G(UK) models	3.50V19-4PR	4.50V17-4PR
G(US) model	3.50H19-4PR	4.50H17-4PR
SF and SG model	3.50H19-4PR	130/90-16 67H

Tyre pressures (cold)

	Front	**Rear**
US models:		
Up to 198 lb (90 kg) load	26 psi (1.8 kg/cm²)	28 psi (2.0 kg/cm²)
198 − 337 lb (90 − 153 kg) load	28 psi (2.0 kg/cm²)	36 psi (2.5 kg/cm²)
337 − 478 lb (153 − 217 kg) load	28 psi (2.0 kg/cm²)	40 psi (2.8 kg/cm²)
Continuous high-speed riding	36 psi (2.5 kg/cm²)	40 psi (2.8 kg/cm²)
UK models:		
Up to 324 lb (147 kg) load	28 psi (2.0 kg/cm²)	36 psi (2.5 kg/cm²)
324 − 463 lb (147 − 210 kg) load	28 psi (2.0 kg/cm²)	40 psi (2.8 kg/cm²)
Continuous high-speed riding	36 psi (2.5 kg/cm²)	40 psi (2.8 kg/cm²)

Wheels

Type	Cast aluminium alloy	Cast aluminium alloy
Rim:		
SF and SG	MT 1.85 × 19	MT 3.00 × 16
All others	MT 1.85 × 19	MT 2.50 × 17

Brakes

Type	Twin hydraulic disc	Single hydraulic disc
Pad thickness (min):		
SG model	6.5 mm (0.26 in)	6.0 mm (0.24 in)
All others	6.0 mm (0.24 in)	6.0 mm (0.24 in)
Disc thickness (min)	6.5 mm (0.26 in)	6.5 mm (0.26 in)
Disc warpage (max)	0.15 mm (0.006 in)	0.15 mm (0.006 in)
Hydraulic fluid	DOT 3 (US) or SAE J1703	

Torque wrench settings

Component	kgf m	lbf ft
Wheel spindle clamp nuts	2.0	14.5
Front wheel spindle nut	10.7	77.4
Rear wheel spindle nut	15.0	108.4
Caliper securing bolt:		
Front	4.5	32.5
Rear	2.6	18.8
Torque rod nut	2.0	14.5
Brake disc nuts	2.0	14.5
Rear hub flange bolts	5.5	40.0

1 General description

All models within the Yamaha XS1100 range are fitted with seven-spoke cast alloy wheels. The E, F and G(UK) model utilise tubed-type tyres, the remainder of the range having tubeless tyres. Tyre size and section depends upon the model and original sales location; the relevant information is given in the Specifications.

Braking is provided by twin front and single rear hydraulically operated disc brakes using single piston calipers.

2 Front wheel: examination and renovation

1   Carefully check the complete wheel for cracks and chipping, particularly at the spoke roots and the edge of the rim. As a general rule a damaged wheel must be renewed as cracks will cause stress points which may lead to sudden failure under heavy load. Small nicks may be radiused carefully with a fine file and emery paper (No 600 – No 1000) to relieve the stress. If there is any doubt as to the condition of a wheel, advice should be sought from a Yamaha repair specialist.

2   Each wheel is covered with a coating of lacquer, to prevent corrosion. If damage occurs to the wheel and the lacquer finish is penetrated, the bared aluminium alloy will soon start to corrode. A whitish grey oxide will form over the damaged area, which in itself is a protective coating. This deposit however, should be removed carefully as soon as possible and a new protective coating of laquer applied.

3   Check the lateral run out at the rim by spinning the wheel and placing a fixed pointer close to the rim edge. If the maximum run out is greater than 2.0 mm (0.080 in), Yamaha recommend that the wheel be renewed. This is, however, a counsel of perfection; a run out somewhat greater than this can probably be accommodated without noticeable effect on steering. No means is available for straightening a warped wheel without resorting to the expense of having the wheel skimmed on all faces. If warpage was caused by impact during an accident, the safest measure is to renew the wheel complete. Worn wheel bearings may cause rim run out. These should be renewed as described in Section 9 of this Chapter.

4   Note that impact damage or serious corrosion on models fitted with tubeless tyres has wider implications in that it could lead to a loss of pressure from the tubeless tyres. If in any doubt as to the wheel's condition, seek professional advice.

3 Front disc brake: checking and renewing the pads

1   To facilitate the checking of brake pad wear, each caliper is provided with an inspection window closed by a small cover. Prise the cover from position and inspect both pads. Each pad has a red wear limit line around its periphery. If either pad has worn down to or past the line, both pads in that set should be renewed. In practice, it is probable that both sets of pads will wear at a similar rate, and therefore the two sets will require renewal at the same time.

2   Removal of the pads is straightforward. The procedure is identical for both calipers, and does not require the hydraulic hose to be disconnected. Remove the two bolts that secure the caliper bracket to front fork leg, and lift the complete unit up off the brake disc. Remove the single bolt which secures the caliper unit to the caliper mounting bracket. Unscrew the crosshead screw from the inner face of the caliper, noting that the screw acts as a detent for the pads. Pull the support bracket from the main caliper and lift both pads from position. Note the various shims and their positions, before removal. If required, pad replacement may be carried out with the caliper bracket attached to the fork leg.

3   Fit new pads by reversing the dismantling sequence. If difficulty is encountered when fitting the caliper over the brake disc, due to the reduced distance between the new pads, use a wooden lever to push the pad on the piston side inwards.

4   In the interests of safety, always check the function of the brakes before taking the machine on the road.

4 Front disc brake: removing, renovating and replacing the caliper units

1   Before either caliper assembly can be removed from the fork leg upon which it is mounted, it is first necessary to drain off the hydraulic fluid. Disconnect the brake pipe at the union connection it makes with the caliper unit and allow the fluid to drain into a clean container. It is preferable to keep the front brake lever applied throughout this operation, to prevent the fluid from leaking out of the reservoir. A thick rubber band cut from a section of inner tube will suffice, if it is wrapped tightly around the lever and the handlebars.

2   Note that brake fluid is an extremely efficient paint stripper. Take care to keep it away from any paintwork on the machine or from any clear plastic, such as that sometimes used for instrument glasses.

3   When the fluid has drained off, remove the caliper mounting bolts, separate the two main caliper components and remove the pads as described in the preceding Section.

4   To displace the piston, apply a blast of compressed air to the brake fluid inlet. Take care to catch the piston as it emerges from the bore – if dropped or prised out with a screwdriver a piston may suffer irreparable damage. Before removing the piston, displace the dust seal which is retained by a circlip.

5   Remove the sleeve and protective boot upon which the caliper unit slides. If play has developed between the sleeve and the caliper, the former must be renewed. Check the condition of the boot, renewing it if necessary.

6   The parts removed should be cleaned thoroughly, using only brake fluid as the liquid. Petrol, oil or paraffin will cause the various seals to swell and degrade, and should not be used under any circumstances. When the various parts have been cleaned, they should be stored in polythene bags until reassembly, so that they are kept dust free.

7   Examine the pistons for score marks or other imperfections. If they have any imperfections they must be renewed, otherwise air or hydraulic fluid leakage will occur, which will impair braking efficiency. With regard to the various seals, it is advisable to renew them all, irrespective of their appearance. It is a small price to pay against the risk of a sudden and complete front brake failure. It is standard Yamaha practice to renew the seals every two years, even if no braking problems have occurred.

8   Reassemble under clinically-clean conditions, by reversing the dismantling procedure. Apply a small quantity of graphite grease to the slider sleeve before fitting the boot. Reconnect the hydraulic fluid pipe and make sure the union has been tightened fully. Before the brake can be used, the whole system must be bled of air, by following the procedure described in Section 8 of this Chapter.

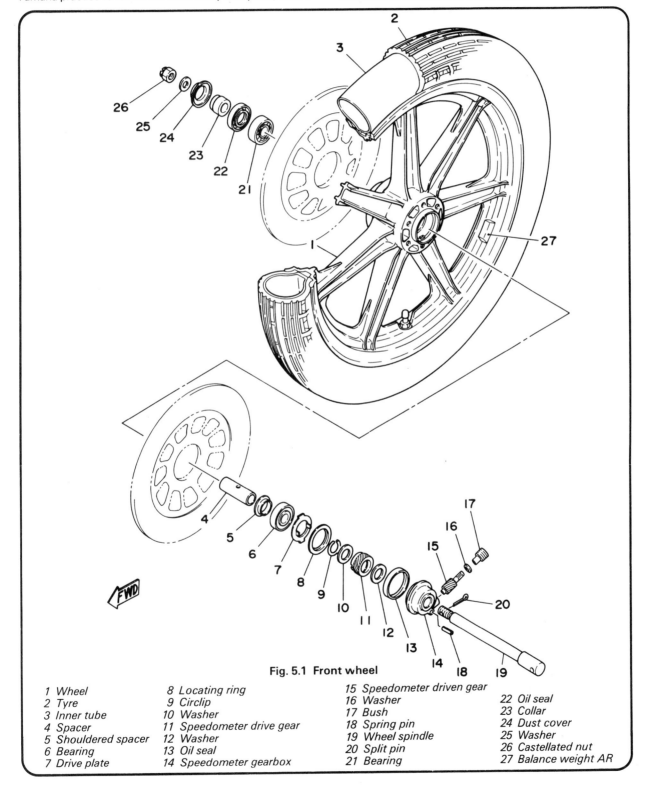

Fig. 5.1 Front wheel

1 Wheel	8 Locating ring	15 Speedometer driven gear	22 Oil seal
2 Tyre	9 Circlip	16 Washer	23 Collar
3 Inner tube	10 Washer	17 Bush	24 Dust cover
4 Spacer	11 Speedometer drive gear	18 Spring pin	25 Washer
5 Shouldered spacer	12 Washer	19 Wheel spindle	26 Castellated nut
6 Bearing	13 Oil seal	20 Split pin	27 Balance weight AR
7 Drive plate	14 Speedometer gearbox	21 Bearing	

3.2a Remove bolt to release caliper from mounting bracket

3.2b Lift caliper assembly clear of bracket ...

3.2c ... to expose pads

3.2d Engraved line denotes maximum wear limit (arrowed)

5 Master cylinder: examination and renewing seals

1   The master cylinder and hydraulic fluid reservoir takes the form of a combined unit mounted on the right-hand side of the handlebars, to which the front brake lever is attached.

2   Before the master cylinder unit can be removed and dismantled, the system must be drained. Place a clean container below each brake caliper unit and attach a plastic tube from the bleed screw of each caliper unit to the container. Lift off the master cylinder cover (cap), gasket and diaphragm, after removing the four countersunk retaining screws. Open the bleed screws one complete turn and drain the system by operating the brake lever until the master cylinder reservoir is empty. Close the bleed screws and remove the tube.

3   Before dismantling the master cylinder, it is essential that a clean working area is available on which the various component parts can be laid out. Use a sheet of white paper, so that none of the smaller parts can be overlooked.

4   Disconnect the stop lamp switch and front brake lever, taking care not to misplace the brake lever return spring. The stop lamp switch is a push fit in the lever stock. The lever pivots on a bolt retained by a single nut. Remove the brake hose by unscrewing the banjo union bolt. Take the master cylinder away from the handlebars by removing the two bolts that clamp it to the handlebars. Take care not to spill any hydraulic fluid on the paintwork or on plastic or rubber

components.

5   Withdraw the rubber boot that protects the end of the master cylinder and remove the snap ring that holds the piston assembly in position, using a pair of circlip pliers. The piston assembly can now be drawn out, followed by the return valve, spring cup and return spring.

6   The spring cup can now be separated from the end of the return valve spring and the main cup prised off the piston.

7   Examine the piston and the cylinder cup very carefully. If either is scratched or has the working surface impaired in any other way, it must be renewed without question. Reject the various seals, irrespective of their condition, and fit new ones in their place. It often helps to soften them a little before they are fitted by immersing them in a container of clean brake fluid.

8   When reassembling, follow the dismantling procedure in reverse, but take great care that none of the component parts is scratched or damaged in any way. Use brake fluid as the lubricant whilst reassembling. When assembly is complete, reconnect the brake fluid pipe and tighten the banjo union bolt.

9   Use two new sealing washers at the union so that the banjo bolt does not require overtightening to effect a good seal. Refill the master cylinder with DOT 3 or SAE J1703 brake fluid and bleed the system of air by following the procedure described in Section 8 of this Chapter.

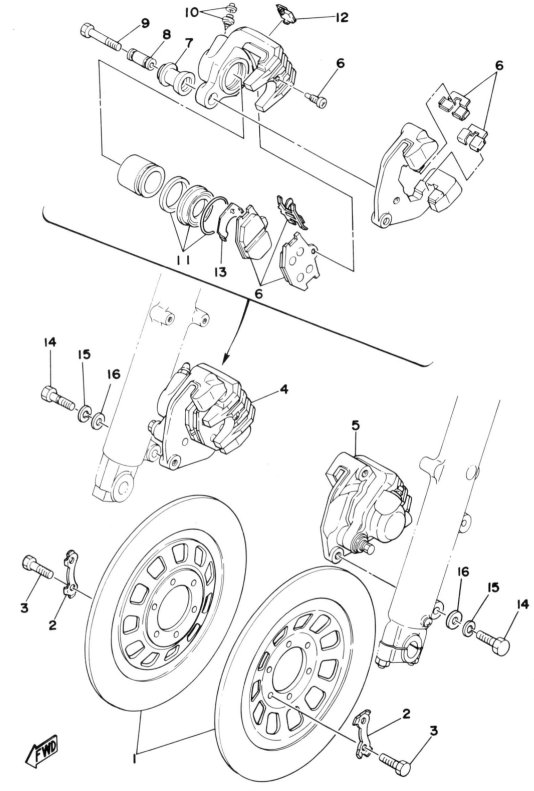

Fig. 5.2 Front brake caliper

1 Front brake disc − 2 off
2 Tab washer − 6 off
3 Bolt − 12 off
4 Right-hand caliper
5 Left-hand caliper
6 Pad set − 2 off
7 Bush − 2 off

8 Sleeve − 2 off
9 Bolt − 2 off
10 Bleed nipple and cap − 2 off
11 Caliper seal assembly − 2 off
12 Pad wear indicator window
      − 2 off

13 Shim − 2 off
14 Bolt − 4 off
15 Spring washer − 4 off
16 Washer − 4 off

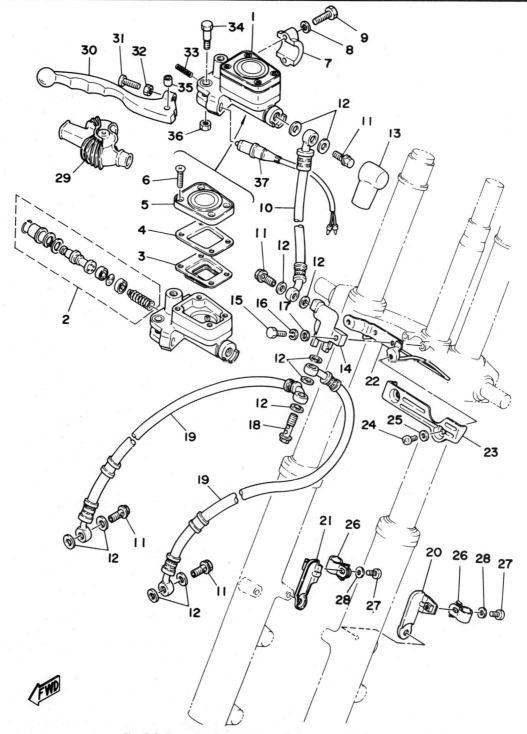

Fig. 5.3 Front brake master cylinder assembly

1 Master cylinder	14 Junction	26 Clamp – 2 off
2 Piston and cup set	15 Bolt	27 Screw – 2 off
3 Diaphragm	16 Spring washer	28 Spring washer – 2 off
4 Diaphragm plate	17 Washer	29 Brake lever cover
5 Reservoir top	18 Banjo union bolt	30 Brake lever
6 Screw – 4 off	19 Lower brake hose – 2 off	31 Screw
7 Master cylinder clamp	20 Left-hand hose retaining clamp	32 Nut
8 Spring washer – 2 off	21 Right-hand hose retaining clamp	33 Spring
9 Bolt – 2 off	22 Cable guide	34 Bolt
10 Upper brake hose	23 Cable clamp front	35 Spacer
11 Banjo union bolt – 4 off	24 Screw – 2 off	36 Nut
12 Washer – 11 off	25 Washer – 2 off	37 Front stop lamp switch
13 Boot		

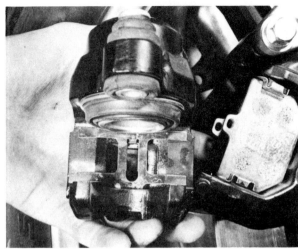

4.8 Check dust seals and anti-squeal shim condition

6   Removing and replacing the brake disc

1   It is unlikely that either disc will require attention until a considerable mileage has been covered, unless premature scoring of the disc has taken place thereby reducing braking efficiency. To remove each disc, first detach the front wheel as described in Chapter 4, Section 2.2 and 3. Each disc is bolted to the front wheel by six bolts, which are secured in pairs by a common tab washer. Bend back the tab washers and remove the bolts to free the disc.
2   The brake disc can be checked for wear and for warpage whilst the front wheel is still in the machine. Using a micrometer, measure the thickness of the disc at the point of greatest wear. If the measurement is much less than the recommended service limit of 6.5 mm (0.26 in) the disc should be renewed. Check the warpage of the disc by setting up a suitable pointer close to the outer periphery of the disc and spinning the front wheel slowly. If the total warpage is more than 0.15 mm (0.006 in) the disc should be renewed. A warped disc, apart from reducing the braking efficiency, is likely to cause juddering during braking and will also cause the brake to bind when it is not in use.

7   Hydraulic brake hoses and pipes: examination

1   External brake hoses and pipes are used to transmit the hydraulic pressure to the caliper units when the front brake or rear brake is applied. The brake hose is of the flexible type, fitted with an armoured surround. It is capable of withstanding pressures up to 350 kg/cm². The brake pipe attached to it is made from double steel tubing, zinc plated to give better corrosion resistance.
2   When the brake assembly is being overhauled, check the condition of both the hose and the pipe for signs of leakage or scuffing, if either has made rubbing contact with the machine whilst it is in motion. The union connections at either end must also be in good condition, with no stripped threads or damaged sealing washers.

8   Bleeding the hydraulic system

1   As mentioned earlier, brake action is impaired or even rendered inoperative if air is introduced into the hydraulic system. This can occur if the seals leak, the reservoir is allowed to run dry or if the system is drained prior to the dismantling of any component part of the system. Even when the system is refilled with hydraulic fluid, air pockets will remain and because air will compress, the hydraulic action is lost.
2   Check the fluid content of the reservoir and fill almost to the top. Remember that hydraulic brake fluid is an excellent paint stripper, so beware of spillage, especially near the petrol tank.
3   Place a clean glass jar below the brake caliper unit and attach a clear plastic tube from the caliper bleed screw to the container. Place some clean hydraulic fluid in the container so that the pipe is always immersed below the surface of the fluid.
4   Unscrew the bleed screw one complete turn and pump the handlebar lever slowly. As the fluid is ejected from the bleed screw the level in the reservoir will fall. Take care that the level does not drop too low whilst the operation continues, otherwise air will re-enter the system, necessitating a fresh start.
5   Continue the pumping action with the lever until no further air bubbles emerge from the end of the plastic pipe. Hold the brake lever against the handlebars and tighten the caliper bleed screw. Remove the plastic tube **after** the bleed screw is closed. Where the front brakes are being bled, attach the pipe to the second caliper and repeat the sequence.
6   Check the brake action for sponginess, which usually denotes there is still air in the system. If the action is spongy, continue the bleeding operation in the same manner, until all traces of air are removed.
7   Bring the reservoir up to the correct level of fluid and replace the diaphragm, sealing gasket and cap. Check the entire system for leaks. Recheck the brake action.
8   Note that fluid from the container placed below the brake caliper unit whilst the system is bled, should not be reused, as it will have become aerated and may have absorbed moisture.

9   Front wheel bearings: examination and replacement

1   Access to the front wheel bearings may be made after removal of the wheel from the forks. Pull the speedometer gearbox out of the hub left-hand boss and remove the dust seal cover and wheel spacer from the hub right-hand side.
2   Lay the wheel on the ground with the disc side facing downward and with a special tool, in the form of a rod with a curved end, insert the curved end into the hole in the centre of the spacer separating the two wheel bearings. If the other end of the special tool is hit with a hammer, the right-hand bearing, bearing flange washer, and bearing spacer will be expelled from the hub.
3   Invert the wheel and drive out the left-hand bearing by inserting a drift of the appropriate size, through the hub. During the removal of either bearing it may be necessary to support the wheel across an open-ended box so that there is sufficient clearance for the bearing to be displaced completely from the hub.
4   Remove all the old grease from the hub and bearings, giving the latter a final wash in petrol. Check the bearings for signs of play or roughness when they are turned. If there is any doubt about the condition of a bearing, it should be renewed.
5   Before replacing the bearings, first pack the hub with new grease. Then drive the bearings back into position, not forgetting the distance piece that separates them. Take great care to ensure that the bearings enter the housings perfectly squarely otherwise the housing surface may be broached. Fit replacement oil seals and any dust covers or spacers that were also displaced during the original dismantling operation.

7.1 Check brake hoses and pipes for signs of leaks

8.3 Bleed tube attached to caliper bleed nipple

9.1a Remove speedometer gearbox from LH side ...

9.1b ... and dust seal/spacer from RH side of wheel

9.5a Bearings are separated by distance tube

9.5b Sealed face of bearing should face outwards

9.5c Grease oil seal lip and fit as shown

9.5d Note location of speedometer drive dog

9.5e Flanged retaining ring is fitted next ...

9.5f ... followed by speedometer drive oil seal

10 Rear wheel: examination, removal and renovation

1   Place the machine on the centre stand so that the rear wheel is raised clear of the ground. Check for rim alignment, spokes etc., as described for the front wheel in Section 2.
2   Removal of the rear wheel should be carried out as described in Chapter 4, Section 9.3-4.

11 Rear wheel bearings: examination and replacement

1   The procedure for the removal and examination of the rear wheel bearings is similar to that given for the front wheel bearings. A heavy dust cover and oil seals are fitted on both sides of the hub. Commence by drifting out the right-hand wheel bearing and bearing spacer. Two bearings placed side by side are fitted on the left of the hub. These should be drifted out together. The double sealed bearing should be fitted on the outside.

11.1a Remove headed spacer ...

11.1b … followed by oil seal

11.1c Bearing is retained by circlip

11.1d Note that sealed face is fitted outwards

11.1e Flanged distance piece fits between bearings

11.1f LH bearing inner race may drop free

11.1g Use large socket to drive bearing home squarely

11.1h LH bearing is of the caged needle roller type

11.1i Note projecting spacer is headed, and is held by seal

11.1j LH inner and outer bearing, and RH bearing. Grease well prior to reassembly

11.1k Remove disc to expose cush drive bolt blanking plugs

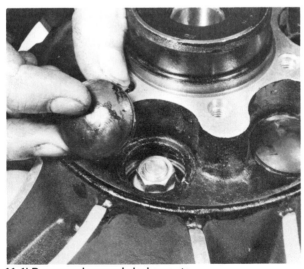

11.1l Remove plugs and slacken nuts ...

11.1m ... to facilitate removal of splined hub unit

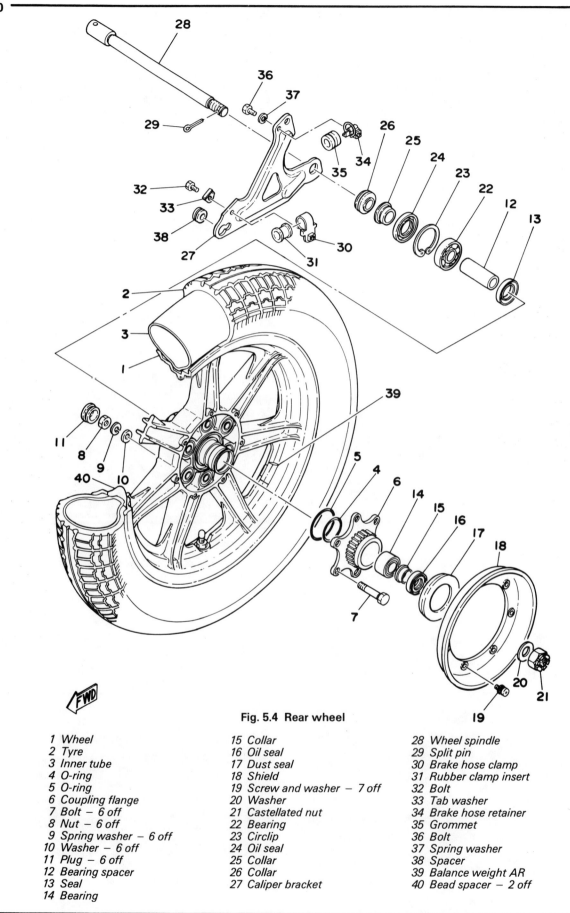

Fig. 5.4 Rear wheel

1 Wheel	15 Collar	28 Wheel spindle
2 Tyre	16 Oil seal	29 Split pin
3 Inner tube	17 Dust seal	30 Brake hose clamp
4 O-ring	18 Shield	31 Rubber clamp insert
5 O-ring	19 Screw and washer – 7 off	32 Bolt
6 Coupling flange	20 Washer	33 Tab washer
7 Bolt – 6 off	21 Castellated nut	34 Brake hose retainer
8 Nut – 6 off	22 Bearing	35 Grommet
9 Spring washer – 6 off	23 Circlip	36 Bolt
10 Washer – 6 off	24 Oil seal	37 Spring washer
11 Plug – 6 off	25 Collar	38 Spacer
12 Bearing spacer	26 Collar	39 Balance weight AR
13 Seal	27 Caliper bracket	40 Bead spacer – 2 off
14 Bearing		

12 Rear disc brake: examination, pad inspection and overhaul

1   The disc and caliper assembly fitted to the rear of the machine are almost identical in design to the units fitted to the front. The procedure for inspection and repair is therefore similar.

2   The caliper may be detached complete with the mounting bracket after removal of the rear wheel and the bracket pivot nut. For normal purposes the caliper may be detached from the support bracket in a manner similar to that of the front caliper.

13 Rear brake master cylinder: removal, examination and renovation

1   The rear brake master cylinder is mounted inboard of the frame right-hand triangulation, and is so placed that the fluid level can be seen readily without the need to remove the side cover. The master cylinder is operated by a foot pedal via an adjustable push rod connected to the pedal shaft by a clevis pin and a split pin.

2   Drain the master cylinder and reservoir, using a similar technique to that described for the front brake master cylinder. The master cylinder reservoir is fitted with a triangular cap, secured by three screws.

3   Disconnect the hydraulic hose at the master cylinder by removing the banjo bolt. Take care not to drop any residual fluid on the paintwork. The master cylinder is retained on the frame lug by two bolts. After removal of the bolt, the cylinder unit may be lifted upwards so that the operating push rod leaves the cylinder. The master cylinder can now be lifted away from the machine.

4   Examination and dismantling of the rear brake master cylinder may be made by referring to the directions in Section 5 of this Chapter. Additionally, the reservoir should be flushed out with clean fluid before refitting.

5   After reassembly and replacement of the rear brake master cylinder components which may be made by reversing the dismantling procedure – bleed the rear brake system of air by referring to Section 8 of this Chapter.

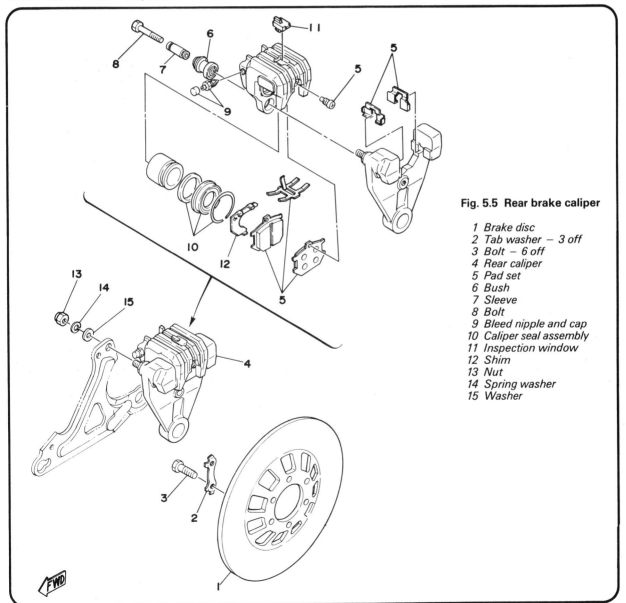

Fig. 5.5 Rear brake caliper

1 Brake disc
2 Tab washer – 3 off
3 Bolt – 6 off
4 Rear caliper
5 Pad set
6 Bush
7 Sleeve
8 Bolt
9 Bleed nipple and cap
10 Caliper seal assembly
11 Inspection window
12 Shim
13 Nut
14 Spring washer
15 Washer

12.1 Inspection window facilitates check of pad condition

12.2 Caliper is retained to bracket by bolt (arrowed)

13.1a Rear brake master cylinder fluid reservoir

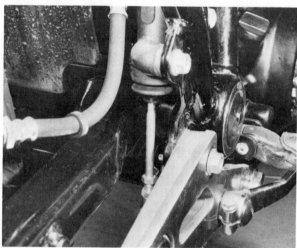

13.1b Cylinder is connected to brake pedal by pushrod

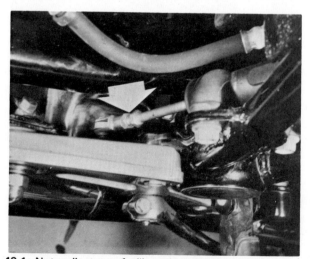

13.1c Note adjustment facility at bottom of pushrod (arrowed)

14 Rear brake pedal height: adjustment

1   The pivot shaft upon which the rear brake pedal is mounted is splined to allow adjustment of the pedal height to suit individual requirements.

2   To adjust the height, loosen and remove the pinch bolt which passes into the rear of the pedal boss. Draw the pedal off the splines and refit it at the required angle. Ideally the pedal should be fitted, so that it is positioned just below the rider's right foot, when the rider is seated normally. In this way the foot does not have to be lifted before the brake can be applied.

3   The upper limit of travel of the brake pedal may be adjusted by means of the bolt and locknut fitted to the pedal pivot mounting bracket. Care should be exercised when lowering the pedal by this method as movement imparted to the master cylinder piston may actuate the brake to a small degree. Free play between the brake push rod and master cylinder should be adjusted to 13 − 15 mm (0.51 − 0.59 in) using the pushrod thread and locknut. Adjustment of the pedal may necessitate readjustment of the rear stop lamp switch.

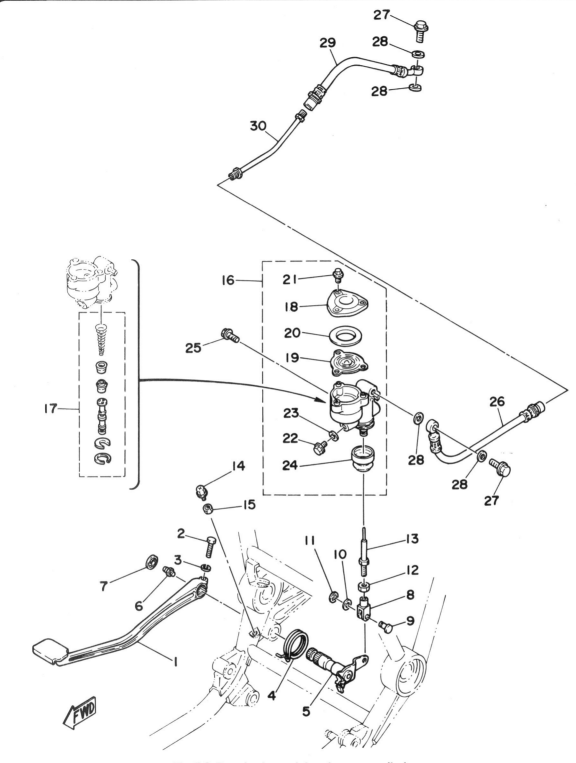

Fig. 5.6 Rear brake pedal and master cylinder

1 Brake pedal
2 Bolt
3 Spring washer
4 Spring
5 Brake pedal shaft
6 Grease nipple
7 Rubber cover
8 Link
9 Clevis pin
10 Washer

11 Circlip
12 Nut
13 Brake rod
14 Screw
15 Adjusting nut
16 Master cylinder assembly
17 Piston and cup set
18 Reservoir cap
19 Diaphragm
20 Packing

21 Bolt – 3 off
22 Bolt
23 Sealing washer
24 Boot
25 Bolt – 2 off
26 Brake hose
27 Banjo union bolt – 2 off
28 Washer – 4 off
29 Brake hose
30 Brake pipe

14.3 Stop bolt allows brake pedal height to be modified

Fig. 5.7 Method of measuring rear brake pedal height and free play

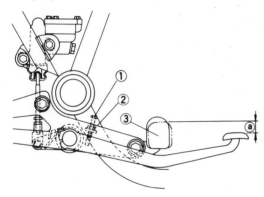

Brake pedal height

a 17 – 23 mm   2 Locknut
(0.67 – 0.91 in)   3 Footrest
1 Adjusting bolt

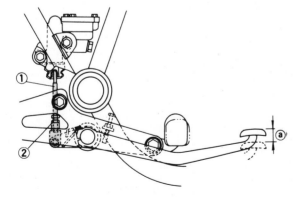

Brake pedal free play

a 13 – 15 mm   1 Push rod
(0.51 – 0.59 in)   2 Locknut

15 Tubed tyres: removal and replacement — E, F and G(UK) models

1   At some time or other the need will arise to remove and replace the tyres, either as the result of a puncture or because a renewal is required to offset wear. To the inexperienced, tyre changing represents a formidable task yet if a few simple rules are observed and the technique learned, the whole operation is surprisingly simple.

2   To remove the tyre from the wheel, first detach the wheel from the machine by following the procedure in Chapter 4, Section 2.1-3 for the front wheel and Section 9.3-4 for the rear wheel. Deflate the tyre by removing the valve insert and when it is fully deflated, push the bead of the tyre away from the wheel rim on both sides so that the bead enters the centre well of the rim. Remove the locking cap and push the tyre valve into the tyre itself.

3   Insert a tyre lever close to the valve and lever the edge of the tyre over the outside of the wheel rim. Very little force should be necessary; if resistance is encountered it is probably due to the fact that they tyre beads have not entered the well of the wheel rim all the way round the tyre.

4   Once the tyre has been edged over the wheel rim, it is easy to work around the wheel rim so that the tyre is completely free on one side. At this stage, the inner tube can be removed.

5   Working from the other side of the wheel ease the other edge of the tyre over the outside of the wheel rim furthest away. Continue to work around the rim until the tyre is free from the rim.

6   If a puncture has necessitated the removal of the tyre, reinflate the inner tube and immerse it in a bowl of water to trace the source of the leak. Mark its position and deflate the tube. Dry the tube and clean the area around the puncture with a petrol-soaked rag. When the surface has dried, apply rubber solution and allow this to dry before removing the backing from the patch and applying the patch to the surface.

7   It is best to use a patch of the self-vulcanising type, which will form a permanent repair. Note that it may be necessary to remove a protective covering from the top surface of the patch, after it has sealed in position. Inner tubes made from synthetic rubber may require a special type of patch and adhesive, if a satisfactory bond is to be achieved.

8   Before replacing the tyre, check the inside to make sure the agent that caused the puncture is not trapped. Check also the outside of the tyre, particularly the tread area, to make sure nothing is trapped that may cause a further puncture.

9   If the inner tube has been patched on a number of past occasions, or if there is a tear or large hole, it is preferable to discard it and fit a new one. Sudden deflation may cause an accident, particularly if it occurs with the rear wheel.

10   To replace the tyre, inflate the inner tube sufficiently for it to assume a circular shape but only just. Then push it into the tyre so that it is enclosed completely. Lay the tyre on the wheel at an angle and insert the valve through the rim tape and the hole in the wheel rim. Attach the locking cap on the first few threads, sufficient to hold the valve captive in its correct location.

11   Starting at the point furthest from the valve, push the tyre bead over the edge of the wheel rim until it is located in the central well. Continue to work around the tyre in this fashion until the whole of one side of the tyre is on the rim. It may be necessary to use a tyre lever during the final stages.

12   Make sure there is no pull on the tyre valve and again commencing with the area furthest from the valve, ease the other bead of the tyre over the edge of the rim. Finish with the area close to the valve, pushing the valve up into the tyre until the locking cap touches the rim. This will ensure the

inner tube is not trapped when the last section of the bead is edged over the rim with a tyre lever.

13   Check that the inner tube is not trapped at any point. Reinflate the inner tube, and check that the tyre is seating correctly around the wheel rim. There should be a thin rib moulded around the wall of the tyre on both sides, which should be equidistant from the wheel rim at all points. If the tyre is unevenly located on the rim, try bouncing the wheel when the tyre is at the recommended pressure. It is probable that one of the beads has not pulled clear of the centre well.

14   Always run the tyres at the recommended pressures and never under or over-inflate. The correct pressures for solo use are given in the Specifications Section of this Chapter.

15   Tyre replacement is aided by dusting the side walls, particularly in the vicinity of the beads, with a liberal coating of french chalk. Washing-up liquid can also be used to good effect.

16   Never replace the inner tube and tyre without the rim tape in position. If this precaution is overlooked there is good chance of the ends of the spoke nipples chafing the inner tube and causing a crop of punctures.

17   Never fit a tyre that has a damaged tread or side walls. Apart from the legal aspects, there is a very great risk of blow-out, which can have serious consequences on any two-wheeled vehicle.

18   Tyre valves rarely give trouble, but it is always advisable to check whether the valve itself is leaking before removing the tyre. Do not forget to fit the dust cap, which forms an effective second seal.

16   Valve cores and caps: tubed tyres

1   Valve cores seldom give trouble, but do not last indefinitely. Dirt under the seating will cause a puzzling 'slow-puncture'. Check that they are not leaking by applying spittle to the end of the valve and watching for air bubbles.

2   A valve cap is a safety device, and should always be fitted. Apart from keeping dirt out of the valve, it provides a second seal in case of valve failure, and may prevent an accident resulting from sudden deflation.

17   Tubeless tyres: removal and replacement – SF, G(US) and SG models

1   It is strongly recommended that should a repair to a tubeless tyre be necessary, the wheel is removed from the machine and taken to a tyre fitting specialist who is willing to do the job or taken to an official Yamaha dealer. This is because the force required to break the seal between the wheel rim and tyre bead is considerable and considered to be beyond the capabilities of an individual working with normal tyre removing tools. Any abortive attempt to break the rim to bead seal may also cause damage to the wheel rim, resulting in an expensive wheel replacement. If, however, a suitable bead releasing tool is available, and experience has already been gained in its use, tyre removal and refitting can be accomplished as follows.

2   To remove the tyre from either wheel, first detach the wheel from the machine by following the procedure in this Chapter, Sections 2 or 9 depending on whether the front or the rear wheel is involved. Deflate the tyre by removing the valve insert and when it is fully deflated, push the bead of the tyre away from the wheel rim on both sides so that the bead enters the centre well of the rim. As noted, this operation will almost certainly require the use of a bead releasing tool.

3   Insert a tyre lever close to the valve and lever the edge of the tyre over the outside of the wheel rim. Very little force should be necessary; if resistance is encountered it is probably due to the fact that the tyre beads have not entered the well of the wheel rim all the way round the tyre. Should the initial problem persist, lubrication of the tyre bead and the inside edge and lip of the rim will facilitate removal. Use a recommended lubricant, a dilute solution of washing-up liquid or french chalk. Lubrication is usually recommended as an aid to tyre fitting but its use is equally desirable during removal. The risk of lever damage to wheel rims can be minimised by the use of proprietary plastic rim protectors placed over the rim flange at the point where the tyre levers are inserted. Suitable rim protectors may be fabricated very easily from short lengths (4 – 6 inches) of thick-walled nylon petrol pipe which have been split down one side using a sharp knife. The use of rim protectors should be adopted whenever levers are used and, therefore, when the risk of damage is likely.

4   Once the tyre has been edged over the wheel rim. It is easy to work around the wheel rim so that the tyre is completely free on one side.

5   Working from the other side of the wheel, ease the other edge of the tyre over the outside of the wheel rim which is furthest away. Continue to work around the rim until the tyre is freed completely from the rim.

6   Refer to the following Section for details relating to puncture repair and the renewal of tyres. See also the remarks relating to the tyre valves in Section 19.

7   Refitting of the tyre is virtually a reversal of the removal procedure. If the tyre has a balance mark (usually a spot of coloured paint), as on the tyres fitted as original equipment, this must be positioned alongside the valve. Similarly, any arrow indicating direction of rotation must face the right way.

8   Starting at the point furthest from the valve, push the tyre bead over the edge of the wheel rim until it is located in the central well. Continue to work around the tyre in this fashion until the whole of one side of the tyre is on the rim. It may be necessary to use a tyre lever during the final stages. Here again, the use of a lubricant will aid fitting. It is recommended strongly that when refitting the tyre only a recommended lubricant is used because such lubricants also have sealing properties. Do not be over generous in the application of lubricant or tyre creep may occur.

9   Fitting the upper bead is similar to fitting the lower bead. Start by pushing the bead over the rim and into the well at a point diametrically opposite the tyre valve. Continue working round the tyre, each side of the starting point, ensuring that the bead opposite the working area is always in the well. Apply lubricant as necessary. Avoid using tyre levers unless absolutely essential, to help reduce damage to the soft wheel rim. The use of the levers should be required only when the final portion of bead is to be pushed over the rim.

10   Lubricate the tyre beads again prior to inflating the tyre, and check that the wheel rim is evenly positioned in relation to the tyre beads. Inflation of the tyre may well prove impossible without the use of a high pressure air hose. The tyre will retain air completely only when the beads are firmly against the rim edges at all points and it may be found when using a foot pump that air escapes at the same rate as it is pumped in. This problem may also be encountered when using an air hose, on new tyres which have been compressed in storage and by virtue of their profile hold the beads away from the rim edges. To overcome this difficulty, a tourniquet may be placed around the circumference of the tyre over the central area of the tread. The compression of the tread in this area will cause the beads to be pushed outwards in the desired direction. The type of tourniquet most widely used consists of a length of hose closed at both ends with a suitable clasp fitted to enable both ends to be connected. An ordinary tyre valve is fitted at one end of the tube so that after the hose has been secured around the tyre it may be inflated, giving a constricting effect. Another possible method of seating beads to obtain initial inflation is to press the tyre into the angle between a wall and the floor. With the airline attached to the valve additional pressure is then applied to

the tyre by the hand and shin, as shown in the accompanying illustration. The application of pressure at four points around the tyre's circumference whilst simultaneously applying the airhose will often effect an initial seal between the tyre beads and wheel rim, thus allowing inflation to occur.

11   Having successfully accomplished inflation, increase the pressure to 40 psi and check that the tyre is evenly disposed on the wheel rim. This may be judged by checking that the thin positioning line found on each tyre wall is equidistant from the rim around the total circumference of the tyre. If this is not the case, deflate the tyre, apply additional lubrication and reinflate. Minor adjustments to the tyre position may be made by bouncing the wheel on the ground.

12   Always run the tyre at the recommended pressures and never under- or over-inflate. The correct pressures for solo use are given in the Specification Section of this Chapter. If a pillion passenger is carried, increase the rear tyre pressure only as recommended.

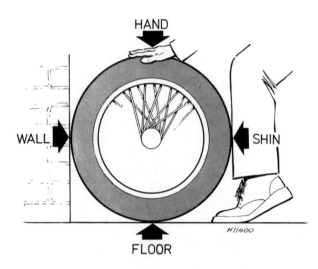

Fig. 5.8 Method of tubeless tyre inflation

---

18   Puncture repair and tyre renewal – tubeless tyres

1   The primary advantage of the tubeless tyre is its ability to accept penetration by sharp objects such as nails etc without loss of air. Even if loss of air is experienced, because there is no inner tube to rupture, in normal conditions a sudden blow-out is avoided.

2   If a puncture of the tyre occurs, the tyre should be removed for inspection for damage before any attempt is made at remedial action. The temporary repair of a punctured tyre by inserting a plug from the outside should not be attempted. Although this type of temporary repair is used widely on cars, the manufacturers strongly recommend that no such repair is carried out on a motorcycle tyre. Not only does the tyre have a thinner carcass, which does not give sufficient support to the plug, but the consequences of a sudden deflation are often sufficiently serious that the risk of such an occurrence should be avoided at all costs.

3   The tyre should be inspected both inside and out for damage to the carcass. Unfortunately the inner lining of the tyre – which takes the place of the inner tube – may easily obscure any damage and some experience is required in making a correct assessment of the tyre condition.

4   There are two main types of tyre repair which are considered safe for adoption in repairing tubeless motor-cycle tyres. The first type of repair consists of inserting a mushroom-headed plug into the hole from the **inside** of the

tyre. The hole is prepared for insertion of the plug by reaming and the application of an adhesive. The second repair is carried out by buffing the inner lining in the damaged area and applying a cold or vulcanised patch. Because both inspection and repair, if they are to be carried out safely, require experience in this type of work, it is recommended that the tyre be placed in the hands of a repairer with the necessary skills, rather than repaired in the home workshop.

5   In the event of an emergency, the only recommended 'get-you-home' repair is to fit a standard inner tube of the correct size. If this course of action is adopted, care should be taken to ensure that the cause of the puncture has been removed before the inner tube is fitted.

6   In the event of the unavailability of tubeless tyres, ordinary tubed tyres may be fitted to these wheel rims. Use tyres of an equivalent type and grade to ensure their suitability. It is recommended that the advice of the tyre manufacturer or a reputable supplier is sought to ensure that a compatible replacement tyre is fitted. **Never** fit a tubeless tyre to a tube-tyre rim.

---

19   Tyre valves: description and renewal – tubeless tyres

1   It will be appreciated from the preceding Sections that the adoption of tubeless tyres has made it necessary to modify the valve arrangement, as there is no longer an inner tube which can carry the valve core. The problem has been overcome by fitting a separate tyre valve which passes through a close-fitting hole in the rim, and which is secured by a nut and locknut. The valve is fitted from the rim well, and it follows that the valve can be removed and replaced only when the tyre has been removed from the rim. Leakage of air from around the valve body is likely to occur only if the sealing seat fails or if the nut and locknut become loose.

2   The valve core is of the same type as that used with tubed tyres, and screws into the valve body. The core can be removed with a small slotted tool which is normally incorporated in plunger type pressure gauges. Some valve dust caps incorporate a projection for removing valve cores. Although tubeless tyre valves seldom give trouble, it is possible for a leak to develop if a small particle of grit lodges on the sealing face. Occasionally, an elusive slow puncture can be traced to a leaking valve core, and this should be checked before a genuine puncture is suspected.

3   The valve dust caps are a significant part of the tyre valve assembly. Not only do they prevent the ingress of road dirt into the valve, but also act as a secondary seal which will reduce the risk of sudden deflation if a valve core should fail.

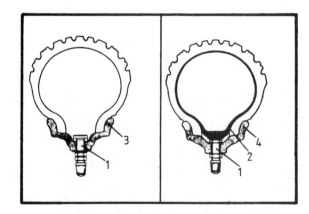

Fig. 5.9 Tubeless and tubed type tyre profile

1 Tyre valve   *3 Wheel (tubeless type tyre)*
2 Inner tube   *4 Wheel (tubed type tyre)*

Tyre removal: Deflate tyre and insert lever in close proximity to tyre valve

Use two levers to work bead over tyre rim

When first bead is clear, remove tyre as shown

Tyre fitting: Replace first bead over rim noting arrow indicating correct direction of rotation

Start second bead under the rim opposite the valve

Work bead under rim towards and each side of valve using lever if necessary

Use lever in final section

Air hose may be required for initial tyre inflation

20 Wheel balancing

1   The front wheel should be statically balanced, complete with tyre. An out of balance wheel can produce dangerous wobbling at high speed.

2   Some tyres have a balance mark on the sidewall. This must be positioned adjacent to the valve. Even so, the wheel still requires balancing.

3   With the front wheel clear of the ground, spin the wheel several times. Each time, it will probably come to rest in the same position. Balance weights should be attached diametrically opposite the heavy spot, until the wheel will not come to rest in any set position, when spun.

4   Machines fitted with cast aluminium wheels require special balancing weights which are designed to clip onto the centre rim flange, much in the way that weights are affixed to car wheels. When fitting these weights, take care not to affix any weight nearer than 40 mm (1.54 in) to the radial centre line of any spoke. Refer to the accompanying diagram.

5   It is possible to have a wheel dynamically balanced at some dealers. This requires its removal.

6   Although the rear wheel is more tolerant to out-of-balance forces than is the front wheel, ideally this too should be balanced if a new tyre is fitted. Because of the drag of the final drive components the wheel must be removed from the machine and placed on a suitable free-running spindle before balancing takes place. Balancing can then be carried out as for the front wheel.

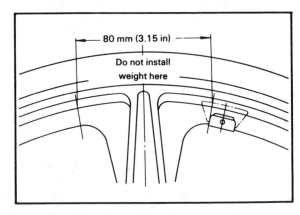

Fig. 5.10 Correct fitting of balance weight

21 Fault diagnosis: wheels, brakes and tyres

Symptom	Cause	Remedy
Handlebars oscillate at low speed	Buckle or flat in wheel rim, most probably front wheel	Check rim for damage by spinning wheel. Renew wheel if not true.
	Tyre pressure incorrect	Check, and if necessary adjust.
	Tyre not straight on rim	Check tyre fitting. If necessary, deflate tyre and reposition.
	Worn wheel or steering head bearings	Check and renew or adjust.
Machine tends to weave	Tyre pressure incorrect	Check, and if necessary adjust. If sudden, check for puncture.
	Suspension worn or damaged	Check action of front forks and rear suspension units. Check swinging arm for wear.
Machine lacks power and accelerates poorly	Front or rear brake binding	Hot disc or caliper indicates binding. Overhaul caliper and master cylinder, fit new pads if required, check disc for scoring or warpage.
Brakes grab or judder when applied gently	Pads badly worn or scored. Wrong type of pad fitted	Renew pads and check disc and caliper.
	Warped disc	Renew.
Break squeal	Glazed pads. Pads worn to backing metal	Sand pad surface to remove glaze then use brake gently for about 100 miles to permit bedding in. If worn to backing check that disc is not damaged and renew as necessary.
	Caliper and pads polluted with brake dust or foreign matter	Dismantle and clean. Overhaul caliper where necessary.
Excessive front brake lever travel or brake pedal travel	Air in system	Find cause of air's presence. If due to leak, rectify, then bleed brake.
	Very badly worn pads	Renew, and overhaul system where required.
	Badly polluted caliper	Dismantle and clean.
Front brake lever/brake pedal feels springy	Air in system	See above.
	Pads glazed	See above.
	Caliper jamming	Dismantle and overhaul.

Chapter 6 Electrical system

Contents

Specifications

Battery

Make	GS
Type	GM18Z-3A
Voltage	12 volts
Capacity	20 ah
Earth (ground)	Negative (−)

Alternator

Make	Hitachi
Type:	
SF model	LD104-04
All others	LD102-04
Output	14v 20A @ 5000 rpm
Field coil resistance	3.5 Ohms ± 10% @ 20°C (68°F)
Stator coil resistance	0.4 Ohms ± 10% @ 20°C (68°F)

Starter motor

Make	Mitsuba
Type	SM-224F
Armature coil resistance	0.007 Ohms @ 20°C (68°F)
Field coil resistance	0.01 Ohms @ 20°C (68°F)
Brush length	12.5 mm (0.492 in)
Wear limit	5.5 mm (0.22 in)
Brush spring pressure	620 ± 60 g (21.87 ± 2.12 oz)
Commutator undercut	0.5 mm (0.02 in)

Regulator/rectifier

Make	Matsushita
Type:	
SF and SG models	RD1143 or SH233
All others	RD1143
Voltage	14.5 ± 0.3 volts
Maximum amperage	4A

Starter relay

Make	Hitachi
Type:	A104-70
Cut-in voltage	6.5 volts
Resistance	3.5 Ohms @ 20°C (68°F)

Bulbs

	UK models	US models
Headlamp:		
E model	60/55W, quartz	65/50W
All others	60/55W, quartz	60/55W, quartz
Parking lamp	4W	–
Tail/stop lamp	5/21W × 2	8/27W × 2
Turn indicator:		
Front	21W × 2	27W × 2 (SF/SG 27/8W × 2)
Rear	21W × 2	27W × 2
Speedometer lamp	3.4W × 2	3.4W × 2
Tachometer lamp	3.4W × 2	3.4W × 2
Neutral indicator	3.4W	3.4W
Oil pressure warning	3.4W	3.4W (SF, combined with headlamp failure warning)
Headlamp failure warning	–	3.4W (except SF)
High beam warning	3.4W	3.4W
Indicator warning	3.4W × 2	3.4W × 2
Fuel level warning	–	3.4W (SF and SG only)
License plate	–	3.8W × 2 (SG only)

1 General description

The Yamaha XS1100 models feature an unusually sophisticated electrical system, sporting a number of components and circuits rarely found on motorcycles. The heart of the system is the three-phase alternator mounted on the right-hand end of the crankshaft. The rectified and regulated output feeds the 12 volt 20 Ah battery and powers the electrical system. The alternator is of the electro-magnetic type in which the rotor poles are energised by internal windings, which draw power via brushes mounted on the alternator cover. This arrangement allows a high output to be obtained from a relatively small alternator.

2 Electrical system testing: general information

1   As already mentioned, the Yamaha XS1100 models feature an unusually sophisticated electrical system incorporating a number of electronic sub-assemblies. These two factors make any testing a rather exacting process which will invariably require the use of some form of test equipment. Simple continuity checks may be made using a dry battery and bulb arrangement, but for most of the tests in this Chapter a pocket multimeter can be considered essential. Many owners will already possess one of these devices, but if necessary they can be obtained from electrical specialists, mail order companies or can be purchased from a Yamaha Service Agent as a 'pocket tester', part number 90890-03104.
2   Care must be taken when performing any electrical test, because some of the electronic assemblies can be destroyed if they are connected incorrectly or inadvertently shorted to earth. Instructions regarding meter probe connections are given for each test, and these should be read carefully to preclude any accidental damage during the test. Note that separate amp, volt and ohm meters may be used in place of the multimeter if necessary, noting that the appropriate test ranges will be required.
3   Where test equipment is not available, or the owner feels unsure of the procedure described, it is recommended that professional assistance is sought. Do not forget that a simple error can destroy a component such as the regulator/rectifier, resulting in expensive replacements being necessary.

4   A certain amount of preliminary dismantling will be necessary to gain access to the components to be tested. Normally, removal of the seat and side panels will be required, with the possible addition of the fuel tank and headlamp unit to expose the remaining components.

3 Charging system: output check

1   Set the multimeter to the 0 – 20 volts dc scale and connect the red positive (+) probe to the positive battery terminal and the black negative (−) probe to the negative battery terminal.
2   Start the engine, and raise the engine speed to about 2000 rpm or slightly more, noting the meter reading. The nominal charging voltage is 14.5 ± 0.3 volts, so a reading of 14.2 – 14.8 volts will indicate that the system is functioning correctly. If the voltage reading is significantly lower than that shown above, carry out the alternator resistance tests described in Section 4 of this Chapter. Important note: on no account should the engine be run when the battery leads are disconnected, because the resultant open voltage can destroy the rectifier diodes.

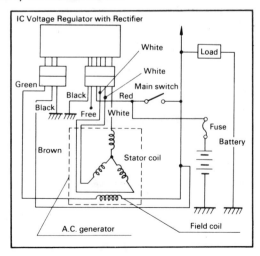

Fig. 6.1 Charging system circuit

4 Alternator: rotor and stator resistance tests

1   If the charging system output has been found to be inadequate (see Section 3) it will be necessary to make a resistance check on the alternator rotor and stator windings. Trace the alternator leads back to the two-pin and four-pin connectors, noting that the two-pin connector serves the field coil windings inside the rotor, whilst the four-pin connector controls the stator connections. The test can be made with the alternator cover in position.

2   Set the multimeter to the ohms × 1 scale. Separate the two connectors and measure the resistance between the green and brown field coil leads at the two-pin connector. A reading of 3.5 ohms ± 10% at 68°F (20°C) should be obtained (3.15 – 3.85 ohms). Note that for the purpose of resistance checks, the polarity of the probe connections can be ignored.

3   Measure the resistance between the three white wires at the four-pin connector, a total of three tests. In each case, a reading of 0.4 ohms ± 10% at 68°F (20°C) should be shown (0.36 – 0.44 ohms). If any of the windings have failed, it will normally show up as a short circuit (zero resistance) or an open circuit (infinite resistance). In either case, the rotor or stator must be renewed unless the fault is caused by broken wiring connections. If the alternator appears to be functioning normally, attention can be turned to the regulator/rectifier unit as described in Section 5.

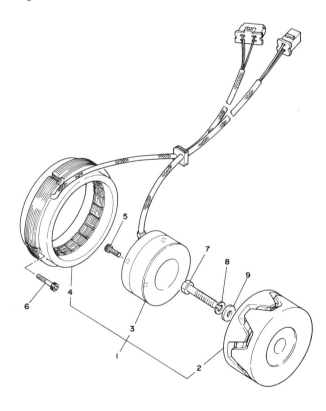

Fig. 6.2 Alternator

1 Alternator assembly
2 Rotor
3 Field coil
4 Stator
5 Allen screw – 3 off
6 Allen screw – 4 off
7 Bolt
8 Spring washer
9 Washer

5 Voltage regulator/rectifier unit: testing

1   The voltage regulator/rectifier unit is a small integrated circuit (IC) housed in a finned alloy casing mounted beneath the frame top tubes. Its function is to convert the alternator output to direct current (dc) from alternating current (ac), this part of the function being executed by the rectifier stage. The regulator stage monitors the drain on the electrical system and controls the alternator voltage output to suit by adjusting the effective power of the electromagnetic rotor. The unit is normally very reliable, there being no possibility of mechanical failure, but it can become damaged in the event of a short circuit in the electrical system or by poor or intermittent battery or earth connections.

5.1 Rectifier/Regulator unit is mounted between frame tubes

Voltage regulator test

2   With the seat and fuel tank removed, trace back along the two sets of leads to the tree-pin (regulator) and six-pin (rectifier) connectors. Note that the test is made with the connectors assembled and the electrical system intact. It is essential that the battery is fully charged during the tests because it will otherwise affect the results obtained. To this end, check that the specific gravity is at 1.260 or more, and if necessary remove the battery for recharging. For full details on the above, refer to Sections 6 and 7. Note that two multimeters are required for the regulator test, each set on the 0 – 20 volts dc scale.

3   Refer to Fig. 6.3 for details of the test connections. The wiring codes (G1, B2 etc) refer to the schematic diagram of the regulator/rectifier unit, Fig. 6.5. Connect the multimeter test probes by inserting them into the appropriate opening of the assembled connector, noting the polarity markings in the diagram. Be very careful not to allow the test probes to short to earth or against each other. In the case of US models fitted with a headlamp relay, remove the headlamp fuse to prevent the lighting circuit from coming on when the engine is started.

4   Switch on the ignition and note the reading on the V2 meter. This should be less than 1.8 volts. Start the engine and check that the V2 reading gradually increases to 9 – 11 volts as the engine speed rises. The V1 reading should rise to 14.2 – 14.8 volts when the engine is started and should stabilise at this level despite variations in engine speed. The accompanying graph shows the relationship of the two voltage readings at various engine speeds. If the readings obtained are significantly outside these limits, the regulator stage must be considered defective and the unit renewed There is no provision for adjustment or repair.

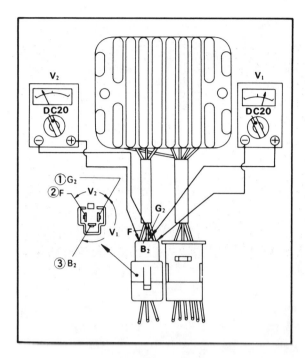

Fig. 6.3 Regulator testing

1 Black   3 Brown
2 Green

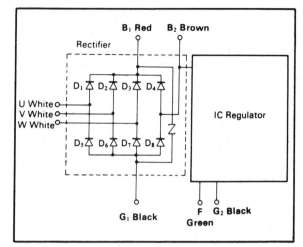

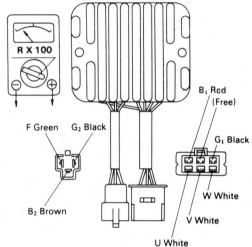

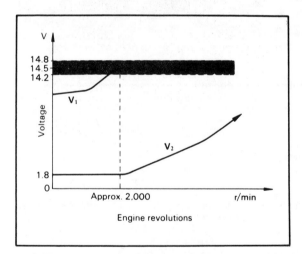

Fig. 6.4 Voltage output graph

Rectifier test

5   The rectifier stage consists of an arrangement of diodes whose function can be likened to that of a one way valve. The object of the test is to ensure that each diode will pass current in one direction only. Refer to Fig. 6.5 which shows a schematic view of the rectifier connections and coded wires which will correspond with those shown in the accompanying table. Work through the test connections shown in the table, noting that if any one diode has failed, the unit must be renewed. Again, no form of repair is possible.

Checking element	Pocket test connecting point		Good	Replace (element shorted)	Replace (element opened)
	(+) (red)	(−) (black)			
D_1	B_1	U	O	O	x
	U	B_1	x	O	x
D_2	B_1	V	O	O	x
	V	B_1	x	O	x
D_3	B_1	W	O	O	x
	W	B_1	x	O	x
D_4	B_1	B_2	O	O	x
	B_2	B_1	x	O	x
D_5	U	G_1	O	O	x
	G_1	U	x	O	x
D_6	V	G_1	O	O	x
	G_1	V	x	O	x
D_7	W	G_1	O	O	x
	G_1	W	x	O	x
D_8	B_2	G_1	O	O	x
	G_1	B_2	x	O	x

O No resistance (continuity)
X High resistance (non-continuity)

Fig. 6.5 Rectifier continuity test chart and meter connections

6 Battery: examination and maintenance

1 A G.S. GM18Z-3A battery is fitted as standard. This battery is a lead-acid type and has a capacity of 20 amp hours.

2 The translucent plastic case of the battery permits the upper and lower levels of the electrolyte to be observed when the battery is lifted from its housing below the dualseat. Maintenance is normally limited to keeping the electrolyte level between the prescribed upper and lower limits and by making sure the vent pipe is not blocked.

3 Unless acid is spilt, as may occur if the machine falls over, the electrolyte should always be topped up with distilled water, to restore the correct level. If acid is spilt on any of the machine, it should be neutralised with an alkali such as washing soda and washed away with plenty of water, otherwise serious corrosion will occur. Top up with sulphuric acid of the correct specific gravity (1.260 – 1.280) only when spillage has occurred. Check that the vent pipe is well clear of the frame tubes or any of the other cycle parts, for obvious reasons. Note the instructions on topping up which are fixed to the top of the battery.

4 If battery problems are experienced, the following checks will determine whether renewal is required. A battery can normally be expected to last for about 3 years, but this life can be shortened dramatically by neglect. In normal use, the capacity for storage will gradually diminish, and a point will be reached where the battery is adequate for all but the strenuous task of starting the engine. It follows that renewal will be necessary at this stage, particularly on late model machines with no emergency kickstart.

5 Remove the flat battery and examine the cell and plate condition near the bottom of the casing. This may prove rather difficult with the translucent-cased original battery. An accumulation of white sludge around the bottom of the cells indicates sulphation, a condition which indicates the imminent demise of the battery. Little can be done to reverse this process, but it may help to have the electrolyte drained, the battery flushed and then refilled with new electrolyte. Most electrical wholesalers have facilities for this work.

6 Warping of the plates or separators is also indicative of an expiring battery, and will often be evident in one or two of the cells. It can often be caused by old age, but a new battery which is overcharged will show the same failure. There is no cure for the problem and the need to avoid overcharging cannot be overstressed.

7 Try charging the suspect battery as described in Section 7. If the battery fails to accept a full charge, and in particular, if one or more cells show a low hydrometer reading, the battery is in need of renewal.

8 A hydrometer will be required to check the specific gravity of the electrolyte, and thus the state of charge. Any small hydrometer will do, but avoid the very large commercial types because there will be insufficient electrolyte to provide a reading. When fully charged, each cell should read 1.280, with little discrepancy between cells. Again, this last check is impractical with the original battery and its single filler hole.

7 Battery: charging procedure

1 A good, safe, charging rate for the 20 amp hour battery is about 1.5 amps over a period of 14 hours. In an emergency a charging rate of 2.0 – 2.5 amps is permissible, at reduced periods of 1 hour and 45 minutes respectively. As a general rule, go for the smallest charging rate available, because this is best for the battery. Avoid 'quick charge' services offered by garages. This will indeed charge the battery rapidly, but will also overheat it and may halve its life expectancy.

6.1 Battery can be removed after releasing strap on LH side

6.2 Battery has single large filler hole

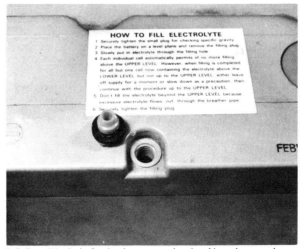

6.8 Small hole is for hydrometer checks. Note instruction label on battery top

2   Make sure that the battery charger connections are correct; red to positive and black to negative. It is preferable to remove the battery from the machine whilst it is being charged and to remove the filler and test plugs. When the battery is reconnected to the machine, the black lead must be connected to the negative terminal and the red lead to positive. This is most important, as the machine has a negative earth system. If the terminals are inadvertently reversed, the electrical system will be damaged permanently. The rectifier will be destroyed by a reversal of the current flow.

3   A word of caution concerning batteries. Sulphuric acid is extremely corrosive and must be handled with great respect. Do not forget that the outside of the battery is likely to retain traces of acid from previous spills, and the hands should always be washed promptly after checking the battery. Remember too that battery acid will quickly destroy clothing. In the author's experience, acid seems partial to nearly new jeans in particular, and experience has shown that it is best to keep well clear of batteries unless old clothing is being worn. Note the following rules concerning battery maintenance.

Do not allow smoking or naked flames near batteries.
Do avoid acid contact with skin, eyes and clothing.
Do keep battery electrolyte level maintained.
Do avoid over-high charge rates.
Do avoid leaving the battery discharged.
Do avoid freezing.
Do use only distilled or demineralised water for topping up.

8   Fuses: location, function and renewal

1   On all models a bank of four fuses is mounted in a plastic fuse box behind the right-hand side cover. The correct fuse ratings are inscribed behind the relevant fuse position and suitable replacements are provided in the box lid. On G(US) and SG models an additional fuse, together with a spare, is mounted in a holding block behind the left-hand side cover. On these machines this is the main fuse for the electrical system.

2   Fuses are fitted to protect the electrical system in the event of a short circuit or sudden surge; they are, in effect, an intentional 'weak link' which will blow, in preference to the circuit burning out.

3   Before replacing a fuse that has blown, check that no obvious short circuit has occurred, otherwise the replacement fuse will blow immediately it is inserted. It is always wise to check the electrical circuit thoroughly, to trace the fault and eliminate it.

4   When a fuse blows while the machine is running and no spare is available, a 'get you home' remedy is to remove the blown fuse and wrap it in silver paper before replacing it in the fuseholder. The silver paper will restore the electrical continuity by bridging the broken fuse wire. This expedient should **never** be used if there is evidence of a short circuit or other major electrical fault, otherwise more serious damage will be caused. Replace the 'doctored' fuse at the earliest possible opportunity, to restore full circuit protection. It follows that spare fuses that are used should be replaced as soon as possible to prevent the above situation from arising.

9   Starter motor: removal, examination and testing

1   The electric starter system forms the main starting system on the XS1100 range, the kickstart arrangement, where fitted, being no more than an emergency backup measure. It is of great importance that the system functions efficiently, because the load placed on the battery is at best, very high. When the starter switch is pressed, a heavy solenoid switch is brought into operation, switching the heavy current to the motor, cranking the engine via a primary shaft mounted roller clutch. As soon as the engine starts the clutch freewheels, disconnecting the starter drive. The clutch will rarely require any attention, a fortunate situation since a considerable amount of dismantling work would be required in the event of its failure. The starter clutch and drive are covered in Section 34 of Chapter 1.

2   In the event of partial or complete starter failure, check the condition of the battery, which should be fully charged, and ensure that the starter solenoid is working (See Section 10). Make sure that all switch and wiring connections are sound. If this fails to effect a cure, proceed as follows.

3   Remove the two bolts which pass through the left hand end of the starter motor cover, which is immediately behind the cylinder block. Remove the single bolt at the right-hand end. Lift away the cover to expose the motor, which can now be withdrawn by pulling it to the left and lifting clear of the casing recess. As the motor comes clear, release the heavy starter motor cable from its terminal.

4   With the motor removed and on the work bench, attention can be turned to those parts most likely to be in need of attention, namely the commutator and brushes. The end cover is retained by the two long screws which pass through the lugs cast on both end pieces. If the screws are withdrawn, the end cover can be lifted away and the brush gear exposed.

5   Lift up the spring clips which bear on the end of each brush and remove the brushes from their holders. Each brush should have a length of 12.5 mm (0.5 in). The minimum allowable brush length is 5.5 mm (0.22 in). If the brush is shorter it must be renewed.

6   Before the brushes are replaced, make sure that the commutator is clean. The commutator is the copper segments on which the brushes bear. Clean the commutator with a strip of glass paper. Never use emery cloth or 'wet-and-dry' as the small abrasive fragments may embed themselves in the soft copper of the commutator and cause excessive wear of the brushes. Finish off the commutator with metal polish to give a smooth surface and finally wipe the segments over with a methylated spirits soaked rag to ensure a grease free surface. Check that the mica insulators, which lie between the segments of the commutator, are undercut. The standard groove depth is 0.5 – 0.8 mm (0.02 – 0.03 in), but if the average groove depth is less than this the armature should be renewed or returned to a Yamaha dealer for re-cutting.

7   Replace the brushes in their holders and check that they slide quite freely. Make sure the brushes are replaced in their original positions because they will have worn to the profile of the commutator. Replace and tighten the end cover, then replace the starter motor and cable in the housing, tighten down and remake the electrical connection to the solenoid switch. Check that the starter motor functions correctly before replacing the compartment cover and sealing gasket.

8   If the motor has given indications of a more serious fault, the armature and field coil winding should be checked using a multimeter set on the resistance scale. To check the armature, set the meter on the ohms × 1 scale, and measure the resistance between each pair of commutator segments. The correct figure is 0.007 ohms at 68°F (20°C). In practice, the test will identify any dead segment. Check for armature insulation faults between each segment and the metal of the armature body. An insulation failure will require the renewal of the armature.

9   Check the field coil winding for resistance between the external terminal and the brush leads. A figure of 0.01 ohms at 68°F (20°C) is to be expected from sound windings. Check the insulation between the windings and the body of the motor.

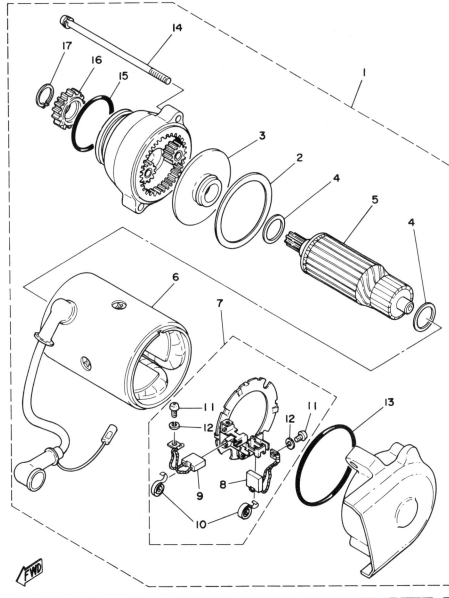

Fig. 6.6 Starter motor

1 Starter motor assembly
2 Gasket
3 End plate
4 Washer
5 Armature
6 Stator
7 Brush retainer assembly
8 Positive brush
9 Negative brush
10 Brush spring − 2 off
11 Screw − 2 off
12 Spring washer − 2 off
13 O-ring
14 Bolt − 2 off
15 O-ring
16 Drive pinion
17 Circlip

8.1 Fuse functions are marked. Spare fuses housed in lid

9.3a Starter motor and cover are retained by three bolts

9.3b Remove motor and disconnect cable

9.4a Remove two retaining screws to release end covers

9.4b Brush cover can be lifted clear

9.5a Brush gear is arranged as shown

9.5b Check brush length and renew if below limit

9.6 Check armature, especially commutator condition

9.7a Opposite end cover houses reduction gears

9.7b Check condition of gear teeth, then grease well

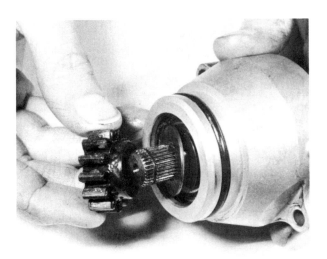

9.7c Drive gear is retained by circlip. Note shims

9.7d Idler gears and centre shaft are removed as shown

9.7e Bearing is retained by wire clip

10 Starter solenoid switch: function and location

1   The starter motor switch is designed to work on the electromagnetic principle. When the starter motor button is depressed, current from the battery passes through windings in the switch solenoid and generates an electromagnetic force which causes a set of contact points to close. Immediately the points close, the starter motor is energised and a very heavy current is drawn from the battery.

2   This arrangement is used for at least two reasons. Firstly, the starter motor current is drawn only when the button is depressed and is cut off again when pressure on the button is released. This ensures minimum drainage on the battery. Secondly, if the battery is in a low state of charge, there will not be sufficient current to cause the solenoid contacts to close. In consequence it is not possible to place an excessive drain on the battery which, in some circumstances, can cause the plates to overheat and shed their coatings. If the starter will not operate, first suspect a discharged battery. This can be checked by trying the horn or switching on the lights. If this check shows the battery to be in good shape, suspect the starter switch which should come into action with a pronounced click. It is located

behind the left-hand side panel and can be identified by the heavy duty starter cable connected to it. It is not possible to effect a satisfactory repair if the switch malfunctions; it must be renewed.

11 Headlamp: bulb renewal and alignment

1   All models except the XS1100 E(US) are fitted with a headlamp containing a removable quartz halogen bulb. The XS1100 E(US) model utilizes a sealed beam unit where the bulb filament is integral with and inseparable from the lens/reflector unit.

2   To gain access to the headlamp bulb or reflector unit it is necessary to release the lens/reflector assembly from the headlamp shell. In the case of E, F and G models, the rectangular unit is retained by two screws which pass up through the underside of the shell. On SF and SG models the two screws are located in the 4 o'clock and 8 o'clock positions, just to the rear of the headlamp rim. After removal of the screws lift the unit away from the shell and disconnect the three-pin connector from the rear of the reflector.

3   On those models fitted with a separate headlamp bulb, note the position of the rubber shroud, and then pull it off to reveal the bulb and retainer. Twist the retainer to free it, remove the spring and lift out the bulb by grasping the terminals or metal body. The bulb is of the quartz halogen type in which a quartz glass envelope is used to permit higher operating temperatures and, therefore, brighter light emission for a given wattage. **Never touch the glass envelope with the fingers,** because the oils and acids on the skin will contaminate the glass surface leading to the formation of hot-spots and a reduced bulb life. If contamination does occur de-natured alcohol should be used as a cleaning agent.

4   On XS1100 E(US) models a sealed beam unit is fitted and thus, if failure occurs, the complete assembly must be renewed. The reflector unit can be detached from the headlamp rim after releasing the pivot screw and adjuster screw.

5   UK models are fitted with a parking lamp. The bulb holder is a simple push fit in the rear of the reflector and the bulb is of the bayonet fitting type.

6   The XS1100 E, F and G models employ a three-way alignment adjustment system. At the rear of the headlamp shell a spring-loaded adjuster provides coarse vertical adjustment, whilst a small screw at the lower front edge of

the rim provides fine vertical adjustment. Horizontal adjustment is by means of a small screw on the top edge of the rim. On the round headlamp fitted to the SF and SG models, vertical adjustment is via an elongated slot in a bracket below the headlamp and is locked by a single screw. A screw in the front edge of the rim gives horizontal alignment.

7   In the UK, regulations stipulate that the headlamp must be arranged so that the light will not dazzle a person standing at a distance greater than 25 feet from the lamp, whose eye level is not less than 3 feet 6 inches above that plane. It is easy to approximate this setting by placing the machine 25 feet away from a wall, on a level road, and setting the dip beam height so that it is concentrated at the same height as the distance of the centre of the headlamp from the ground. The rider must be seated normally during this operation and also the pillion passenger, if one is carried regularly.

8   Most other areas have similar regulations controlling headlamp beam alignment, and these should be checked before any adjustment is made.

10.1 Starter solenoid is mounted behind RH side panel

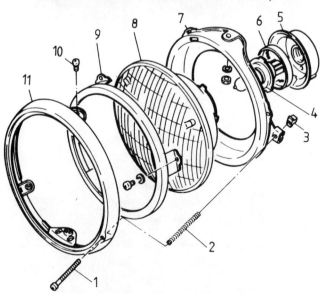

Fig. 6.8 Headlamp – SF and SG models

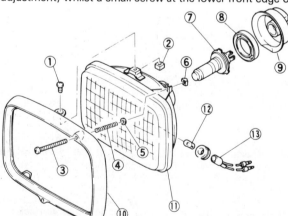

Fig. 6.7 Headlamp – quartz halogen type (sealed beam type is similar)

1 Screw	5 Washer	9 Dust cover
2 Nut	6 Nut	10 Rim
3 Adjusting screw	7 Bulb	11 Reflector unit
4 Spring	8 Bulb retainer	12 Pilot bulb
		13 Pilot bulb holder

1 Adjusting screw	5 Dust cover	9 Unit retaining
2 Spring	6 Bulb retainer	bracket
3 Nut	7 Mounting bracket	10 Screw
4 Bulb	8 Reflector unit	11 Rim

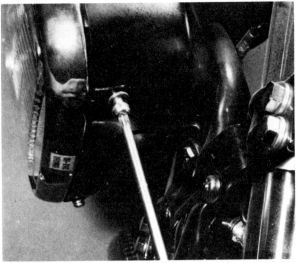

11.1 Headlamp lens/reflector unit is retained by two screws

11.2a Remove unit and unplug bulb connector

11.2b Remove rubber shroud, noting 'top' marking

11.2c Twist retaining ring and remove spring

11.3 Handle bulb as shown. **Never** touch bulb envelope

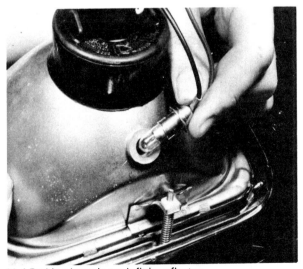

11.4 Parking lamp is push fit in reflector

11.5a Screw on underside (arrowed) provides coarse vertical adjustment

11.5b Fine vertical adjustment screw

11.5c Horizontal adjustment screw

12 Reserve lighting system and headlamp relay: US models only

1   The US models of the XS1100 are equipped with a relay which automatically switches the headlamp circuit on when the machine is started, irrespective of the position of the handlebar switch. In addition, the reserve lighting system is designed to sense a bulb filament failure, switching automatically to a sound bulb filament whilst illuminating the headlamp failure warning lamp on the instrument panel. In the event of failure, refer to the circuit diagram (Fig. 6.10a,b,c) and follow the following flow chart during the fault diagnosis procedure.

Headlight condition	Headlight failure indicator light	Reserve lighting function
Normal	Comes on (very dim)	—
High beam faulty	Comes on	Low beam comes on
Low beam faulty	Comes on	High beam comes on at low brilliance

Fig. 6.9 Reserve lighting system function

13 Stop and tail lamp: replacing bulbs

1   In the event of a bulb failure, renewal is a straightforward matter involving the removal of the plastic lens. Release the two retaining screws and lift the lens away. One or two bulbs are fitted depending on the model. The double filament bulbs fitted have a simple bayonet fitting with offset pins to ensure that they are fitted correctly. It is good practice to check that both the tail and brake filaments operate properly before setting off on a journey. This should be an habitual check made whilst the engine is warmed up, particularly on single bulb models.

2   If problems with constantly blowing bulbs are experienced it is often due to a poor earth or power connection to the filament concerned. Check that all connections are secure and clean. The bulb can also fail due to vibration, in which case there will be no blackening of the envelope as in the case of a blown bulb. Try to trace and eliminate the source of vibration to prevent further occurrences.

13.1 Rear lamp bulb is offset pin bayonet fitting

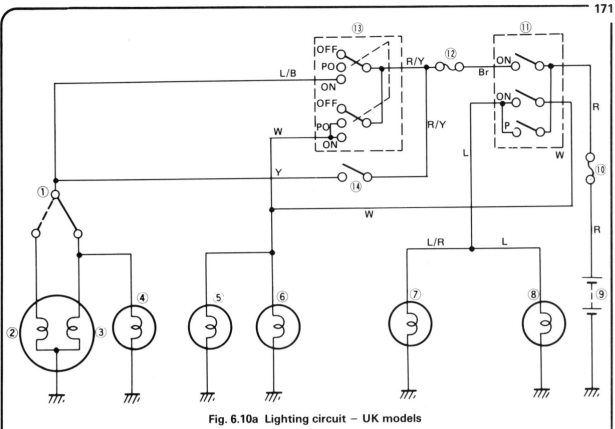

Fig. 6.10a Lighting circuit – UK models

1 Dip switch
2 Dip beam
3 High beam
4 High beam indicator
5 Meter lamp
6 Meter lamp
7 Parking lamp
8 Tail/stop lamp
9 Battery
10 Main fuse
11 Main switch
12 Headlamp fuse
13 Lighting switch
14 Passing switch

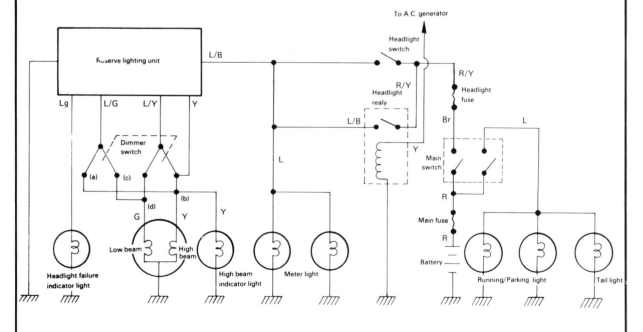

Fig. 6.10b Lighting circuit – E(US) model

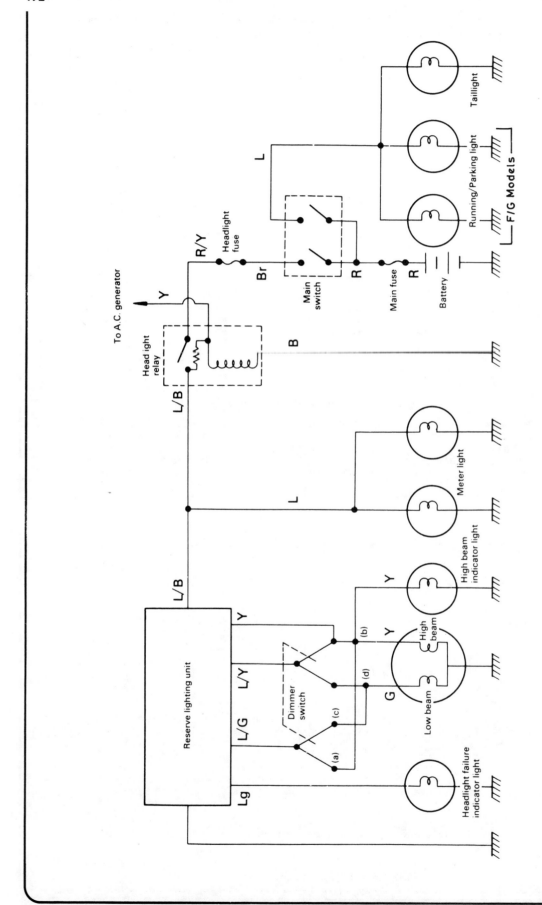

Fig. 6.10c Lighting circuit – F, SF, G and SG models (All US)

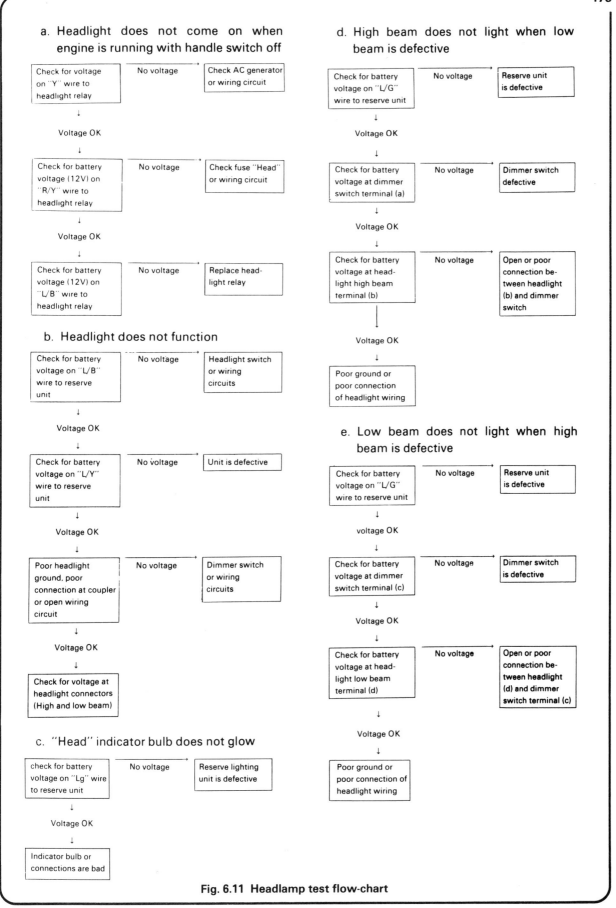

a. Headlight does not come on when engine is running with handle switch off

Check for voltage on "Y" wire to headlight relay → No voltage → Check AC generator or wiring circuit

↓ Voltage OK ↓

Check for battery voltage (12V) on "R/Y" wire to headlight relay → No voltage → Check fuse "Head" or wiring circuit

↓ Voltage OK ↓

Check for battery voltage (12V) on "L/B" wire to headlight relay → No voltage → Replace headlight relay

b. Headlight does not function

Check for battery voltage on "L/B" wire to reserve unit → No voltage → Headlight switch or wiring circuits

↓ Voltage OK ↓

Check for battery voltage on "L/Y" wire to reserve unit → No voltage → Unit is defective

↓ Voltage OK ↓

Poor headlight ground, poor connection at coupler or open wiring circuit → No voltage → Dimmer switch or wiring circuits

↓ Voltage OK ↓

Check for voltage at headlight connectors (High and low beam)

c. "Head" indicator bulb does not glow

check for battery voltage on "Lg" wire to reserve unit → No voltage → Reserve lighting unit is defective

↓ Voltage OK ↓

Indicator bulb or connections are bad

d. High beam does not light when low beam is defective

Check for battery voltage on "L/G" wire to reserve unit → No voltage → Reserve unit is defective

↓ Voltage OK ↓

Check for battery voltage at dimmer switch terminal (a) → No voltage → Dimmer switch defective

↓ Voltage OK ↓

Check for battery voltage at headlight high beam terminal (b) → No voltage → Open or poor connection between headlight (b) and dimmer switch

↓ Voltage OK ↓

Poor ground or poor connection of headlight wiring

e. Low beam does not light when high beam is defective

Check for battery voltage on "L/G" wire to reserve unit → No voltage → Reserve unit is defective

↓ voltage OK ↓

Check for battery voltage at dimmer switch terminal (c) → No voltage → Dimmer switch is defective

↓ Voltage OK ↓

Check for battery voltage at headlight low beam terminal (d) → No voltage → Open or poor connection between headlight (d) and dimmer switch terminal (c)

↓ Voltage OK ↓

Poor ground or poor connection of headlight wiring

Fig. 6.11 Headlamp test flow-chart

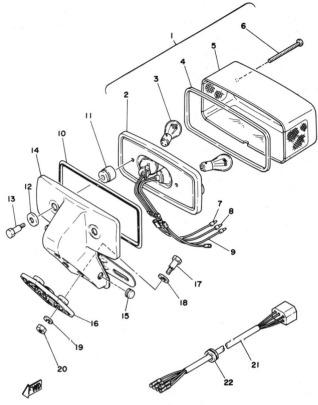

Fig. 6.12 Tail lamp

1 Tail lamp assembly
2 Bulb retaining plate
3 Bulb – 2 off
4 Rubber seal
5 Lens
6 Screw – 2 off
7 Blue lead
8 Yellow lead

9 Black earth lead
10 Seal
11 Grommet – 2 off
12 Washer – 2 off
13 Bolt – 2 off
14 Tail lamp and license plate bracket
15 Grommet – 2 off

16 Damping block
17 Bolt – 3 off
18 Washer – 3 off
19 Spring washer – 3 off
20 Nut – 3 off
21 Lead
22 Lead grommet

14 Flashing indicator lamps: bulb renewal

1 The flashing indicators, or turn signals, are mounted on stalks to the front and rear of the machine. In the case of the XS1100 E, F and G models, the front stalks are clamped to projections on the lower fork yoke, whilst on the SF and SG models, the front stalks double as the headlamp shell mountings. The rear units are attached to the frame to the rear of the dualseat on all models.

2 The lens is retained by two screws and should be removed to gain access to the bulb, should renewal be required. In the event of problems other than blown bulbs, check that the feed and earth connections are sound. Do not forget that problems may be traced to the flasher relay or to the self-cancelling circuit.

3 Note that F and G(US) models are equipped with twin filament bulbs in the front indicators to allow them to double as parking lights. This does not materially affect bulb renewal.

15 Flasher relay: location and renewal

1 The flasher relay unit is located behind the right-hand side cover and is supported on anti-vibration mountings made of rubber.

2 If the flasher unit is functioning correctly, a series of audible clicks will be heard when the indicator lamps are in action. If the unit malfunctions and all the bulbs are in working order, the usual symptom is one initial flash before the unit goes dead; it will be necessary to replace the unit complete if the fault cannot be attributed to any other cause.

14.2 Indicator bulbs are bayonet fitting

15.1 Indicator relay is mounted below fuse box

16 Hazard warning system: description and testing – G(US) and SG models

1   A hazard warning lamp switch is incorporated in the left-hand handlebar switch assembly. When the switch is operated all four indicator lamps flash simultaneously, controlled by a separate relay unit. The system will function whether the main switch is in the 'Off', 'On' or 'P' position.
2   Should the system become inoperative follow the check sequence given here. Place the main switch in the 'On' position and select the right-hand and then left-hand flashing indicators using the normal indicator control. If all is well, the bulbs and the wiring from the handlebar switch to the bulbs are in good condition. This leaves the switch and flasher relay and the wiring from the main fuse to the relay unit or switch as possible suspects.
3   To check the switch disconnect the 6-pin connector from the left-hand handlebar switch. Make a continuity test, using a multimeter or battery and bulb arrangement, across the dark brown, dark green, and brown/yellow wires. With the switch in the 'Off' position non-continuity (infinitely high resistance) should be found; with the switch in the 'On' position continuity (little or no resistance) should be found. If these test results are not met the switch and wiring should be checked carefully. If no fault is found it must be assumed that the hazard flasher relay unit has malfunctioned. The relay unit is located behind the left-hand side cover and is supported in a rubber mounting. In the event of failure no repair is possible; the unit must be renewed.

17 Self-cancelling circuit: description and testing

1   With the exception of machines sold in Germany all XS1100 models are equipped with an ingenious electro-mechanical system which will automatically cancel the flashing indicators after a predetermined distance and/or time has elapsed. In practice, the indicators should switch off after 10 seconds or after 150 metres (164 yards) have been covered. Both systems must switch off before the indicators stop, thus at low speeds the system is controlled by distance, whilst at high speeds, elapsed time is the controlling factor.
2   A speedometer sensor measures the distance covered from the moment that the switch is operated. After the

150 metres have been covered, this part of the system will reset to off. The flasher cancelling unit starts a ten second countdown from the moment that the switch is operated. As soon as both sides of the system are at the off position, the flashers are cancelled. If required, the system may be overridden manually by depressing the switch inwards.
3   In the event of malfunction, refer to Fig. 6.13a,b which shows the circuit diagram for the self-cancelling system. The self-cancelling unit is located beneath the dualseat, next to the air intake trunking. Trace the output leads to the 6-pin connector and disconnect it. If the ignition switch is now turned on and the indicators will operate normally, albeit with manual cancelling, the flasher relay, bulbs, wiring and switch can be considered sound.
4   To check the speedometer sensor, connect a multimeter to the white/green and the black leads of the wiring harness at the 6-pin connector. Set the meter to the ohms × 100 scale. Release the speedometer cable at the wheel end and use the projecting cable end to turn the speedometer. If all is well, the needle will alternate between zero resistance and infinite resistance. If not, the sender or the wiring connections will be at fault.
5   Connect the meter probes between the yellow/red lead and earth, again on the harness side of the 6-pin connector. Check the switch and associated wiring by turning the indicator switch on and off. In the off position, infinite resistance should be shown, with zero resistance in both on positions.
6   If the above tests reveal no obvious fault in the indicator circuits or the indicators will work only as a manually operated arrangement, the self cancelling system is inoperative and the unit will require renewal.

18 Speedometer and tachometer heads: replacement of bulbs

1   Bulbs fitted to each instrument illuminate the dials during the hours of darkness when the headlamp is switched on. All bulbs fitted to either instrument head have the same type of bulb holder which is a push fit in the instrument base.
2   Access to the bulbs and holders is gained by removing the nuts and washers which secure the rubber mounted instruments to their protective outer cases. Disconnect the drive cables and lift each instrument up and pull out the bulb holders.

17.2a Instruments are secured by domed nut ...

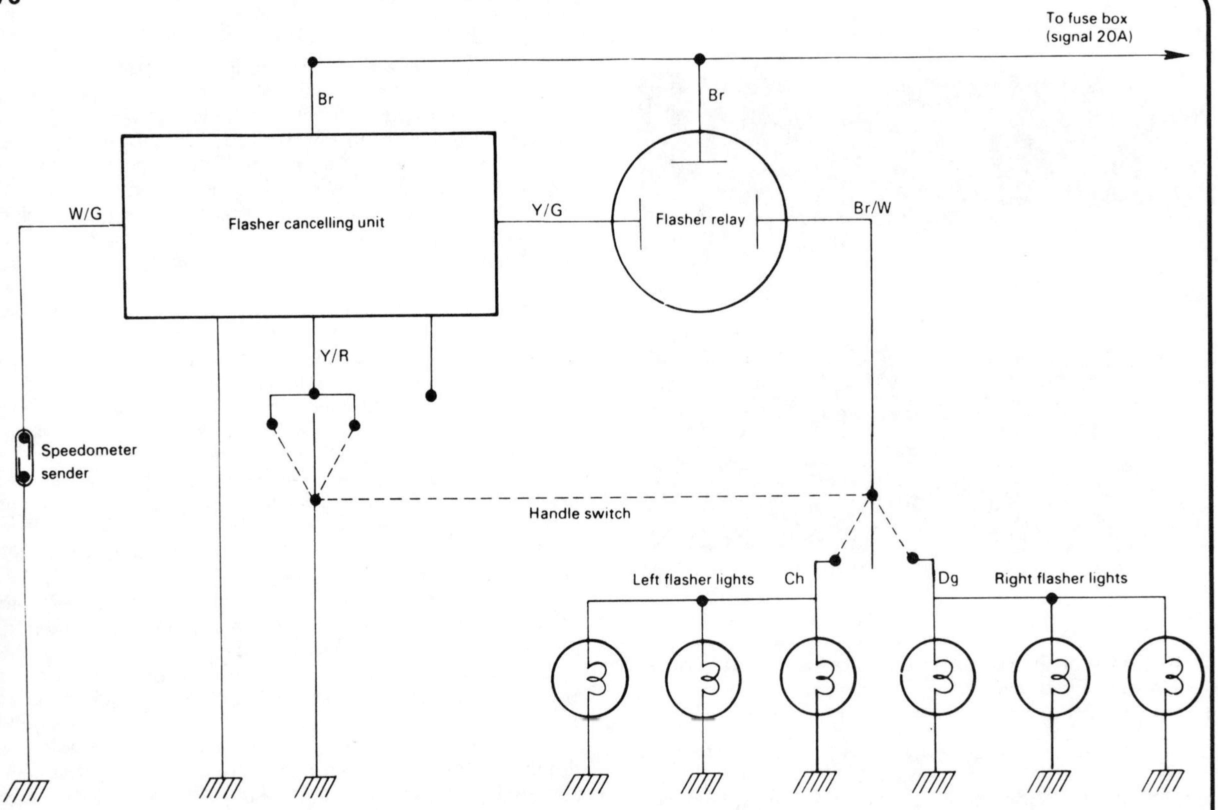

To fuse box
(signal 20A)

Br

Br

Flasher cancelling unit

W/G

Y/G

Flasher relay

Br/W

Y/R

Speedometer
sender

Handle switch

Left flasher lights   Ch   Dg   Right flasher lights

Fig. 6.13a Self-cancelling indicator circuit

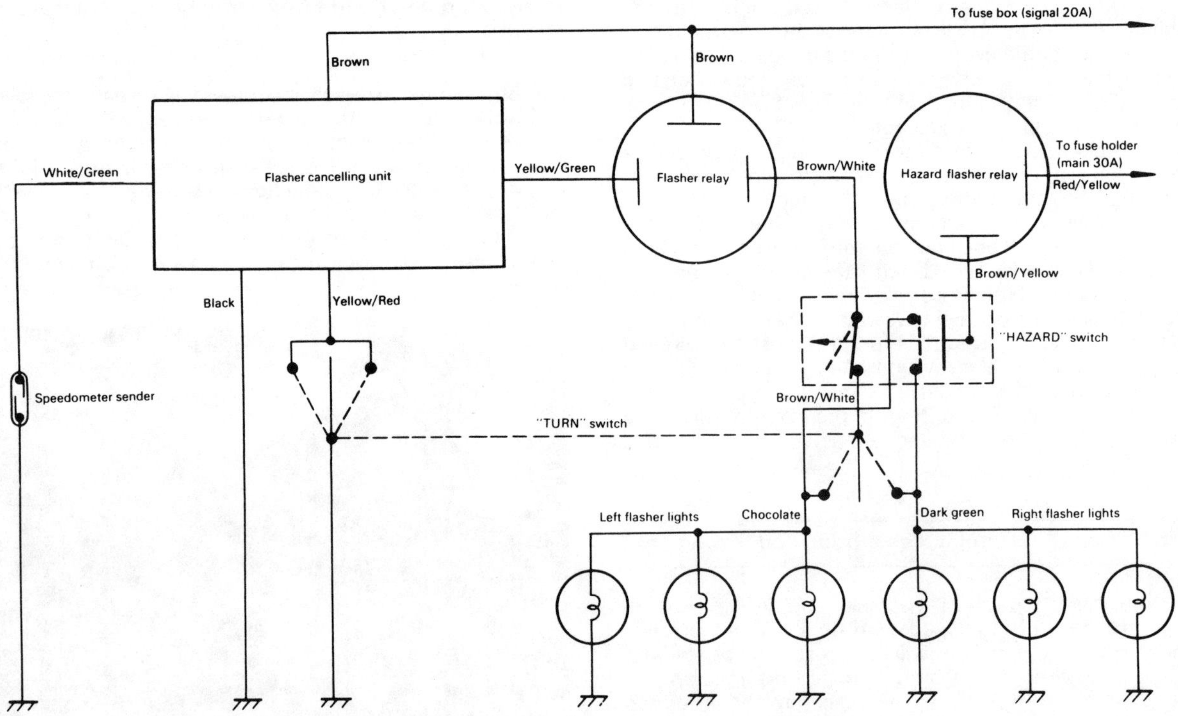

To fuse box (signal 20A)

Brown

Brown

Flasher cancelling unit

White/Green

Yellow/Green

Flasher relay

Brown/White

Hazard flasher relay

To fuse holder
(main 30A)

Red/Yellow

Brown/Yellow

Black

Yellow/Red

"HAZARD" switch

"TURN" switch

Brown/White

Speedometer sender

Brown/White

Left flasher lights   Chocolate   Dark green   Right flasher lights

Fig. 6.13b Self-cancelling indicators and hazard warning lamp circuit — G and SG (US models)

17.2b ... and anti-vibration rubber insert

17.2c Bulbholders are push fit in cases

18.1 Warning lamp panel is secured by screws from underside

19 Indicator panel lamps

1   An indicator lamp panel which holds the various warning bulbs is fitted between the speedometer and tacho-meter heads. To gain access to the bulbs remove the two screws (E, F and G) or four screws (SF and SG) which pass through the upper cover and lift the cover away, over the ignition switch barrel. Each bulb is a screw fit in the one piece holder.

20 Fuel gauge: operation and testing

1   All XS1100 models are equipped with a fuel gauge which monitors the fuel level in the tank. A float-operated sender unit consists of a variable resistor (E, F and G models) which controls the position of the fuel gauge needle in the tachometer face. On the SF model, a tank-mounted sender unit switches on a low fuel level warning lamp, again built into the tachometer.

Fault finding – E, F and G models
2   Refer to the accompanying diagrams for details of the fuel gauge sender resistances at various levels. Start by

removing the headlamp unit to gain access to the tachometer connector. Set a multimeter to the 0 – 20 volts dc position and measure the various voltages as described below, with the ignition switched on.
3   If the fuel tank sender unit is faulty, it will be necessary to remove and drain the fuel tank. Place the tank upside down on a soft blanket or similar to protect the paintwork. Remove the four bolts which retain the sender, taking great care not to damage the float or float arm as they are withdrawn. Using a multimeter, check the sender unit resistances at the various positions indicated in Fig. 6.14. If the unit is outside the specified limits or erratic in operation, it must be renewed.

Fault finding – SF and SG models
4   A similar test procedure is employed when checking the SF and SG model fuel warning lamp circuit. Remove the headlamp unit to expose the tachometer wiring connector, and carry out the following test sequence with the ignition switched on. The test meter should be set to 0 – 20 volts dc.

5   If the sender unit appears to be at fault, check the resistance between the green wire and the black wire of the unit. A reading of 1500 ± 100 ohms at 77°F (25°C) should be obtained. If it is outside these limits, renew the sender unit.

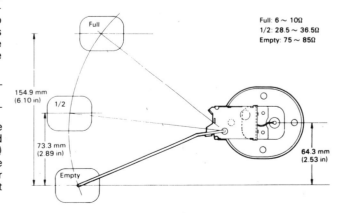

Fig. 6.14 Fuel tank level gauge mechanism

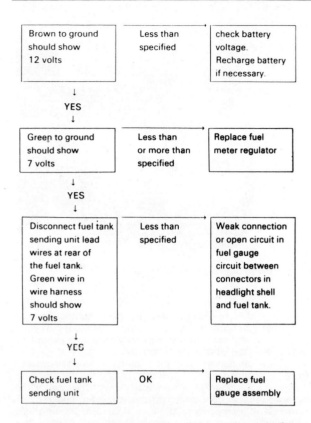

Brown to ground should show 12 volts	Less than specified	check battery voltage. Recharge battery if necessary.

↓
YES
↓

Green to ground should show 7 volts	Less than or more than specified	Replace fuel meter regulator

↓
YES
↓

Disconnect fuel tank sending unit lead wires at rear of the fuel tank. Green wire in wire harness should show 7 volts	Less than specified	Weak connection or open circuit in fuel gauge circuit between connectors in headlight shell and fuel tank.

↓
YES
↓

Check fuel tank sending unit	OK	Replace fuel gauge assembly

Fig. 6.15 Fuel gauge test flow-chart – except SF and SG models

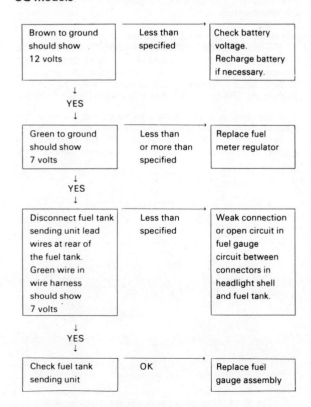

Brown to ground should show 12 volts	Less than specified	Check battery voltage. Recharge battery if necessary.

↓
YES
↓

Green to ground should show 7 volts	Less than or more than specified	Replace fuel meter regulator

↓
YES
↓

Disconnect fuel tank sending unit lead wires at rear of the fuel tank. Green wire in wire harness should show 7 volts	Less than specified	Weak connection or open circuit in fuel gauge circuit between connectors in headlight shell and fuel tank.

↓
YES
↓

Check fuel tank sending unit	OK	Replace fuel gauge assembly

Fig. 6.16 Fuel warning lamp test flow-chart – SF and SG models

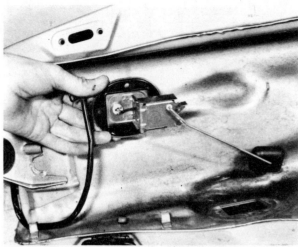

19.3 Fuel gauge sender unit can be removed for testing

21 Horn: location and examination

1   Depending on the model, one or two horns are fitted, each of which is suspended from a flexible steel strip bolted to the frame below the petrol tank.
2   The type of horn fitted has no external means of adjustment. If it malfunctions, it must be renewed; it is a statutory requirement that the machine must be fitted with a horn in working order.

22 Ignition switch: removal and replacement

1   The combined ignition and lighting master switch is mounted in the warning light panel mounting plate.
2   If the switch proves defective it may be removed after detaching the warning light cover and unscrewing the two mounting screws. Disconnect the two wiring sockets connecting the switch to the loom.
3   Reassembly of the switch can be made in the reverse procedure as described for dismantling. Repair is rarely practicable. It is preferable to purchase a new switch unit, which will probably necessitate the use of a different key.

23 Stop lamp switch: adjustment

1   All models have a stop lamp switch fitted to operate in conjunction with the rear brake pedal. The switch is located immediately to the rear of the crankcase, on the right-hand side of the machine. It has a threaded body giving a range of adjustment.
2   If the stop lamp is late in operating, slacken the locknuts and turn the body of the lamp in an anti-clockwise direction so that the switch rises from the bracket to which it is attached. When the adjustment seems near correct, tighten the locknuts and test.
3   If the lamp operates too early, the locknuts should be slackened and the switch body turned clockwise so that it is lowered in relation to the mounting bracket.
4   As a guide, the light should operate after the brake pedal has been depressed by about 2 cm (¾ inch).
5   A stop lamp switch is also incorporated in the front brake system. The mechanical switch is a push fit in the handlebar lever stock. If the switch malfunctions, repair is impracticable. The switch should be renewed.

24 Handlebar switches: general

1   Generally speaking, the switches give little trouble, but if necessary they can be dismantled by separating the halves which form a split clamp around the handlebars. Note that the machine cannot be started until the ignition cut-out on the right-hand end of the handlebars is turned to the central 'Run' position.
2   Always disconnect the battery before removing any of the switches, to prevent the possibility of a short circuit. Most troubles are caused by dirty contacts, but in the event of the breakage of some internal part, it will be necessary to renew the complete switch.
3   Because the internal components of each switch are very small, and therefore difficult to dismantle and reassemble, it is suggested a special electrical contact cleaner be used to clean corroded contacts. This can be sprayed into each switch, without the need for dismantling.

25 Neutral indicator switch: location and removal

1   A switch is incorporated in the gearbox which indicates via a small light in the warning console when neutral gear has been selected. The switch is screwed into the base of the gearbox. In the event of failure the switch may be unscrewed without draining the transmission oil. Disconnect the switch lead by unscrewing the central cross-head screw. Note that the switch is prone to shear if it is overtightened.

26 Tachometer: testing

1   As mentioned previously, an electronic impulse tachometer is fitted, and is arranged to sense the pulses in one of the alternator coils. These instruments are normally very reliable, a happy state of affairs because no adjustment or repair is practicable. In the event of tachometer failure, go through the following test sequence, having removed the headlamp unit and separated the tachometer wiring connector.

27 Auxiliary power outlet and fuse

1   An auxiliary power outlet is fitted behind the right-hand side panel and is provided to facilitate the connection of electrical accessories. It has its own fuse, rated at 10A and of the slo-blo type which can withstand occasional surges. No accessory or combination of accessories should exceed its maximum rated output of 12 volts, 50W. Note that if radios or tape players are connected, they must be protected by their own separate in-line fuse to protect their internal circuitry from damage. The terminal fuse **will not** protect the equipment.

28 Instrument panel dimmer control – G(UK) model only

1   The G(UK) model of the XS1100 features a dimmer control by means of which the intensity of the instrument panel illumination can be varied. To operate the control the trip meter reset knob is pulled outwards and turned clockwise to increase brightness or anti-clockwise to decrease brightness. The knob controls a rheostat, or variable resistor, incorporated in the instrument panel circuit.
2   If a fault develops in the control circuit, remove the headlamp to gain access to the speedometer connector block. Disconnect the connector and measure the voltage on the wiring harness side using a multimeter set on the $0 - 20$ volts dc scale. Connect the positive $(+)$ probe to the blue lead and the negative $(-)$ probe to the black lead. A reading of 1 volt minimum to 10.5 volts maximum should be obtained with the ignition and light switches on. If a fault is indicated, check the control unit as described below.
3   Disconnect the three-pin connector block and measure the resistance between the W/Y (white/yellow) and W/Br (white/brown) terminals. A resistance of 100 ohms $\pm$ 10% should be indicated. Repeat the resistance test between the W/Y (white/yellow) and W/L (white/blue) terminals, checking that the resistance changes from $0 - 100$ ohms as the control knob is moved.

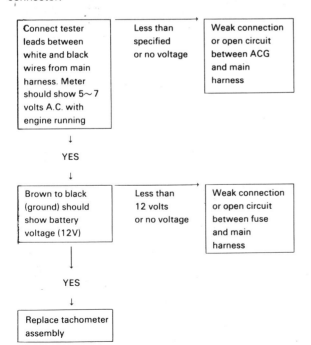

Fig. 6.17 Tachometer test flow-chart

22.2 Combined ignition switch and steering lock

24.1 Switches can be separated for examination and cleaning

25.1 Neutral indicator switch is fitted as shown

26.1 Tachometer is of electronic impulse type

27.1 Auxilliary terminal has its own fuse

29 Fault diagnosis: electrical system

Symptom	Cause	Remedy
Complete electrical failure	Blown fuse	Check wiring and electrical components for short circuit before fitting a new fuse. Check battery connections, also whether connections show signs of corrosion.
Dim lights, horn inoperative	Discharged battery	Recharge battery with battery charger and check whether alternator is giving correct output (electrical specialist).
Constantly 'blowing' bulbs	Vibration, poor earth connection	Check whether bulb holders are secured correctly. Check earth return or connections to frame.
Sub-system failure	—	Refer to relevant section in main text.

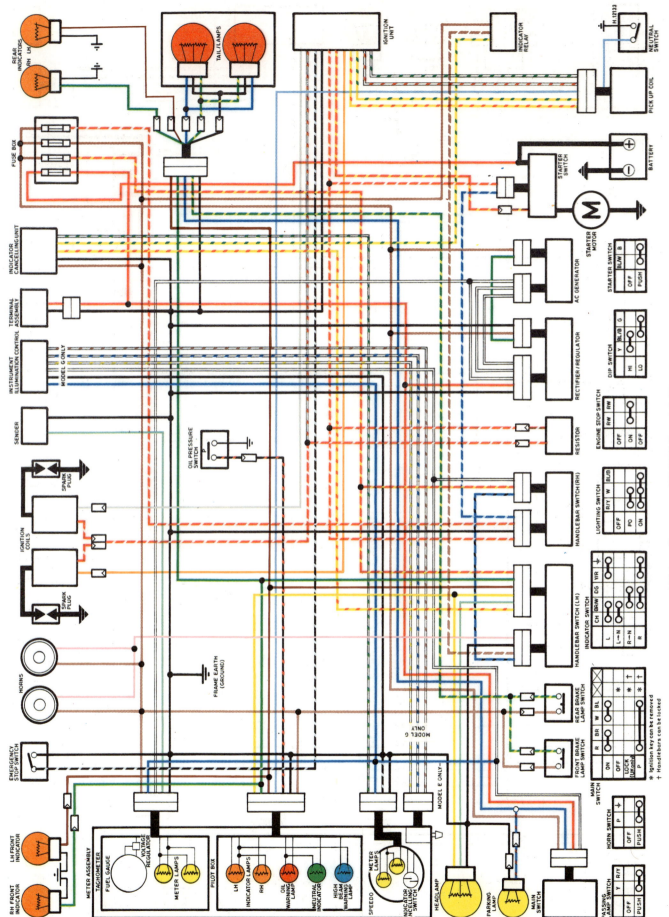

Wiring diagram – XS1100 E and G UK model

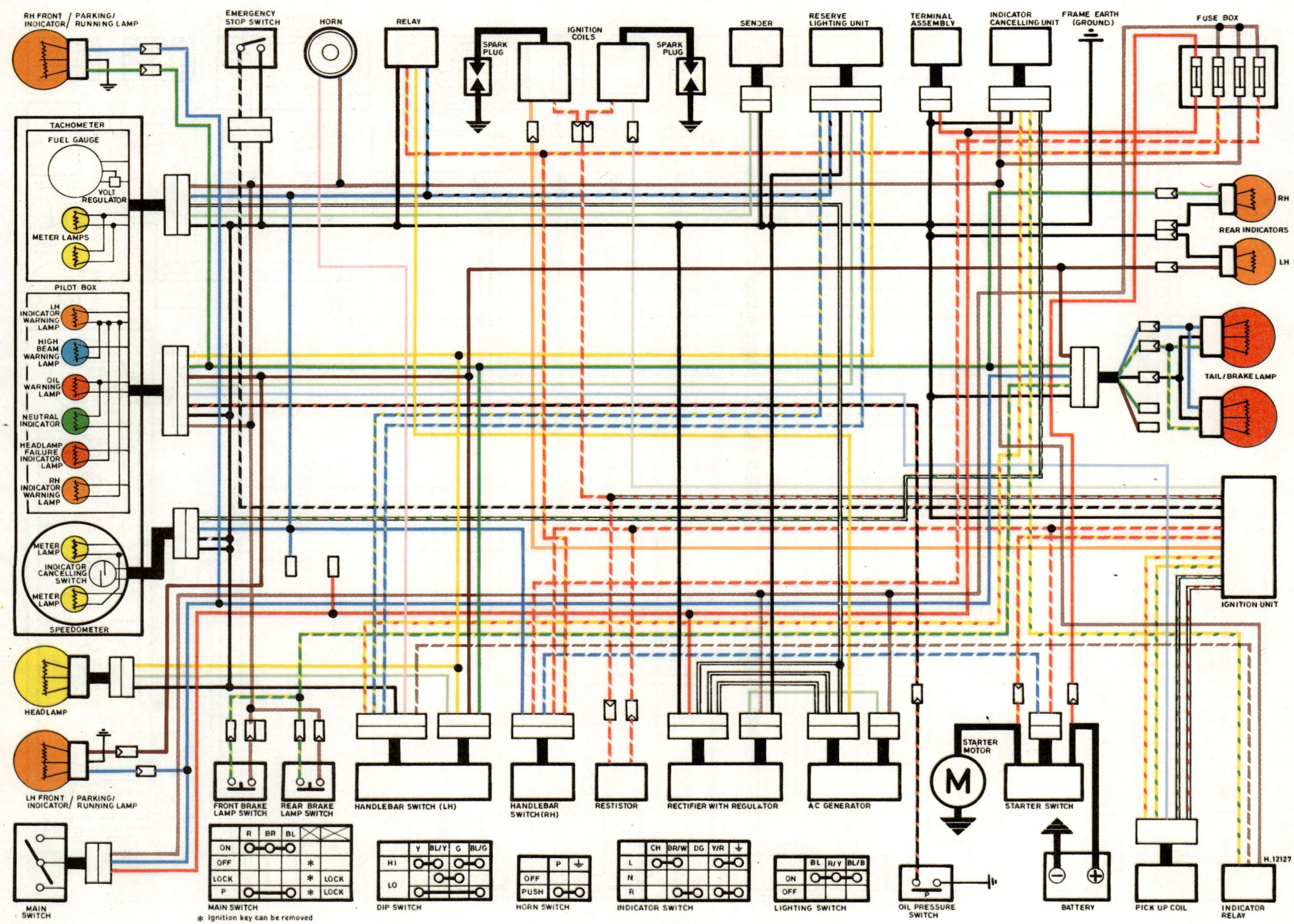

Wiring diagram – XS1100 E and F US model

FUSE BOX

RH / **REAR INDICATORS** / **LH**

TAIL/BRAKE LAMP

IGNITION UNIT

INDICATOR RELAY

PICK UP COIL

BATTERY

FRAME EARTH (GROUND)

INDICATOR CANCELLING UNIT

STARTER SWITCH

TERMINAL ASSEMBLY

STARTER MOTOR

OIL PRESSURE SWITCH

RESERVE LIGHTING UNIT

AC GENERATOR

SENDER

RECTIFIER WITH REGULATOR

SPARK PLUG

IGNITION COILS

RESISTOR

SPARK PLUG

HANDLEBAR SWITCH (RH)

RELAY

HANDLEBAR SWITCH (LH)

HORN

REAR BRAKE LAMP SWITCH

EMERGENCY STOP SWITCH

FRONT BRAKE LAMP SWITCH

RH FRONT / INDICATOR / PARKING / RUNNING LAMP

TACHOMETER | **FUEL GAUGE** | **VOLT REGULATOR** | **METER LAMPS** | **PILOT BOX** | **LH INDICATOR WARNING LAMP** / **HIGH BEAM WARNING LAMP** / **OIL WARNING LAMP** / **NEUTRAL INDICATOR** / **HEADLAMP FAILURE INDICATOR** / **RH INDICATOR WARNING LAMP** | **METER LAMP** / **INDICATOR CANCELLING SWITCH** / **METER LAMP** | **SPEEDOMETER** | **HEADLAMP** | **LH FRONT / INDICATOR / PARKING / RUNNING LAMP** | **MAIN SWITCH**

LIGHTING SWITCH

	BL	R/Y	BL/B
ON			
OFF			

INDICATOR SWITCH

	CH	BroW	DG	Y/R
L				
N				
R				

HORN SWITCH

	P	⊥	
OFF			
PUSH			

DIP SWITCH

	Y	BL/Y	G	Br/G
HI				
LO				

MAIN SWITCH

	R	BR	BL	
ON				
OFF			LOCK	
LOCK				LOCK
P				

* Ignition key can be removed

H.12127

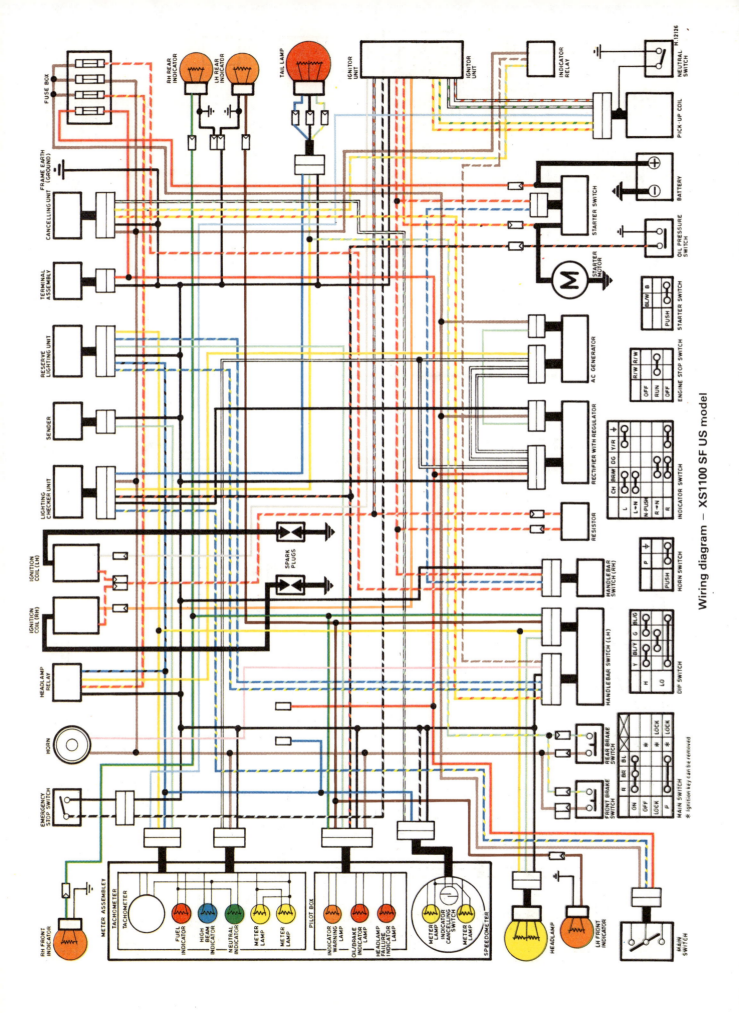

Wiring diagram – XS1100 SF US model

H.12126

NEUTRAL SWITCH

PICK-UP COIL

BATTERY

OIL PRESSURE SWITCH

STARTER MOTOR

| | BL/W | B |
| PUSH | | |

STARTER SWITCH

	R/W	R/W	
OFF			
RUN			
OFF			

ENGINE STOP SWITCH

	CH	BRW	DG	Y/R	+
L					
L→N					
N→PUSH					
R→N					
R					

INDICATOR SWITCH

	+	
PUSH		

HORN SWITCH

	Y	BL/V	G	BL/G
H				
LO				

DIP SWITCH

	R	BR	BL	
ON				
OFF			LOCK	LOCK
LOCK			*	*
P			*	*

MAIN SWITCH

* Ignition key can be removed

FUSE BOX

RH REAR INDICATOR

LH REAR INDICATOR

TAIL LAMP

IGNITOR UNIT

IGNITOR UNIT

INDICATOR RELAY

FRAME EARTH (GROUND)

CANCELLING UNIT

TERMINAL ASSEMBLY

RESERVE LIGHTING UNIT

SENDER

LIGHTING CHECKER UNIT

IGNITION COIL (LH)

IGNITION COIL (RH)

SPARK PLUGS

AC GENERATOR

RECTIFIER WITH REGULATOR

RESISTOR

HANDLEBAR SWITCH (RH)

HANDLEBAR SWITCH (LH)

HEADLAMP RELAY

HORN

EMERGENCY STOP SWITCH

STARTER SWITCH

REAR BRAKE SWITCH

FRONT BRAKE SWITCH

RH FRONT INDICATOR

METER ASSEMBLEY

TACHOMETER

TACHOMETER

FUEL INDICATOR

HIGH BEAM INDICATOR

NEUTRAL INDICATOR

METER LAMP

METER LAMP

PILOT BOX

INDICATOR WARNING LAMP

OIL/BRAKE INDICATOR LAMP

HEADLAMP FAILURE INDICATOR LAMP

METER LAMP

INDICATOR CANCELLING SWITCH

METER LAMP

SPEEDOMETER

HEADLAMP

LH FRONT INDICATOR

MAIN SWITCH

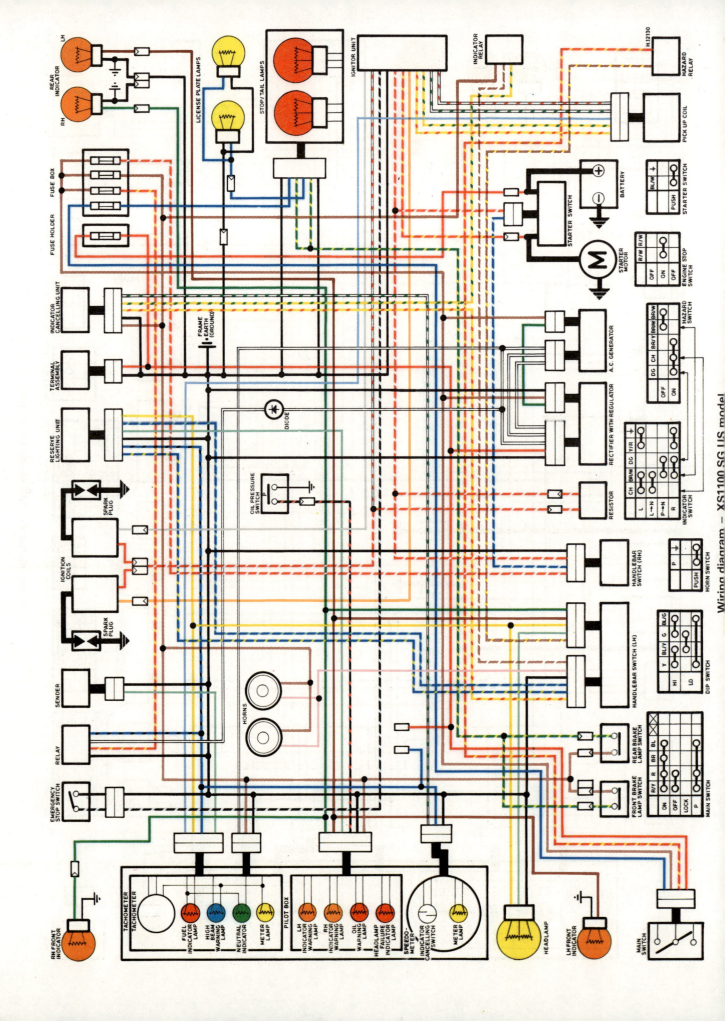

Wiring diagram – XS1100 SG US model

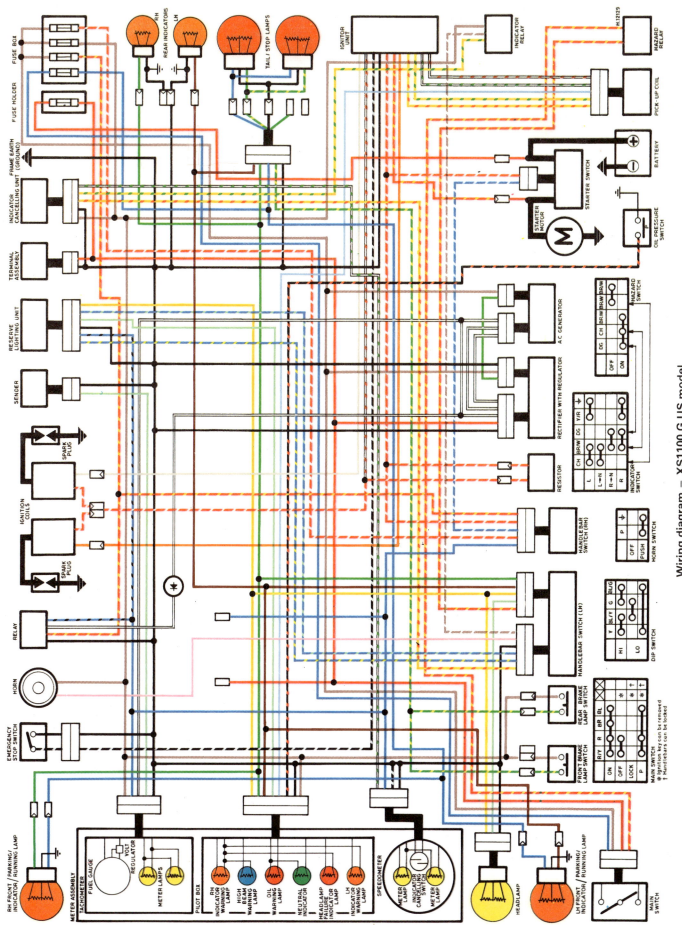

Wiring diagram – XS1100 G US model

Conversion factors

Length (distance)
Inches (in)	X	25.4	= Millimetres (mm)	X 0.039	= Inches (in)
Feet (ft)	X	0.305	= Metres (m)	X 3.281	= Feet (ft)
Miles	X	1.609	= Kilometres (km)	X 0.621	= Miles

Volume (capacity)
Cubic inches (cu in; in^3)	X	16.387	= Cubic centimetres (cc; cm^3)	X 0.061	= Cubic inches (cu in; in^3)
Imperial pints (Imp pt)	X	0.568	= Litres (l)	X 1.76	= Imperial pints (Imp pt)
Imperial quarts (Imp qt)	X	1.137	= Litres (l)	X 0.88	= Imperial quarts (Imp qt)
Imperial quarts (Imp qt)	X	1.201	= US quarts (US qt)	X 0.833	= Imperial quarts (Imp qt)
US quarts (US qt)	X	0.946	= Litres (l)	X 1.057	= US quarts (US qt)
Imperial gallons (Imp gal)	X	4.546	= Litres (l)	X 0.22	= Imperial gallons (Imp gal)
Imperial gallons (Imp gal)	X	1.201	= US gallons (US gal)	X 0.833	= Imperial gallons (Imp gal)
US gallons (US gal)	X	3.785	= Litres (l)	X 0.264	= US gallons (US gal)

Mass (weight)
Ounces (oz)	X	28.35	= Grams (g)	X 0.035	= Ounces (oz)
Pounds (lb)	X	0.454	= Kilograms (kg)	X 2.205	= Pounds (lb)

Force
Ounces-force (ozf; oz)	X	0.278	= Newtons (N)	X 3.6	= Ounces-force (ozf; oz)
Pounds-force (lbf; lb)	X	4.448	= Newtons (N)	X 0.225	= Pounds-force (lbf; lb)
Newtons (N)	X	0.1	= Kilograms-force (kgf; kg)	X 9.81	= Newtons (N)

Pressure
Pounds-force per square inch (psi; lbf/in^2; lb/in^2)	X	0.070	= Kilograms-force per square centimetre (kgf/cm^2; kg/cm^2)	X 14.223	= Pounds-force per square inch (psi; lbf/in^2; lb/in^2)
Pounds-force per square inch (psi; lbf/in^2; lb/in^2)	X	0.068	= Atmospheres (atm)	X 14.696	= Pounds-force per square inch (psi; lbf/in^2; lb/in^2)
Pounds-force per square inch (psi; lbf/in^2; lb/in^2)	X	0.069	= Bars	X 14.5	= Pounds-force per square inch (psi; lbf/in^2; lb/in^2)
Pounds-force per square inch (psi; lbf/in^2; lb/in^2)	X	6.895	= Kilopascals (kPa)	X 0.145	= Pounds-force per square inch (psi; lbf/in^2; lb/in^2)
Kilopascals (kPa)	X	0.01	= Kilograms-force per square centimetre (kgf/cm^2; kg/cm^2)	X 98.1	= Kilopascals (kPa)

Torque (moment of force)
Pounds-force inches (lbf in; lb in)	X	1.152	= Kilograms-force centimetre (kgf cm; kg cm)	X 0.868	= Pounds-force inches (lbf in; lb in)
Pounds-force inches (lbf in; lb in)	X	0.113	= Newton metres (Nm)	X 8.85	= Pounds-force inches (lbf in; lb in)
Pounds-force inches (lbf in; lb in)	X	0.083	= Pounds-force feet (lbf ft; lb ft)	X 12	= Pounds-force inches (lbf in; lb in)
Pounds-force feet (lbf ft; lb ft)	X	0.138	= Kilograms-force metres (kgf m; kg m)	X 7.233	= Pounds-force feet (lbf ft; lb ft)
Pounds-force feet (lbf ft; lb ft)	X	1.356	= Newton metres (Nm)	X 0.738	= Pounds-force feet (lbf ft; lb ft)
Newton metres (Nm)	X	0.102	= Kilograms-force metres (kgf m; kg m)	X 9.804	= Newton metres (Nm)

Power
Horsepower (hp)	X	745.7	= Watts (W)	X 0.0013	= Horsepower (hp)

Velocity (speed)
Miles per hour (miles/hr; mph)	X	1.609	= Kilometres per hour (km/hr; kph)	X 0.621	= Miles per hour (miles/hr; mph)

Fuel consumption*
Miles per gallon, Imperial (mpg)	X	0.354	= Kilometres per litre (km/l)	X 2.825	= Miles per gallon, Imperial (mpg)
Miles per gallon, US (mpg)	X	0.425	= Kilometres per litre (km/l)	X 2.352	= Miles per gallon, US (mpg)

Temperature

Degrees Fahrenheit (°F) $= (°C \times \frac{9}{5}) + 32$

Degrees Celsius (Degrees Centigrade; °C) $= (°F - 32) \times \frac{5}{9}$

It is common practice to convert from miles per gallon (mpg) to litres/100 kilometres (l/100km), where mpg (Imperial) x l/100 km = 282 and mpg (US) x l/100 km = 235

Metric conversion tables

Inches	Decimals	Millimetres	Millimetres to Inches		Inches to Millimetres	
			mm	Inches	Inches	mm
1/64	0.015625	0.3969	0.01	0.00039	0.001	0.0254
1/32	0.03125	0.7937	0.02	0.00079	0.002	0.0508
3/64	0.046875	1.1906	0.03	0.00118	0.003	0.0762
1/16	0.0625	1.5875	0.04	0.00157	0.004	0.1016
5/64	0.078125	1.9844	0.05	0.00197	0.005	0.1270
3/32	0.09375	2.3812	0.06	0.00236	0.006	0.1524
7/64	0.109375	2.7781	0.07	0.00276	0.007	0.1778
1/8	0.125	3.1750	0.08	0.00315	0.008	0.2032
9/64	0.140625	3.5719	0.09	0.00354	0.009	0.2286
5/32	0.15625	3.9687	0.1	0.00394	0.01	0.254
11/64	0.171875	4.3656	0.2	0.00787	0.02	0.508
3/16	0.1875	4.7625	0.3	0.01181	0.03	0.762
13/64	0.203125	5.1594	0.4	0.01575	0.04	1.016
7/32	0.21875	5.5562	0.5	0.01969	0.05	1.270
15/64	0.234375	5.9531	0.6	0.02362	0.06	1.524
1/4	0.25	6.3500	0.7	0.02756	0.07	1.778
17/64	0.265625	6.7469	0.8	0.03150	0.08	2.032
9/32	0.28125	7.1437	0.9	0.03543	0.09	2.286
19/64	0.296875	7.5406	1	0.03937	0.1	2.54
5/16	0.3125	7.9375	2	0.07874	0.2	5.08
21/64	0.328125	8.3344	3	0.11811	0.3	7.62
11/32	0.34375	8.7312	4	0.15748	0.4	10.16
23/64	0.359375	9.1281	5	0.19685	0.5	12.70
3/8	0.375	9.5250	6	0.23622	0.6	15.24
25/64	0.390625	9.9219	7	0.27559	0.7	17.78
13/32	0.40625	10.3187	8	0.31496	0.8	20.32
27/64	0.421875	10.7156	9	0.35433	0.9	22.86
7/16	0.4375	11.1125	10	0.39370	1	25.4
29/64	0.453125	11.5094	11	0.43307	2	50.8
15/32	0.46875	11.9062	12	0.47244	3	76.2
31/64	0.484375	12.3031	13	0.51181	4	101.6
1/2	0.5	12.7000	14	0.55118	5	127.0
33/64	0.515625	13.0969	15	0.59055	6	152.4
17/32	0.53125	13.4937	16	0.62992	7	177.8
35/64	0.546875	13.8906	17	0.66929	8	203.2
9/16	0.5625	14.2875	18	0.70866	9	228.6
37/64	0.578125	14.6844	19	0.74803	10	254.0
19/32	0.59375	15.0812	20	0.78740	11	279.4
39/64	0.609375	15.4781	21	0.82677	12	304.8
5/8	0.625	15.8750	22	0.86614	13	330.2
41/64	0.640625	16.2719	23	0.09551	14	355.6
21/32	0.65625	16.6687	24	0.94488	15	381.0
43/64	0.671875	17.0656	25	0.98425	16	406.4
11/16	0.6875	17.4625	26	1.02362	17	431.8
45/64	0.703125	17.8594	27	1.06299	18	457.2
23/32	0.71875	18.2562	28	1.10236	19	482.6
47/64	0.734375	18.6531	29	1.14173	20	508.0
3/4	0.75	19.0500	30	1.18110	21	533.4
49/64	0.765625	19.4469	31	1.22047	22	558.8
25/32	0.78125	19.8437	32	1.25984	23	584.2
51/64	0.796875	20.2406	33	1.29921	24	609.6
13/16	0.8125	20.6375	34	1.33858	25	635.0
53/64	0.828125	21.0344	35	1.37795	26	660.4
27/32	0.84375	21.4312	36	1.41732	27	685.8
55/64	0.859375	21.8281	37	1.4567	28	711.2
7/8	0.875	22.2250	38	1.4961	29	736.6
57/64	0.890625	22.6219	39	1.5354	30	762.0
29/32	0.90625	23.0187	40	1.5748	31	787.4
59/64	0.921875	23.4156	41	1.6142	32	812.8
15/16	0.9375	23.8125	42	1.6535	33	838.2
61/64	0.953125	24.2094	43	1.6929	34	863.6
31/32	0.96875	24.6062	44	1.7323	35	889.0
63/64	0.984375	25.0031	45	1.7717	36	914.4

Index

Printed by
Haynes Publishing Group
Sparkford Yeovil Somerset
England